THE POLITICAL ECOLOGY OF EDUCATION

The Political Ecology of Education

Brazil's Landless Workers' Movement and the Politics of Knowledge

DAVID MEEK

WEST VIRGINIA UNIVERSITY PRESS / MORGANTOWN

ISBN
Cloth 978-1-949199-75-8
Paper 978-1-949199-76-5
Ebook 978-1-949199-77-2

Library of Congress Control Number: 2020015459

Book and cover design by Than Saffel / WVU Press
Cover image by David Meek

To all the landless farmers in Brazil and the marginalized producers throughout the world, who see agroecology and critical food systems education as a pathway to a more food sovereign future.

Contents

Acknowledgments

I first came to southeastern Pará, Brazil, a decade ago to begin the research for this book. In the intervening period, I and this project have benefitted immensely from a diverse network of support. The research began as part of my doctoral studies at the University of Georgia. I would first like to thank my co-chairs Pete Brosius and Julie Velásquez Runk. Pete's strong support in negotiating funding opportunities was critical to remaining in and returning to the field. Similarly, his enthusiasm for the project's novel synthesis of political ecology and critical education has kept me motivated throughout the writing process. Julie's careful feedback, mentorship, and experience have been pivotal along the journey. This project has been shaped by our many conversations on research ethics, the politics of remote sensing, and geographic theory. Many thanks to my committee members Ted Gragson, Diane Napier, and Wendy Wolford for their support and feedback. I owe a great debt to Wendy, in particular, for her insights, time, and mentorship over the years. I still remember visiting Wendy in Chapel Hill, where she pushed me to think about political participation in novel ways. These and her other critical insights were instrumental in honing my research design and analyses.

Much of the success of this project is also attributed to the assistance and friendship of my colleagues at several institutions in Brazil. I would first like to recognize Bernardo Mançano Fernandes, who continues to be my principal academic mentor, an intellectual inspiration, and an exemplar of engaged scholarship. I would also like to thank Ligia Terezinha Lopes Simonian of the Núcleo de Altos Estudos Amazônicos (NAEA) at the University of Pará for the institutional support that was necessary for this research. At the Federal Institute of Pará-Rural Campus of Marabá, I would like to send particular thanks to Dalcione Lima Marinho for his commitment to supporting this project as a friend, colleague, and activist. I would be remiss if I did not offer a big thumbs-up to the entire Educação do Campo collective at the Federal University of South and Southeastern Pará, and in particular Fernando Michelloti, Haroldo da Souza, and Bruno Malheiro for all of the critical discussions and for demonstrating what an allied academic looks like by example.

Whereas I could easily devote this entire acknowledgment section to the following two individuals, for brevity, and fairness, it must suffice to say that without the assistance of two particular individuals in Brazil, there is no chance this research would ever have gotten off the ground, much less been successful. Dan Baron Cohen and Manoela Souza are tireless activists in the region where I conducted my fieldwork and were instrumental in facilitating my introduction to the 17 de Abril settlement. The groundwork they did before I arrived for my first stint of pilot research in 2009 ensured a smooth landing and set the stage for a lifelong series of friendships. Over the years they have been intellectual and personal advisers, providing support on all matters of life in Brazil, and in movement. I am forever indebted to their friendship and magnanimity.

This research was made possible by generous funding and in-kind donations from numerous organizations. In chronological order, pilot research funding was supplied by the Latin American and Caribbean Studies Institute's Tinker Award and the Janice Steingruber award through the University of Georgia's Department of Anthropology. In-kind donations of satellite imagery were provided by both Digital Globe, as part of the American Society for Photogrammetry and Remote Sensing's GeoEye prize, as well as Digital Globe, as part of their 8-band challenge. Dissertation funding was provided by the National Science Foundation (BCS #1060888), the Fulbright Program, and the Social Science Research Council. Particular thanks go out to Deborah Wilson at NSF, Daniella Sarnoff at SSRC, and Jody Dudderar at Fulbright for their patience and commitment to my research during the funding negotiation process. Extra special thanks go out to Patricia Grijo for her administrative and personal support throughout my time in Brazil, particularly during the difficult times of my daughter's illness while in the field.

This book is the product of an immense, and deeply rewarding, cross-pollination of ideas. I was fortunate enough to begin this project in lockstep with a number of phenomenal critical food systems scholars. Jahi Chappell, Teresa Mares, Laura-Anne Minkoff Zern, Lindsay Naylor: y'all are just amazing human beings and have pushed me to engage with theory and representation in ways I never would have imagined. Hopefully, you'll be pleased to find many of your ideas tucked into the book's various nooks and crannies. I will always be grateful for the intellectual community we built in the trenches. Developing a political ecology of education framework was never a singular project. Teresa Lloro-Bidart, Joseph Henderson, and Becky Zarger were instrumental in mapping out the contours of this perspective in the early years. Thanks to the above characters, along with Nicolas Stahlein, Sophie Moore, Robert Fletcher, Fern Thompsett, Eli Meyerhoff, who participated in the production of a special issue of *Journal of Environmental Education* on the political ecology of education (2017; 48, no. 4). An extra special thanks goes out to Becky Tarlau, who has been a close intellectual collaborator and accomplice over the years; thanks for inspiring me to remain politically engaged and helping to imagine and actualize the transformative potential of critical food systems education.

My family has most certainly been along for the ride throughout this research, having joined me on numerous extended field seasons in the 17 de Abril. Annabelle and Miles: those experiences, while challenging (still very, very sorry about that broken leg), were hopefully formative. Perhaps my biggest debt goes to Lesley Jo, who perhaps did not sign up for a year in the Amazon while actively dissertating with a young baby, but who rose to the challenge, learning Portuguese, and starting her own research project; my hat will forever be off to you. Much appreciation and love to my parents who have continually supported me in my education and research, and broader family, many of whom visited Brazil, providing an important space for processing these experiences.

My most heartfelt thanks go out to all those MST activists, farmers, and everyday friends who live in the agrarian reform encampments and settlements throughout the 17 de Abril in particular, but throughout southeastern and northern Pará as well. Thank you for putting up with endless questions, critically reflecting on your experiences and dreams, and welcoming my family and me into your homes and lives. My hope is that in this book I've been able to mobilize your voices to ask difficult but necessary questions and help advance a broader process of social change.

Part I

Conceptions of the World

CHAPTER 1

It Wasn't Supposed to Be This Way

"We need to reflect on why we are no longer producing food," Isabel remarked, as she poured steaming hot coffee into an old jelly jar. Isabel is a secondary school teacher in an agrarian reform settlement of the Brazilian Landless Workers' Movement (O Movimento dos Trabalhadores Rurais Sem Terra, or MST). The MST is Latin America's largest agrarian social movement. MST members tactically occupy land to push the state for agrarian reform, and at the same time they are pushing the boundaries of food systems education. Isabel, like many other educators in this movement, encourages her students to critically reflect on the dominant agroindustrial system and how it structures farmers' lives in her community. She teaches these students about sustainable agriculture, helping them design agricultural systems around ecological principles. Isabel believes these critical forms of agroecological education can help her community become more food sovereign—more in control over its own food system. Through my discussion with Isabel, I begin to untangle the book's main themes, which are the role of critical forms of food systems education in shaping political participation, commonsense understandings of agriculture, and the landscape itself. Isabel's voice opens this chapter because her narrative illustrates what is at stake in this book: the survival of her community, the future of the movement, and the viability of sustainable agriculture in the Amazon.

Isabel painted a picture of her community in dire straits. She gestured up a street of largely abandoned houses and into the distance where a cattle pasture extends to the horizon (figs. 1.1 and 1.2). "It wasn't supposed to be this way," she tells me. "No, our comrades, our brothers and sisters did not die in the struggle for this." Isabel lives in an agrarian reform settlement known as the 17 de Abril (April 17). This community, consisting of 690 families, was born out of one of Brazil's most violent agrarian conflicts. On April 17, 1996, gunmen massacred nineteen rural landless workers who were occupying highway PA-150 in Eldorado dos Carajás, Pará. Following the massacre, the government created a

Figure 1.1. Abandoned dreams

type of planned community, known as an agrarian reform settlement, in this corner of the rural Brazilian Amazon for the survivors. Among them were Isabel's father and approximately two thousand other MST members. Nineteen activists sacrificed their lives for a dream, but it was not a vision of abandoned houses and degraded cattle pasture. Their aspiration was for land to live on and to farm..

Isabel was particularly dismayed by the current state of agricultural production in this settlement and how far her community had moved from its founding vision. Isabel's father originally joined the movement to get access to land and engage in small-scale subsistence agriculture. Yet since the founding of the settlement two decades ago, he and most community members had transitioned from subsistence crops to export-oriented dairy production, a development that didn't sit well with Isabel, who told me, "What you have here are essentially mini-*fazendas* [large farms], with tons of cattle. You won't find a single lemon tree, or a banana tree, or any pineapple. . . . No, it is just cattle. Just pasture." Isabel lamented the disjuncture between the settlement's reality and the movement's model of food sovereignty.

The MST holds an agroecological vision for its settlements: land should be used for small-scale diversified peasant agriculture, should involve no

Figure 1.2. The promised land?

pesticides or genetically modified organisms, and should contribute significantly to the subsistence of the household. The MST legitimizes its land occupations in part by arguing that its members will take unproductive land and make it fruitful, replacing environmentally damaging forms of production with more ecologically benign practices. This position is essential to the movement's success because Brazil's 1988 federal constitution states that land must have a socially productive function, or it can be expropriated and redistributed as part of a process of agrarian reform (Clauses 22–25 of Article 5).[1] There are three components to land's social function. First, land must be utilized in a manner that is "rational and adequate" (Ondetti 2016: 31). Second, existing landowners must comply with labor laws, such as not maintaining workers in a state of forced servitude. As I will highlight in chapter 5, the presence of forced labor shaped both the landscape in southeastern Pará and the legitimacy with which the MST was able to acquire illegally worked land and decolonize it. Last, land must contribute to sustainable development while not degrading the environment.

Debates about the concept of productivity have long been at the core of the broader struggle for agroecology and against industrial agriculture in diverse international contexts. Industrial advocates hold that organic agriculture has low yield and that large-scale monocultures, consisting of high-yielding varieties or genetically modified crops fed by chemical fertilizers and treated with chemical pesticides, are necessary to achieve the output required to feed the world's growing population. Rosset (1999) critiques this singular focus on yield (output of a single crop per area), suggesting that the concept of "total output," which accounts for the aggregate yield of growing multiple crops together, is better suited for traditional production systems. Drawing on this logic, Weis (2010: 336) proposes "throwing out the dominant conception of agricultural productivity." Various studies support this position, demonstrating that while unit output of a particular crop might be higher when grown in monoculture, the unit of total food per hectare is frequently higher for agroecological plots (Grain 2014; Sampson 2019).[2] Similarly, debates about agricultural production indices make invisible the contribution of agroecological methods to household food security. Agroecology plays an important role in ensuring a balanced diet, as "minor crops," such as wild plants and animals from around farms, which are often produced for household consumption and not measured as part of official statistics, contribute essential micronutrients that are associated with greater food security and overall nutrition (Ogle et al. 2001; Roos et al. 2003). While not providing new data on whether or not agroecology is more productive than conventional agriculture, this book contributes to these broader debates by exploring the diverse challenges to agroecology taking root, even among its most vocal advocates.[3]

From the movement's perspective, MST members are supposed to depart from the dominant model of agriculture—which in southeastern Pará consists of intensive cattle ranching. Many would rightly argue that raising cattle is a "productive" form of agriculture—particularly in a country with a high rate of beef consumption and export. Yet "while cattle are food," Isabel noted, "they're not the proposal that the movement has—the movement's vision is that you receive a piece of land, and you use it for agriculture. Not exclusively for ranching; maybe a few cattle, in order to derive a little milk." Tapping my knee to make sure I'm paying attention, Isabel emphasized, "We need to ask ourselves this question: why is it our settlement, *our movement*, doesn't have agricultural production?" Here, Isabel drew my attention to how the settlement's shift away from subsistence agriculture tracks the fate of the movement itself within this community, which many believe has departed on a large scale from its original ideals.

Figure 1.3. The fate of political space in the 17 de Abril

For Isabel, and many others, the settlement was at an existential cross-roads. In a resigned tone, Isabel told me "the 17 de Abril settlement has lost its identity, its sense of purpose. Today, there's no more unity. *Companheiros* don't have any unity anymore. People are called together to do something collectively—few people agree to do it." Raising her shoulders, and putting up her hands in a sign of bewilderment, she asked me, "Where is the struggle? Where is the movement?" The answer was, "It's over." Spaces that have been carved out by, and for, the movement, such as the Che Guevara Cultural Center, have been largely abandoned and serve as dismal reminders of an alternate future (fig. 1.3).

Many in the community believed that within the next decade, the flag of the movement would literally be taken down from the central square and the school, where it flies, tattered, in the sun. Removing the MST's signature red flag from these places would be a highly symbolic action, indicating the community's rejection of the MST and the end of the movement's presence in the settlement. While this would be an emblematic act in any MST settlement, its symbolism would be particularly heavy in the 17 de Abril because this settlement, more than any other, symbolizes the movement's struggle, born as it was out of the massacre of Eldorado dos Carajás. The existence of the settlement is the materialization of the MST's struggle for agrarian reform; it exemplifies that there will need to be sacrifices, often grave ones, but that truly radical visions of transforming land concentration, resisting agribusiness, and bringing a new agroecological vision of production into existence are possible. The settlement's reality—characterized by the slow death of both political participation and agriculture—was particularly disturbing for Isabel because the MST intended that this settlement would be an exemplar of its success. As Isabel told me, beginning with carefully metered words for emphasis,

> We . . . were . . . supposed . . . to . . . be . . . a . . . model. . . . A model for the other encampments and settlements. Imagine if everything was functioning and producing today; if the settlement members were producing rice, producing *farinha* [manioc flour], producing milk to make cheese and yogurt. This would have been a developed area; there would have been jobs for everyone, people would have been flocking to the 17 de Abril to work, you wouldn't have had one single youth leaving in search of work in the cities. No, they would have worked here, and remained here, because it would have been developed. But no, this didn't happen. We were supposed to be a model.

Isabel's concerns extend beyond the settlement, speaking to broader questions about the long-term political viability of the MST as a broader national-scale movement. To be successful in their aims of pushing the state for agrarian and education reform, the MST's members must be personally invested in collective struggles. Yet youth increasingly want nothing to do with the movement. Instead, they are spellbound by the allure of jobs in the nearby cities, the newest cell phones, and designer clothes. The 17 de Abril, which was founded two decades ago, might be seen as a bellwether for MST settlements throughout the country. As founders of this community age, they describe themselves as "tired" and are stepping back from active political participation in the movement, expecting their children to compensate. A hand-painted wooden sign in the settlement's central square captures this broad injunction: "We did our part, now it is your turn." Yet most youth are not heeding the call. If the MST cannot mobilize the next generation in the 17 de Abril, what will become of it at a national scale?

What is in jeopardy is not just the future of the 17 de Abril settlement, or even that of the MST, but also the viability of small-scale agriculture in the Brazilian Amazon. Approximately half of the original founders of the 17 de Abril settlement have left the land. Wealthy newcomers have flocked to the community, buying up ten to fifteen adjacent parcels, recapitulating the very process of land concentration against which the MST explicitly orients its activism. These processes of agrarian change underscore the challenges of bringing an agroecological vision of Amazonian development into existence.

Isabel is on the front lines of this broad struggle for the future of her community, the MST, and sustainable agriculture in the Amazon. She and various other teachers in the settlement understand that contemporary rural education has a role to play in agrarian change. As they described it, the state education system implicitly devalues rural areas and livelihoods while valorizing urban ones. Education can serve as a driver of agrarian change, pushing youth from rural areas to urban ones. Yet Isabel and other teachers within the settlement are trying to help usher in a new vision of education, which I term critical food systems education (Meek and Tarlau 2016). This approach combines critical pedagogy, agroecology, and food sovereignty. Isabel is involved in various forms of critical food systems education, ranging from seed banks, school gardens, and agroforestry projects to student-centered agroecological cooperatives. Critical food systems education is central to the agrarian future of the settlement; although the community is plagued by increasingly high rates of food insecurity, Isabel and others are seeking to help make the settlement more food sovereign by promulgating agricultural diversification, value-added production, and worker-owned cooperatives. Critical food systems education is also pivotal to the future of the MST; workshops, field trips, and extracurricular activities cultivate the political identities of rural youth, forming the next generation of individuals who will, with any luck, self-identify as *Sem Terra* (landless) and be willing to carry on the struggle. Last, critical food systems education seeks to bring a different model of Amazonian agrarian development into existence; Isabel and other educators are committed to propagating an Amazonian vision of agroecology, making visible largely unknown regional agroecological practices, and arguing for their social, economic, and environmental sustainability. Isabel exemplifies a critical food systems educator because she is educating for food sovereignty. Yet Isabel also repurposes education to bring a different—and more food sovereign—vision of the world into existence.

Critical food systems education has the capacity to shape the future of more than the 17 de Abril settlement, MST, and small-scale farming in the Amazon; it has the potential to connect educators, students, and grassroots organizations throughout the Global North, and between the North and South, as part of a broader food sovereignty movement. This potential is grounded in the increasing ubiquity of food systems education courses and initiatives in colleges and universities as well as primary and secondary schools throughout the world. Their rise can be linked to different phenomena, including societies' interest in local foods, concerns with pesticides and genetically modified organisms (GMOs), and the prevalence of nutrition-related chronic disease. Yet many have critiqued certain forms of food systems education, such as garden-based learning, because of its deeply embedded racial and class biases (Flowers and Swan 2012; Rosing 2012; Sumner 2013). As an example, food systems educators frequently teach using the local and a variety of related concepts, such as terroir and the foodshed, as a way of reconnecting students to the food system. White wealthy liberals frequently lead garden-based learning initiatives in the United States, and it is primarily, although certainly not exclusively, children from similar backgrounds who are getting their hands dirty, restricting the transformative potential of these pedagogies. The case of the MST causes us to rethink what Guthman (2008) refers to as the "politics of the possible," or one's perceived repertoire of viable tactics and visions for political-economic and social change. The politics of the possible within traditional food systems education is largely limited to shaping the purchasing choices of future white middle-upper-class consumers (Holt-Gimenez and Shattuck 2011). If, as Isabel told me, "our purpose as educators is to transform the food system," then we need to ask, how can food systems education move away from producing consumer subjects and toward the production of collective agents who are transgressive, using food knowledge and agricultural practice to systematically dismantle the system itself? This book offers valuable lessons about how to advance food sovereignty through education in diverse contexts. It is not just peasant movements that are developing critical forms of food systems education; food justice organizations, such as Detroit's Food Warriors Youth Development Program and Oakland's East Bay Urban Farmer Field School, are advancing educational initiatives that focus on agroecological skills, community building, and leadership development (Meek et al. 2017). By paying close attention to how Isabel and other movement educators build partnerships within the federal university system, gain access to funding for movement courses, and direct student research toward movement needs, we can collectively reimagine the politics of the possible for food systems education.

Based upon Isabel's portrait, it might seem that the politics of the possible is quite bleak both in the 17 de Abril and for the movement at large. Throughout Brazil, critics pronounce the MST a failure when its smallholder farmers are found producing with chemical fertilizers, not waving the movement's flag, or attending schools outside their communities. From that critical perspective, there is perhaps little value in studying education or agriculture within the MST. Yet I hold the opposite view. These apparent contradictions—and they are recognized as such by those within the MST—provide in themselves the rationale for careful study, as these experiences are pedagogical (Tarlau 2015). Drawing upon sociologist Erik Olin Wright, the MST's agroecological education experiments are worthy of analysis as "real utopias." The concept of a real utopia appears to be an inherent contradiction, as utopias are fantastical imaginaries built on social and political ideals, existing outside of the confines of economic constraints. Yet spaces such as the movement's encampments and settlements are where the MST's members forge new types of social relations; they are where activists "envision the counters of an alternative social world that embodies emancipatory ideals" (Wright 2013: 9). These spaces in many ways represent "practical experiments in new forms of life" in which "there is a real sense of subversive energy, freedom and possibility" (Free Association 2011: 33). While these utopias are far from perfect, they are real. By studying the struggles and victories of the 17 de Abril's residents, we gain novel insight into how the MST is advancing a new vision of society based in cooperative relations and new forms of social organization and production.

Theorizing the Intersection of Politics, Ecology, and Education

Isabel's narrative highlighted the transformative potential of critical food systems education for the future of the 17 de Abril, the MST, and small-scale farming in the Amazon. Here I expand on her perspective to describe the theoretical framework I use to make sense of how politics, economics, and ecology shape critical food systems education in the MST.

The politics of knowledge are pivotal to understanding Isabel's original question: "why we are no longer producing food." As Goldman and colleagues (2011) define them, the politics of knowledge are the processes involved in the production, circulation, and application of knowledge. Central to these processes are questions of how political economy—both at a large scale in terms of national visions of agricultural modernization, but also at a smaller scale in the form of specific agricultural credit initiatives—capitalizes the production of particular forms of knowledge, agricultural practices, and the environment itself.

The politics of knowledge have long been at the core of political ecology. For example, as Roderick Neumann argues in the opening to the now-classic work *Making Political Ecology*, "The environment and how we acquire, disseminate, and legitimate knowledge about it are highly politicized, reflective of relations of power, and contested" (2005: 1).[4] Yet despite this focus on the politics of knowledge in political ecology, the role of education in forging and disseminating this knowledge has, rather paradoxically, remained largely underexplored from within this interdisciplinary subfield.[5]

In this book I develop a perspective I refer to as *the political ecology of education* to shed light on how political economy, education, and the environment intersect to mediate agrarian change in the 17 de Abril settlement. This perspective draws upon three basic definitions of traditional political ecology and applies them to an analysis of how education shapes conceptions of nature, agricultural practices, and control over natural resources.

First, Greenberg and Park (1994, 6), in their seminal article in the *Journal of Political Ecology*, characterize political ecology as a synthesis "of political economy, with its insistence on the need to link the distribution of power with productive activity and ecological analysis with its broader vision of bio-environmental relationships." Drawing upon this definition, I offer a fresh analysis of how particular funding mandates, and the policies that promote them, either differentially enable or preclude particular pedagogical practices and the effects of these on the diffusion of particular conceptions of nature and productive activities.

Second, Stott and Sullivan's (2000: 5) conception of political ecology emphasizes the need to deconstruct "particular narratives to suggest that accepted ideas of degradation and deterioration may not be simple linear trends that tend to predominate." I employ their conception in two ways. Development programs, I will subsequently show, promote particular types of knowledge and associated agricultural practices, which ultimately result in environmental degradation, at the expense of other forms of environmental knowledge that might promote sustainability. Second, I draw upon this work to analyze how education can provide students with skills in critical readings of landscapes, empowering them to question histories of landscape change and their role within those narratives (Gruenewald 2003).

Third, Hempel (1996: 150), in a sweeping study of environmental governance, defines political ecology as "the study of interdependence among political units and of interrelationships between political units and their environment." Political institutions are understood broadly in this context as entities of the state, including both public universities and research centers. I apply Hempel's perspective to education, engaging in a close examination of the reciprocal relations between educational units, the political entities that sustain them financially and ideologically, and how particular forms of knowledge surrounding the environment are coproduced.

These traditional definitions and thematic foci provide important elements toward building a political ecology of education. To quickly summarize, these are the importance of political economy (Greenberg and Park 1994), the relations between political circumstances and environmental degradation (Stott and Sullivan 2000), and the interconnections among political institutions (Hempel 1996). Building upon these various aspects, I describe a political ecology of education herein as one attuned to how the distribution of power and resources among interconnected political and cultural entities mediates pedagogical processes—from tacit to formal learning—affecting access and control to natural resources, interactions with the cultural landscape, and conceptions of nature-society relationships.

This framework is not simply a move of esoteric theoretical self-positioning but rather one I developed as agroecologists and critical agrarian scholars are increasingly turning to education as a mechanism to scale up agroecology. Beyond the academy, La Vía Campesina emphasizes the internal importance of education as a process of collective organization, critical consciousness raising, and technical skill development (La Vía Campesina 2017). Reflecting on how education contributes to political mobilization, McCune and Sánchez (2019: 595) ask "what human, political, and technical qualities our cadre needs in order to (collectively) take agroecology to scale?" Drawing upon the political ecology of education perspective informs this critical question in three ways. First, it shows that students require an understanding of the linkages between political economy and the scaling of agroecological education. As I detail in chapters 5 and 6, knowing how to negotiate governmental policies and credit initiatives can enable the scaling up of educational initiatives, such as novel degree programs and access to financial packages to support agroecological transitions. Second, it demonstrates that students must understand how the ecological history of the landscape can structure their efforts to implement these agroecological lessons. In chapter 2, I synthesize remote sensing analyses with ethnographic accounts to explore how spatialized histories of state-driven land exploitation beginning in the 1960s continue to provide obstacles to MST students actualizing their agroecological vision. Third, thinking with this framework suggests that students must develop a capacity to negotiate cultural politics, or advancing agroecology may be disregarded as an imposition. In chapters 2 and 7, I draw upon this framework to explore how histories of extension failures have jaded settlement residents to the point where agroecology is seen as an external mandate rather than a grassroots vision. Beyond the 17 de Abril, the political ecology of education provides agroecologists, critical agrarian scholars, and movements a concrete way to analyze how the distribution of power and resources influences agroecological education and the policies and politics through which it can advance food sovereignty.

Isabel's narrative brought up thorny questions surrounding the constraints facing ongoing political mobilization, the depopulation of the countryside, and the contradictory role of education in peasant societies. To begin addressing these questions, I next synthesize insights from this framework with those from agrarian, postcolonial, and Gramscian studies. Taken together, this synthetic theoretical perspective provides the lenses necessary to analyze the ethnographic data and understand the possibilities and pitfalls of critical food systems education in the 17 de Abril.

Agroecological Education and the Agrarian Question

The 17 de Abril's residents are constantly grappling with a fundamental tension: does one stay working on the land or abandon it and move to a nearby urban center?[6] This question plagues not only those living in the 17 de Abril settlement but peasants throughout the world. Scholars refer to this as the "agrarian question" and have actively debated it for more than a century.[7] This book contributes to the debate by analyzing the role of education in both depeasantization and repeasantization—two processes intertwined with the agrarian question. Depeasantization consists of smallholders abandoning rural livelihoods and migrating to urban centers (Araghi 1995). Repeasantization, by contrast, involves smallholders becoming more autonomous and in turn more peasantlike by employing agroecological practices, including diversifying their farming, reducing off-farm inputs, and creating feedback loops between different forms of production (Van der Ploeg 2012).

Education, I learned through this research, is a force that can propel both depeasantization and repeasantization. Conventional forms of state-designed education denigrate rural areas and cultural traditions while simultaneously valorizing urban ones, weakening connections between the peasantry and the land. Yet one of the most surprising realizations of this research was that education need not destabilize rural society, provided that it is thoughtfully constructed; critical food systems education can valorize peasants' relations to the land. Education matters to understanding the agrarian question in southeastern Pará because it is tied to both the death and the rebirth of the peasantry. I argue that Isabel and other educators are advancing repeasantization through critical food systems education. In this corner of the Amazon, MST educators like Isabel train rural students to critically deconstruct the taken-for-granted assumption that farming is an unviable livelihood. They also help their students develop new relationships to the land, emphasizing the importance of agroecological practices and cooperative forms of production. Agroecological education in the 17 de Abril settlement, as well other educational sites throughout the region, shapes the future of contemporary peasants, a group that is not a relic of the past but rather fluid and, importantly, expanding.

Decolonization and the Politics of Agroecological Education

The connections between decolonization, education, and agroecology are at the core of this book. I argue that decolonization is necessary to create an education system that advances agroecology, peasant culture, and sustainable livelihoods. Herein I define decolonization as a material and epistemological process through which historically marginalized groups deconstruct colonial systems of knowledge and land access and management and rebuild sovereignty over knowing, being, and engaging with the natural world. I base this definition upon my reading of the broader "decolonial turn," which is not a single theoretical school, social movement, or identity group but rather a constellation of views that understand coloniality as an ongoing problem in the modern era and decolonization and decoloniality as unfinished processes (Mignolo 2009; Maldonado-Torres 2011; Ndlovuu-Gatsheni 2015).[8] More specifically, my analysis of decolonization is explicitly grounded in an extensive corpus of scholarship that has and continues to emerge through the modernity/coloniality/decoloniality project (Pérez 1999; Escobar 2010; Mignolo and Walsh 2018). This largely Latin American initiative argues that non-Eurocentric forms of knowing and being, emanating from indigenous, peasant, and other groups on the periphery, are powerful alternatives to the ecologically destructive forces of colonial modernity.

My usage of decolonization is both similar to and different from many indigenous perspectives (Alfred 2009). For various indigenous groups and critical scholars, decolonization centers upon deconstructing colonial ideologies, which hold that Western knowledges and understandings of history are unassailable (Tuhiwai Smith 2012). Decolonization from this vantage requires dismantling the colonial social and psychological structures and discourses that are embedded in the mind (Fanon 1967), and continue to preclude indigenous sovereignty. Yet decolonization from this perspective does much more than deconstruct; it is a culturally grounded process of valorizing traditional knowledge systems, practices, and ways of being (Pirbhai-Illich et al. 2017). To decolonize necessitates we reexamine our basic understandings of history and knowledge, asking epistemological questions about how we arrived at such knowledge and doing the difficult work of changing the misconceptions, prejudice, and assumptions surrounding indigenous peoples (Tuhiwai Smith 2012). My usage differs from that of Tuck and Yang (2012: 1): "Decolonization brings about the repatriation of indigenous land and life; it is not a metaphor for other things we want to do to improve our societies and schools." They argue that social justice advocates, despite their best intentions, mobilize the concept as a metaphor and that white, immigrant, postcolonial, and other oppressed peoples inadvertently advance settler colonialism by framing their struggles around decolonization. From this perspective, decolonization is an explicitly indigenous-led process directed towards the repatriation of native lands, the dissolution of colonial social and psychological structures of oppression, and the creation of spaces within which indigenous groups can prefigure sovereign futures.

Critical scholars and indigenous groups will likely argue—and perhaps correctly so—that it is an inherent contradiction to describe a movement—such as the MST—as advancing decolonization, when it itself is engaged in the explicit colonization of land. While the territories occupied by MST activists are former *fazendas* and not currently inhabited by indigenous groups, much of the land that the movement has won through struggle was unquestionably indigenous territory in recent history. Similarly, the ways in which the MST frames its struggle, ranging from narratives of "land for those who will work it" to the symbolism of its flag, which shows a white male and a white female farmer with their left fists in the air, contributes to the invisibilizing of indigenous land rights and struggles. The MST's arguments about the concentration of land and the need for its redistribution obfuscate both those histories of indigenous dispossession, but also the origins of that land, which was and is indigenous. MST members, who in my research proudly described themselves as "pioneers" on a "frontier" (terms that would be highly problematic for many indigenous groups), can be seen as engaged in settler colonialism; their intention is to build permanent lives on these new territories, engaging in a process of home and place remaking that is predicated upon settler sovereignty (Tuck and Yang 2012; Grande 2015). In this context, agrarian reform movements, regardless of their politics, may not be considered by some as engaged in decolonization because their ultimate end is not the repatriation of indigenous land, but rather the furthering of settler colonialism (Snelgrove et al. 2014).

These are undoubtedly messy contradictions, but ultimately I believe that they are productive ones for both critical scholars and movements of diverse orientations. Rather than "domesticating decolonization" (Tuck and Yang 2012: 3), I believe that my usage of the concept will help more fully actualize indigenous groups' transformative vision by helping restructure a discussion of the "politics of the possible," or the perceived repertoire of forms of political change individuals think of as actual possibilities (Guthman 2011). Analyzing the interconnections between the decolonization of land and knowledge within the MST does the work of opening the doors within the movement itself to thorny debates concerning the radical potential of indigenous-peasant coalitions for structural agrarian reform (Gaztambide-Fernández 2012).

We can contribute to such a broader project of solidarity by recognizing that decolonization is a shared struggle among indigenous and peasant movements. These diverse groups are united around the need to restructure material and subjective relations to land, to deconstruct the social and psychological structures of colonialism, and to bring new visions of modernity into existence. Land for many indigenous groups, as well as nonindigenous peasants, has ontological primacy. It is an assemblage of relations of obligations and identity; land mediates how individuals understand their subjectivities and engage with others and the natural world in nondominating and nonexploitative relations. If decolonial struggles are united in their broad relation to land, then they are also unified in their commitment to transforming the "colonial relation," which consists of cumulative manifestations of interlocking axes of oppression, such as patriarchy, white supremacy, heteronormativity, and totalizing understandings of state power (Coulthard 2014). The object of transformation for both indigenous and peasant movements is the colonial relation, a scaling out that emphasizes a background context of similar structural relations of oppression. Lastly, indigenous and peasant movements share a drive to dismantle the legacy of colonialism on the mind (Fanon 1967). Colonialism created psychological structures of prejudice and self-negation, which colonized peoples throughout the world have long internalized. Decolonizing the mind requires epistemically delinking from modernity and the assumed primacy of Eurocentric knowledge and simultaneously epistemically reconnecting with subaltern forms of knowledge as a process of developing alternative futures in the present (Quijano 2007; Mignolo and Walsh 2018).

Schools are a central location to explore how decolonization can advance such a visionary political and ecological project. Educational institutions have historically served as a colonizing force, controlling "what knowledge-making is allowed, disavowed, devalued or celebrated" (Mignolo 2009: 176). Schools and universities have functioned as instruments of colonialism because they train individuals who will be epistemologically obedient. Yet my research shows that schools and other spaces of learning can also serve as powerful decolonizing instruments, challenging assumptions of agricultural modernization and singular conceptions of what constitutes scientific knowledge. The various educational institutions that I analyze in this book are all spaces of epistemic disobedience. They valorize peasant systems of agrarian knowledge and practice, training students to delink from the "magic of the Western idea of modernity, ideals of humanity and promises of economic growth and financial prosperity" (Mignolo 2009: 161). I believe that teaching about agroecology, studying agroecology, discussing agroecology with one's family, practicing agroecology on one's land all constitute epistemic disobedience because these are processes of liberating what critical scholar and activist Vandana Shiva (1993) aptly terms the "monoculture of the mind." Shiva's phrasing is powerfully symbolic; it highlights how Western modernity is colonized by a homogenous epistemology in which only particular Western conceptions of empirical knowledge exist but also importantly that landscapes defined by monoculture are a product of this singular mentality. One of the major lessons I learned in my research is that decolonization is not just a process of transforming the relations of knowledge production in schools but also a much broader project of transforming dominant conceptions of livelihoods and landscapes.

Education, Hegemony, and Emerging Conceptions of the World

The diverse writings of early twentieth-century Italian political theorist Antonio Gramsci provide a lens through which to analyze how different ways of comprehending and inhabiting the world come into being, how they persist, and how might they be transformed (Crehan 2002: 72).[9] The MST's agroecological imaginary—characterized by cooperative values, agricultural diversification, and social justice—is what Gramsci would term a "conception of the world," a practical way of understanding, living in, and transforming society.[10] Hegemonic forms of "common sense" that normalize and perpetuate existing systems of production constrain the advance of this novel conception of the world. But how does one unlearn common sense to advance emerging conceptions of the world? For Isabel, MST state leaders, and Gramsci, the answer must involve education.[11]

Education is a key element of both hegemony as well as how alternative social systems can come to power.[12] Schools are not neutral; they serve an explicitly political and economic function by supporting the powerful groups in society and their hegemonic systems of production. Alternative forms of education—attentive to the needs of and controlled by subaltern populations—are both for the MST and for Gramsci of the utmost importance in the struggle for transforming common sense.

In this section, I have highlighted how critical food systems education can slow the depopulation of the countryside and contribute to repeasantization. For this to occur, knowledge must be decolonized and common sense transformed. In the next section I introduce the MST, highlighting why its struggles over land and knowledge are interconnected. I show that the MST's critical food systems education initiatives arose out of its shift in the 1990s toward agroecology and role in creating a national education reform movement, which has proved instrumental in accessing financing for the movement's courses.

The Dual Struggles over Land and Knowledge

In 2003, six hundred MST activists occupied a Monsanto experimental agricultural farm in Ponta Grossa, Paraná, Brazil, destroying transgenic plots. These MST members set up an encampment and held their occupation of this Monsanto site for one year. In May 2004, they rechristened the seized Monsanto territory the Chico Mendes Center for Agroecology and began engaging in agroecological education. These interrelated actions—the occupation and subsequent transformation of territory into an education center—illustrate how the struggles over land and knowledge are interconnected for the MST.

Both land and education have historically been concentrated in the hands of Brazil's ruling class. The country has one of the highest concentrations of property ownership in the world, with a Gini coefficient of land distribution at 0.872 (IBGE 2006).[13] While this level of inequity stems from colonial land grants and nineteenth-century land laws (Hall 1990), contemporary neoliberal agroindustrial policies and development projects have perpetuated it (Hecht 1993; Green 2003; Wolford 2005). Similar to the historically inequitable distribution of land is the geographic disparity in education provision (Plank 1996). Public financing of education in Brazil has been directed toward wealthy urban centers. This dynamic is particularly evident in intraregional analyses, which highlight that rural municipalities in the country's impoverished North and Northeast historically receive a sixth of the resources as those in the urban South (Gadotti 1992). The Brazilian ruling class has long governed both land and education toward a dual set of aims: maintaining a consolidated agrarian structure and an education system that explicitly valorizes urban areas. The consolidation of land and knowledge has been part of a larger state project of defining who has power and access to rights within society.

Since Brazil's founding constitution of 1824, social differences surrounding access to land and knowledge have been core defining elements of what it means to be a political citizen in Brazil. While the 1824 constitution guaranteed citizenship to all free-born residents, irrespective of race and religion, rights have never been equitable. Rather, access to land and power have historically intersected to structure active participation in the electoral process. The first republican constitution (1891) employed gender and literacy as constraints to limit political citizenship to educated male residents, structuring inequality by denying the inclusion of nonwhites and women, who are national citizens, in the political process (Holston 2011: 341).

The resulting political system is defined by differentiated citizenship whereby social differences—such as education, gender, ownership of land—that do not structure national membership are used to distribute disparate resources and rights to different groups of citizens (Holston 2011: 341). This legalized system of structural inequality—which is grounded upon unequal access to both land and education—was slowly transformed in certain spaces through civil society forces during the twentieth century. The 1964 land law created a right to land for the rural landless, setting up a redistributive land reform program. In 1988, the revised constitution, which had been drafted by a diverse constellation of social movements and activists, placed an emphasis on the educational rights of the illiterate citizenry—from school-age children through adults. Beyond being simply responsible for providing basic education in line with global dictates, the state became tasked with offering education that supports the country's immense sociocultural diversity. Pushing the state to fulfill its responsibility to redistribute unused agricultural land and ensure culturally relevant education would become one of the defining struggles for emerging grassroots social movements.

The MST is an agrarian social movement that is composed of marginalized peasants who became politically mobilized out of a desire for agricultural land. MST members first identify unused agricultural land and then pressure the government to expropriate it by squatting and forming encampments (Wolford 2010). If these MST members are successful, the government will create an agrarian reform settlement. This tactic of squatting has historically worked fairly well for the MST's members, as the Brazilian constitution states that land must have a social value.

The movement's origination is frequently explained as related to three factors. First, there was a common social grievance for land. Landless workers shared a common experience of marginalization, and this collective grievance structured their objectives, tactics, and strategies. Second, various organizations, particularly those involved with the Catholic Church, provided institutional resources (McCarthy and Zald 1977; Jenkins 1983). During Brazil's repressive military dictatorship, the Catholic Church provided meeting spaces to agrarian activists, spaces from which the movement would begin emerging. Third, a political opportunity for mobilization opened alongside the fall of the Brazilian dictatorship (Tarrow 1998). As the regime began to crumble, spaces and moments opened up where nascent movements could engage in public actions.[14] While this "genesis story" explains many macro-level processes, Wolford (2004) argues it is not attuned to the complex politics of place and does not account for important questions, such as who joined the movement and what were their motivations. Through multisited ethnographic research in the country's South and Northeast, Wolford found that rationales for resistance were grounded in "spatial imaginaries," or particular understandings of space, such as notions of private property, that shape social life.

Although the MST originated in the early 1980s, it was not until the 1990s that it began to "green" itself by beginning to debate agroecology as a political and practical set of strategies. This greening was tactical. The MST had historically pressured the Brazilian government to expropriate land for peasant use, employing the argument that the lands were being "unused." However, increasing transnational investment in Brazilian agriculture in the 1990s resulted in a large percentage of Brazil's idle land being converted to agrofuel monocrop plantations (McMichael 2010; Novo et al. 2010). According to Rosset and Martinez-Torres (2012: 6), the MST, in turn, reframed their argument "by contrasting the ecological and social wasteland of agribusiness plantations ('green deserts') with a pastoral vision of agroecologically farmed peasant lands, conserving biodiversity, keeping families in the countryside, and producing healthy food for local markets ('food sovereignty')." Agroecology's importance continued to grow within the MST throughout the 1990s, as MST groups across the country debated how it could be used to advance food sovereignty and serve as a strategy of resistance to the agroindustrial model.[15] At the MST's 2005 national congress, eleven thousand members formally ratified agroecology as the movement's foundation for small-scale farming (Altieri and Toledo 2011). Since then, the MST has utilized critical forms of food systems education to advance agroecology throughout the country.

The MST has long prioritized education—both within the formal education system as well as through its own nonformal leadership courses—for ideological and practical reasons. Caldart (2006) identifies three reasons why the MST advocates education as a practical means toward social transformation. First, education helps landless families recover dignity and a sense of purpose. Second, education enables the construction of a collective movement identity. Third, the MST uses education to train its activists in the political ideals and agroecological practices of the movement. The MST's approach to education is informed by Brazilian pedagogue Paulo Freire's critical pedagogy (1973). Two Freirean principles that ground the MST's pedagogy are conscientization and praxis. Conscientization refers to learning to perceive social, economic, and political contradictions and to take action against that oppression. Praxis is the action and reflection on the world in order to change it. One way the MST emphasizes the links between conscientization and praxis is that school curricula should arise organically out of, and deal explicitly with, the problems that students identify in their settlements.

The MST has a complicated relationship with the state in terms of education provision. Although the MST sees education as the responsibility of the state, it believes that education within settlements should incorporate the movement's ideals and principles. At the site of a land occupation, known as an encampment, MST members will frequently build a temporary school as one of the first structures (Camini 2009). These early schools are important locations for movement organizing and frequently are sites where MST-oriented pedagogy is quite strong. If the movement is successful in pressuring the government to create a settlement, education will become more formalized as the state builds a municipal school. Yet over time the movement's presence within the school frequently begins to dissipate. The reasons for this are varied. Sometimes educators stop participating in the movement and as a result are reluctant to include MST pedagogical methods and subjects within their classes. Similarly, the inclusion of state and corporate curricula that are not attuned to rural realities frequently complicates the MST's presence in the school.

The MST addresses this lack of culturally relevant curricula through its vocal position in an umbrella movement for education reform known as Educação do Campo. This phrase can be translated as "Education of the Countryside" (Tarlau 2015), but its meaning is broader, signifying a system of education developed by and relevant to the everyday realities of those in the countryside. The Educação do Campo movement is a movement of movements, "defined by its demands for quality and free education from infancy through university, and the construction of a distinctly rural school that is guided by a vision of rural development, which is based in social justice, agricultural cooperation, environmental respect, and the valuing of rural culture" (Munarim 2008: 61). The movement comprises the MST, the Movement of Those Affected by Dams, Movement of Rural Women, Movement of Small Farmers, and syndicates linked to the Confederation of Agricultural Workers, as well as various local and regional NGOs and other civil society organizations.[16] The Educação do Campo movement is a major force in shaping rural education opportunities for agrarian reform settlement inhabitants. It has helped create a new emphasis within Brazilian educational policy and pedagogy toward locally relevant rural education as opposed to homogenous national programs that do not attend to local diversity in geography, culture, and history (Comilo and Brandão 2010; Breitenbach 2011).

Education is part and parcel of the MST's call for ecological and agrarian citizenship. Ecological citizenship sutures environmental concerns, surrounding health and sustainability, to conventional conceptions of citizenship. Here, the liberal emphasis on rights (e.g., the right to a clean water) is combined with a civic emphasis on responsibility (e.g., the responsibility to consume livestock by purchasing ethically raised products) (Wittman 2010: 283). Ecological citizenship can be envisioned as simultaneously an environmental discourse and a normative vision for actions directed toward environmental and social justice. Education, through the struggle for Educação do Campo, becomes a process of advancing both the rights and the responsibilities of ecological citizenship. It is a means of articulating a shift in broader consciousness related to the intersection of the environment and a healthy citizenry. Educação do Campo seeks to connect concerns about the sustainability of the family to the health of the agricultural and ecological systems and—particularly in the present political moment—the civic democracy of the nation. Environmental concerns surrounding access to land are part and parcel of those surrounding equity in education. One way the Educação do Campo movement has pressured the state to fulfill its responsibilities surrounding educational and environmental citizenship is through the National Program for Education in Agrarian Reform (O Programa Nacional de Educação na Reforma Agrária, or PRONERA).

PRONERA, which was launched in 1998, offers funding for institutional partnerships between agrarian social movements and educational organizations (Molina 2003). PRONERA provides financial support for the education of movement members at levels ranging from basic literacy to graduate studies. Over nearly two decades, PRONERA has enabled thousands of rural youth and adults to attain basic literacy training, high school diplomas, university degrees, and professional certificates in a wide range of subjects—from law to geography, medicine, and agroecology (Silva et al. 2011). I pay particularly close attention to PRONERA throughout this book as an example of how political economy mediates educational opportunities, environmental knowledge, and relations to place.

The example of the Monsanto occupation and this brief introduction to the MST illustrate how agrarian reform and critical forms of food systems education are intricately connected. By ripping out an experimental GMO plot—established to advance forms of knowledge linked to agricultural modernization—and replacing it with an agroecological education center, the MST demonstrates that it is not exclusively engaged in the "battle over land per se, but also very much in a battle over ideas" (Rosset and Martinez-Torres 2012). Perhaps nowhere in Brazil is the contest over these interrelated resources as vaulted as in Amazônia. I now draw upon the political ecology of education perspective to disentangle the historical trajectory of the MST in the Amazon, demonstrating that the conflict over land that gave birth to the 17 de Abril settlement is intertwined with the development of critical food systems education opportunities throughout the country.

Coming to the Amazon

Over the last fifty years, southeastern Pará has been defined by interrelated waves of political, economic, ecological, and educational change (Foweraker 1981; Hecht and Cockburn 1989; Schmink and Wood 1991; Brown and Purcell 2005). A major drought in the Northeast of Brazil during the late 1960s proved to be a turning point for Amazonian development policies (Mahar 1979). Brazilian president Medici visited the Northeast's drought-affected areas, proclaiming that the country would "take a people without land to a land without people," a declaration that led to the first National Integration Plan (Plano de Integração National, or PIN). The PIN sought to develop, exploit, and settle the Amazonian region, which the government felt was impeding the country's development because of its alleged unproductivity (Lisansky 1990: 9). Two principal aspects of this plan were the commencement of a large-scale road network across Amazônia, starting with the Transamazônica Highway, and a large-scale colonization plan not unlike the westward expansion of the early United States. The government intended to resettle thousands of northeastern landless farmers on either side of the highway through these two projects (Moran 2019). Colonization was the government's attempt to circumvent the land problem, moving the landless to Amazônia and leaving larger property structures intact (Almeida 1992).

The MST was a latecomer to agrarian reform in Amazônia. Whereas state-led agrarian reform has been occurring there since the 1970s, it was not until the early 1990s that the MST began mobilizing in the state of Pará. One reason for this delay was that the MST wanted the government to conduct agrarian reform throughout the country, not simply using Amazônia as a sink for migration (Wright and Wolford 2003). However, the MST began mobilizing in southeastern Pará in the early 1990s in part because of widespread social grievances of marginalized mine workers.[17]

The early 1980s were a boom period in southeastern Pará. Migrants flocked from Brazil's Northeast to work in the Carajás mine, which would soon become the largest iron ore mine in the world. Many of 17 de Abril's founders narrated similar histories.[18] They first came to Pará from the northeastern state of Maranhão to work in the mine. However, they found the working conditions perilous and left the mine, moving to nearby urban centers.

During the early 1990s, the MST began to organize these *garimperos* and other marginalized workers. All of the pioneers I spoke with recounted an identical story of entering the movement: they remember MST state leaders driving a car with loudspeakers on the roof around these frontier cities, announcing that the poor should occupy unused land because it was their right. These marginalized individuals were not seasoned activists nor particularly familiar with the MST, its ideology, or its broader vision of agrarian reform. They simply wanted a piece of land to work and a decent life. The MST's call for "land for those who will work it" resonated with them. Thousands of individuals signed an official ledger, indicating their desire to enter the struggle for land. They established an encampment on the outskirts of Curionópolis and unknowingly became subjects in what would become one of Brazil's most historic land conflicts.

The drama began unfolding when the MST state leaders delivered a petition to the National Institute of Colonization and Agrarian Reform (INCRA), arguing that the state should expropriate an unproductive fazenda (farm) in the municipality of Eldorado dos Carajás known as Fazenda Macaxeira and use the land to create an agrarian reform settlement. INCRA denied that this fazenda was unproductive and offered to settle those encamped in another existing settlement project. Yet the MST was discontent with this offer, and on April 15, 1996, MST activists began the 685-kilometer march to the state capital in protest. On April 16 the group reached the city of Eldorado dos Carajás and blockaded highway PA-150 at a sharp bend in the road, known locally as the S-curve. A spokesperson from INCRA arrived and brokered a deal whereby the MST would reopen the highway in exchange for transportation to Marabá, where they could discuss their demands with INCRA's superintendent. However, when the MST learned the next day (April 17) that INCRA had no intention of providing transportation or engaging in dialogue, the thousands of activists reoccupied the highway. Several hours later, two battalions of military police arrived, surrounding the roadblock from both directions. Although the exact events that transpired remain disputed, it is clear that the military police opened fire and killed nineteen MST members.[19]

From a political ecology perspective, the massacre of Eldorado do Carajás can be understood as part of a larger pattern of land violence that has come to characterize Amazônia. In Brazil between 1980 and 2003, a total of 1,671 rural landless activists were murdered during land conflicts (Simmons 2005). More than half of these murders occurred in Amazônia, and the overwhelming majority in southeastern Pará (Simmons 2005: 308). This Amazonian "land war" is not just a late twentieth-century phenomenon but can be understood as a regional place-based process with historical antecedents in the War of Canudos (1821), Ronco de Abelha rebellion (1851), Quebra-Quilos rebellion (1874), Contestado rebellion (1912), and various other agrarian conflicts (Simmons 2004). Seen through the lens of resource abundance, these conflicts characterize the region because of a persistent tension between resource abundance and scarcity. The abundance of natural resources, such as rubber and Brazil nuts, fomented rapid settlement. Additionally, the perceived abundance of land in the Amazon in comparison with the concentration of land in other parts of Brazil provided the incentive for a largely landless population to migrate to Amazônia. However, due to inequitable patterns of landownership in the Amazon, in reality land is not abundant but actually scarce because powerful groups hold the land, frequently relying upon fraudulent land titles (Fearnside 2001). From a political ecology perspective, the Amazonian land war is a place-specific process that is at once grounded in conflicting local histories of resource use but also tied to larger-scale processes of land concentration and material transformation that are mediated by political and economic power (Peluso and Watts 2001). The Eldorado dos Carajás massacre played a particularly important role in shaping the political ecology of education at the local, regional, and national scales.

In the aftermath of the massacre, the Brazilian government was under intense domestic and international pressure to increase its pace of creating settlements as well as its public policies for agrarian reform (Vanden 2007). Brazilian social movements seized on this political opportunity. The Educação do Campo movement "hitched a ride" (*carona*) along with the various other political demands the MST was making during the aftermath of the massacre (Tarlau 2015: 1162). At the national scale, for example, it pushed for the development of the PRONERA, which became pivotal in funding many of the degree programs created through partnerships between the MST and federal universities. At a regional scale, following the massacre the MST held massive protests, in which approximately ten thousand people encamped for months at a stretch, on multiple occasions, in front of the regional branch of INCRA (SR-27) in Marabá. These encampments were pivotal spaces where MST members demanded increased educational opportunities—ranging from basic literacy training to graduate programs. More than simply pressuring the state for educational resources, the MST was actively calling for locally relevant education. The massacre plays a pivotal role in how politics, ecology, and education intersect in southeastern Pará. This land conflict, like many others in the Amazon, was fomented by both the ongoing tension between the abundance and scarcity of resources and rapid demographic change associated with the expansion of capital and the extraction of mineral resources. This frontier conflict created a political opportunity, which MST activists were able to harness to make marked multiscalar advancements in their struggle for endogenous education. Exemplifying their success, the MST and its interlocutors have developed a constellation of agroecological education spaces throughout southeastern Pará.

I now turn to introduce the series of educational sites that I focus upon in this book and the methods that I utilized in my research. I begin with a personal vignette, which highlights how the spatial nature of agroecological knowledge production within the MST structured my methodology. Although I began my research intending to focus only on the 17 de Abril settlement, I quickly realized that the production of agroecological knowledge in this settlement is highly interconnected with other educational institutions. I adapted my methods to focus on the material and epistemological relations between these sites, gaining the crucial insights that the MST is bringing an emerging vision of agroecological education to scale and constituting in the process a new knowledge frontier.

Spaces and Methods of Movement

Breakfast this morning is a dinner roll, cup of *farinha* (dried manioc), and incredibly sweet coffee. I stand in line with thirty MST students, shuffling between stations to pick up our meal. We're in the city of Marabá to participate in a critical cartography workshop, learning to map sites of conflict between agribusiness and peasant forms of production. I sip coffee as I stand chatting with Francesca, a professor who is facilitating the workshop.

We discuss the frenetic pace that MST activists face in always traveling to these events. The MST's three-week national leadership school ended last week. Next week, we will all be busy with the MST's National Youth Journey. Francesca muses, "It is a part of the rhythm of the movement to be constantly going to these events." Movement characterizes life within the MST; activists are almost always in motion, traveling to meetings, workshops, actions, and short courses. Frequent movement signals the relation between spaces. In this section I outline the methods I used to explore the interconnections between these spaces.

Multisited research has become increasingly common in contemporary ethnographic scholarship (Marcus 1995; Falzon 2009; Coleman and von Hellermann 2012). At an early stage of my fieldwork I realized that my MST informants were rarely in the 17 de Abril settlement for very long. As activists, they told me that they needed to be "walking with the movement" (*andando com o movimento*), which meant actively participating in its various events. Due to their lives of perpetual movement, it was necessary to accompany these activists as they moved between the MST's various educational spaces. By necessity, my research design became defined by Rocheleau's (2008: 724) methodology of "seeing multiple." I focused on the "kaleidoscope of . . . situations, locations, and experience" that those in the 17 de Abril navigate in their everyday lives. By exploring the material and epistemological relations between this settlement and four other agroecological education sites, I began to uncover how expanding networks of power, political economy, and social struggle produce a frontier of knowledge.

The sites of this research are a series of five agroecological education spaces (fig. 1.4). Having already introduced the 17 de Abril settlement, I now briefly introduce each of the other four sites that appear in this book. The first educational space is the Federal University of South and Southeastern Pará (UNIFESSPA), located in Marabá.[20] Although a federal university, UNIFESSPA has the physical appearance of a hybrid academic-political space. Glittering tile mosaics depicting scenes of political protest with the caption "Never be quiet" adorn the buildings. This ornamentation highlights the ideological and physical presence of social movements within this university. UNIFESSPA is a central space of epistemic disobedience on this knowledge frontier. Many of its courses are grounded in an alternative epistemology that valorizes peasant knowledge, experience, and visions of agroecological production. UNIFESSPA professors have worked together with various social movements to develop undergraduate degree programs in agronomy, history, literature, and pedagogy, as well as graduate certificate programs focused on agroecology. In the chapters that follow, I highlight UNIFESSPA's role in helping to build opportunities at

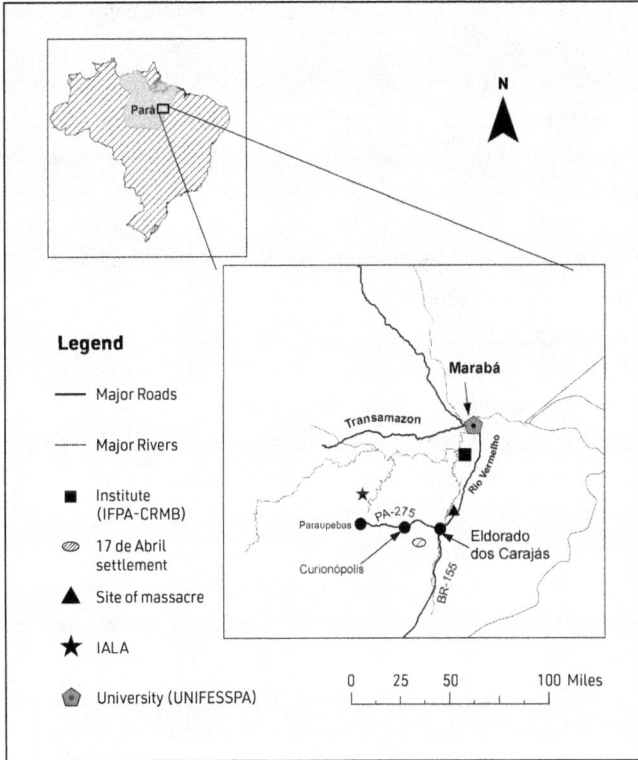

Figure 1.4. Siting agroecological education on the knowledge frontier

a regional scale for agroecological education (chapter 5) and explore the construction of territorial consciousness in its graduate certificate course on the Agrarian Question, Agroecology, and Amazônia (chapter 6). Several educators from the 17 de Abril's municipal school were participating in this certificate course during my research period.

The second site is the Federal Institute of Education, Science, and Technology of Pará–Rural Campus of Marabá (IFPA-CRMB), which is a vocational agricultural high school. It is located on 354 hectares of the MST's 26 de Março settlement, approximately an hour and a half drive from the 17 de Abril settlement. The school offers an agroecological high school program. A cohort of students from the 17 de Abril were doing their high school studies at the IFPA-CRMB during this research. I draw upon the history of the IFPA-CRMB to explore the relationships between the decolonization of land and knowledge (chapters 5 and 6) and the potential for education to structure the future of the peasantry (chapter 7).

The Agroecological Institute of Latin America–Amazônica (Instituto Latino Americano de Agroecologia–Amazônica, or IALA) is the third agroecological education space I focus on. IALA is located in the MST's Palmares II settlement on the outskirts of Paraupebas. IALA is one node in La Vía Campesina's global network of more than forty agroecological training centers.[21] IALA is intended to be a space where agrarian reform inhabitants can participate in formal educa-tion programs at the high school, college, and graduate levels as well as informal courses where rural activists can meet to exchange experiences. During this research IALA was one location where the UNIFESSPA's graduate certificate course on the Agrarian Question, Agroecology, and Amazônia took place. I draw upon the example of IALA to highlight the ways in which universities and social movements co-constitute new forms of political education (chapters 5 and 7).

The fourth and final agroecological educational space is the S-curve in highway PA-150 where the 1996 massacre of Eldorado dos Carajás occurred. Since 2006 this site has been the location of a "pedagogical encampment." Each April hundreds of activists from across the state camp for a week on the sides of this highway. The days are packed with pedagogical activities intended to mold the youth into committed activists. Students wake up at five o'clock and begin singing political songs. They then engage in activities, such as group meal preparation, intended to impart collective values. The rest of the day is filled with seminars that focus on topics such as gender, agroecology, and the nature of agribusiness. The pedagogical encampment itself is interconnected with the three previous critical agroecological education spaces. For example, the entire cohort of seventy-five students from the IFPA-CRMB participates in the week-long encampment, wearing their school uniforms.

These four agroecological education spaces are inherently interconnected. The relations are both material as well as epistemological. Political-economic processes—such as education funding programs like PRONERA—create link-ages between the sites. For example, both the IFPA-CRMB program and the UNIFESSPA graduate certificate course were funded by PRONERA; it was this funding that created material connections between the sites, bringing students from the 17 de Abril to the IFPA-CRMB, UNIFESSPA, and IALA. The politics of knowledge also create tight interconnections between these sites. Professors from UNIFESSPA, teachers from the IFPA-CRMB, and leaders from IALA were all present at the encampment, giving lectures and facilitating workshops. Throughout this book I highlight the material and epistemological relations that connect these spaces and subjects.

Methods in Movement

I recorded the voices, struggles, and visions in this book over a period of seventeen months of ethnographic fieldwork spread over five research periods. I employed a variety of methods to understand the opportunities and constraints toward educating for food sovereignty and how patterns of political participation and landscape change structure students' engagement in these learning opportunities. My primary methods were ethnographic, spatial, and quantitative.

While traveling between the various field sites, I realized that I was encountering the same students, teachers, and professors at diverse MST educational events. I began to grasp that there were important material and epistemological interconnections between the various spaces of agroecological knowledge production in the region, and I turned to ethnographically focus on these linkages. Through interviews with students, teachers, professors, and movement leaders, I gathered data on the role of partnerships between the MST and the state in the creation of courses. Oral histories helped me understand individuals' life trajectories and how, in complicated ways, these mapped on to the region's politics and ecology. I worked extensively with two teachers from the 17 de Abril settlement school who participated as students in UNIFESSPA certificate program at IALA and one student from the 17 de Abril settlement who was participating in the IFPA-CRMB vocational high school program. With each of these three individuals I conducted repeated semistructured interviews that focused on the students' respective learning processes within these two educational programs. These interviews yielded rich data concerning the importance of critical food systems education in the struggle for food sovereignty as well as the constraints of entrenched cattle ranching culture.

Part of the life of the movement is participating in the movement's political meetings, which are a common occurrence in the 17 de Abril. These are pivotal spaces where a dozen or so individuals debate competing visions and strategies for educational and agrarian change. Living in the settlement and being available to attend these extemporaneous meetings, which often lasted late into the night, helped me disentangle the at once political, ecological, and educational struggle behind transforming systems of agricultural production. Being a present observer, one who returned year after year to live in the settlement, also helped me develop the trust necessary to access more intimate moments, such as when MST activists grappled with the contradictions in their broader community and within themselves, which were constraining the movement's struggle.

Returning to conduct research in the settlement over multiple years provided a unique opportunity to gather data on how individuals, institutions,
and landscapes transform. Over the course of seven years, I watched my young
teenage activist friends become parents, learning how they grappled with the
choice of to stay on the land or leave. As politically agnostic school administrators replaced their activist counterparts, I came to understand the ebb and flow
of the movement's presence in the school. Government financing programs
also came and went, shifting land management practices and the contours of
the landscape itself.

I worked closely with multitemporal and multispectral spatial data to
map out these processes of land use and landscape change. I searched for
historic aerial photographs in twelve different archives of conservation, development, mining, and military organizations in Rio de Janeiro, São Paulo,
Belém, and Marabá. Through this archival work, I ultimately uncovered an
aerial photographic map index and associated hard copy aerial photographs
from a late 1960s aerial survey of the Tocantins-Xinguara region.[22] These data
illuminated for me that the process of land conversion to cattle pasture commenced at least thirty years before the MST got access to the land. To expand
this time series, I obtained five cloud-free satellite images from 1985 to 2009
(LANDSAT).[23] I conducted participatory mapping of farmers' land in the 17
de Abril, collecting ground-truthed GPS points from primary and secondary
and forest cover, agroforestry plantings, subsistence agriculture fields, pas-
tures, and recently burned fields. I used these data to develop a classification
guide, extracting the spectral signatures for each respective land cover class.
With this guide I performed a supervised classification on the LANDSAT time
series data. These data highlight that the historical trajectory of land use and
land cover change in the settlement is nearly identical to the larger municipality. I combine these spatial data alongside those from the semistructured
interviews and oral histories, generating a multiscalar and multitemporal
perspective on how political economy and the history of the landscape shape
processes of agrarian change.

Lastly, I sought to provide broader context for the ethnographic data by
conducting a survey of 47 percent of all household heads in the community
($N = 330$). Through this survey, I gathered data on demographics, political
participation, agroecological practices, and education. Five trained research
assistants administered this survey by first dividing the settlement into five
areas of comparable population and then conducting a convenience sample by
going house to house. I present descriptive statistics derived from these data

to buttress ethnographic accounts of agroecology, political participation, and land use practices.

The Politics, Potential, and Pitfalls of Research with the MST

For more than two decades, extensive academic research has been conducted on, alongside, and with Brazil's MST. International and Brazilian scholars external to the movement have engaged in much of this research, shedding light on everything from the spatialized histories of social mobilization to the role of dance and theater in pedagogy and the constraints facing agroecological production (Wolford 2004; Ondetti 2008; Comilo and Brandão 2010; Tarlau 2013). However, the MST has long been concerned with questions surrounding the political and ethical implications of the research process. As Moraes and Witcel (2014: 53)—two activist-scholars from within the MST—note, the question of research brings up the issue of "who is doing research and what is the objective of these researchers? There is no neutrality in research. We believe that research is either done with the intention of contributing to the process that is being studied, or it is done from the position of a different social class. Depending on the ideological point of view of the researcher, the research itself takes a certain tone. It can contribute to the process of struggle, of practice and reflection; it can also provoke concern, indignation, provocation—depending on the intention of the researcher." The MST's concern with the politics of research tracks a broader critical scholarship on the epistemologies, ethics, and methodologies of activist research (Maxey 1999; Bevington and Dixon 2005).

The process of working with the MST has been one of constant self-reflection and negotiation. As a scholar interested in agroecology's capacity to help achieve food sovereignty through advancing cooperative systems of production, I was very conscious about not allowing my political and ideological leanings to lead to proposing particular actions. Moraes and Witcel (2014: 53) once again help to clarify this distinction: "The role of a researcher is not to impose her ideas, to lecture, or to 'bring' consciousness to the movement, or to dictate actions based on what she is most appropriate." My positionality was a source of confusion and debate within the community. For some activists, my ultimate purpose was to help advance community development through bringing projects, literally agricultural credit, into the community. These discussions were challenging in that they called me to question my role within the community and the ways in which I was either engaged or not in advancing its struggles. As Moraes and Witcel (2014: 54) indicate on this dynamic,

> Researchers must interact with the reality they are researching, and their insertion into this reality must be connected to practice. Consciousness and knowledge must be constructed through a process of action and reflection, which must have a connection to real social processes. Capturing the conflicts and contradictions of reality opens the way to ruptures and changes. This is the job of the researcher; to allow herself to be educated by the experience she is living. In truth, what a researcher brings us is a dimension of the everyday life of one particular community, from the perspective of that community's dreams, aspirations, and hopes.

Informed by the MST's vision, my objective was not to "bring development" but rather to help shine light on the "conflicts and contradictions of reality." I sought to give a voice to the settlement's hopes and challenges and ultimately potential methods of transformative social and ecological change by negotiating these educational spaces and research processes alongside emerging MST youth leaders.

The findings of this book will be of no surprise to the community members of the 17 de Abril or the MST's leadership because the research process has been grounded in a process of dialogue. Interview questions and survey instruments were reviewed by activists, and ethical approval of the research protocol was obtained from the University of Georgia and Federal University of Pará prior to conducting field research. In 2009 and 2011 the settlement's president provided written endorsement of the research protocol. In 2015, upon a return visit to the settlement following my extended research period, I discussed research results with the community in an open forum, which was publicly advertised through the community radio and at the vocational agroecological institute where I had conducted research. I met separately with the settlement's governing council as well as the state's MST leaders to discuss the major findings and implications of the research.

Motivated by these research relationships, I have become increasingly involved in thinking about how to advance the movement's objectives. I now serve on the National Coordinating Collective of the Friends of the MST—a solidarity organization that supports the MST—and am a founding member of the Scholars' Collective, which is seeking to develop a protocol for activist scholars interested in working with the MST. All of these moments for increased engagement began with the discussions I had with community members and state MST leaders, who pushed me to think about the politics of engagement in new ways.

Seeing Multiple

The eight chapters of the book are divided into two broad sections, taking seriously Rocheleau's (2008) call to "see multiple." Part I—Conceptions of the World—consists of four chapters and focuses on the 17 de Abril. In chapter 2, I analyze how the relation between the political economy of knowledge and that of land management is a long-standing tension in the 17 de Abril settlement and one of the characteristics of the frontier itself. Through oral histories of several settlement residents, I explore the community's struggle with state-sponsored agricultural projects and how many of these have failed for lack of proper training. In chapter 3, I analyze why the 17 de Abril's school epitomizes the conflict between different forms of knowledge on the frontier and show that these different visions hold serious implications for the future of the movement. The community is undergoing rapid demographic change, and many youth don't identity as Sem Terra or understand the history of the struggle. Educators aspire to foster these youths' political identities by creating learning opportunities centered on the politics of memory. Chapter 4 focuses on youths' difficult choice of "to stay in or to leave" the 17 de Abril settlement. The settlement itself is at crossroads: while some parts of the village are increasingly abandoned, the settlement remains the manifestation of a dream for many—a quiet and safe rural space won through struggle and a space that is part of a broader project of transformation. This chapter analyzes how the settlement's youth make sense of these competing and sometimes complementary visions of development in the 17 de Abril.

The second section—Terrain of Ideologies—focuses on the interconnections between the multiple sites of agroecological knowledge production throughout the region. In chapter 5, I analyze the development of a knowledge frontier in southeastern Pará—from the period of the opening of the southeastern Amazon in the early 1970s to the present day. The objective of this chapter is to depict how a regional movement for Educação do Campo has developed—a movement that provides extensive opportunities for critical training in agroecology. In chapter 6, I examine the porous spatial boundaries between civil society and the state in producing critical agroecological knowledge. This chapter highlights the relational epistemological and material interconnections between the IFPA-CRMB, UNIFESSPA, IALA, and the 17 de Abril school. The interconnections between the informal learning, the politics of knowledge, and the future of the peasantry are the focus of chapter 7, which centers upon the MST's pedagogical encampment. By chapter 8, it might seem that the story of the 17 de Abril is anything but a happy one. Born from Brazil's most violent massacre of landless workers, the settlement's history has by many accounts, including those of its own inhabitants, been a series of failures. Yet for every contradiction there are moments, perhaps even incipient patterns, of resistance. The book concludes with an ethnographic portrait of several "reverse" trends, including development of new encampments by the settlement's youth and their efforts to create cooperatives.

CHAPTER 2

The Struggle on the Land

Coming to the Amazon

"How did you arrive here?" This was a loaded question for those who lived in agrarian reform settlements in the Brazilian Amazon. I never met a native Paraense (one born in the Brazilian state of Pará) among the settlement's founders; rather, all of the *pioneiros* (pioneers) were migrants. As I quickly learned, these stories of migration were textured tales, undergirded by seismic shifts in the region's political economy and ecology.

This chapter focuses on the process through which marginalized individuals in Brazil's Amazon became part of Latin America's most successful social movement, survived one of Brazil's most violent and highly publicized rural massacres, and went on to form the 17 de Abril settlement. However, it's about more than simply the trajectories through which individuals came to found the 17 de Abril agrarian reform settlement of Brazil's Landless Workers' Movement (MST). Rather, it's about the loss of food sovereignty in this community and how structural forces have created both preconditions and obstacles for the MST's agroecological education initiatives. Neither the agroecological or educational objectives of the movement are guaranteed. They are conditioned by the history of failed development initiatives, agricultural subsidies, and demographic shifts associated with migration. This chapter provides an analysis of the political ecology of education in the 17 de Abril. This involves extricating the historical, spatial, social, and environmental factors that structured this community, and how these features constrained the realization of the MST's vision of food sovereignty and its educational initiatives.

As Isabel, a teacher and member of the MST, asked in chapter 1, "Why is it that our movement, our settlement, doesn't have agricultural production?" In this chapter I attempt to answer Isabel's question by exploring how intersecting processes of demographic, political-economic, and ecological changes structured the landscape that the pioneers encountered upon receiving land following the 1996 massacre. This land was not pristine wilderness when the MST's members arrived; it had been used for nearly half a century as cattle pasture, and this constrained these pioneers' land management options. Landscapes, and land use decisions, cannot be seen in a vacuum apart from the confluence of politics and ecology; the hegemony of cattle ranching and the difficulty MST members face in advancing agroecology in its wake need to be understood in the light of broader social and spatial processes that constrained settlement residents' choices. I begin this chapter with a narrative collected from Charlés, a thirty-three-year-old teacher in the Oziel Alves Pereira municipal primary and secondary school, located in the 17 de Abril settlement. Charlés's story is anything but unique; rather, virtually all of the pioneers' oral histories share its central aspects.

When asked how he came to the 17 de Abril settlement, Charlés laughed. "It's a long story, man, wow," pausing for a moment, collecting his thoughts; he continues, "Well, we are all from Piauí [a state in Brazil's Northeast]. We came to Pará during the era of Serra Pelada." Pausing again, Charlés looks me in the eye: "Do you understand?" Charlés's question was about not whether I understood the words but rather their broader historical and political-economic significance. After gathering the necessary clarification, he immediately proceeded to tell me that "this was during that time of the gold fever; there was a huge migration." In January 1979 a child found a six-gram gold nugget while swimming in a small river on a farmer's land in southeastern Pará. The farmer, Genésio Ferreira da Silva, hired a geologist to explore whether the gold nugget was part of a larger deposit. The results were staggering: Silva's land contained one of the largest untapped gold deposits in the world. News of the discovery spread like wildfire throughout Brazil. Within weeks, more than twenty-five thousand miners were sifting through ore by hand, and over the next few years approximately a hundred thousand miners migrated to the southeastern Amazon from areas all throughout the country. Like many of 17 de Abril's pioneers, Charlés's father was one of these miners. Charlés, who would have been only six months old at the time, imagined his father's words upon hearing the news: "He told us: 'We're going to go follow the gold, we're going to go search for gold.'" Charlés slowed down and accented his words, underscoring his father's rationale: "We lived in the interior of Piauí: the land was *dry, poor land*, there was *no way to survive* in the way that we envisioned, and so my father said, 'We're going to go and do this.'"[1]

These migrants did not initially find their envisioned prosperity upon arriving in Pará. Working conditions at the Serra Pelada mine were incredibly difficult. There weren't machines to extract the gold from the ground, and

Charlés's father was one of thousands of recent migrants who were tasked with carrying sacks of ore up perilous bamboo ladders. Brazilian photographer Sebastião Salgado's shocking black-and-white images provide textured insight into migrants' experiences during this period. In one image, a barely clad miner holds one hand to his chest while gripping the barrel of a security guard's automatic weapon with the other. In another, swirling masses of bodies clamor up slick, muddy hillsides with sacks of minerals dangling behind their backs, strung over their foreheads. The trials and tribulations of working in the mine ultimately paid off at least in the short term: Charlés's father earned enough money to buy a small house in the nearby city of Curionópolis. He worked at Serra Pelada during the week and would spend the weekend at home with his family in the small city. Charlés's father, like many of the settlement's founders who worked in the mine during the early 1980s, didn't remain there for long; the work was just too difficult. The physical and mental challenges were frequently recounted to me by the founders of the community. Their descriptions of exhaustion and toil point to the impact of economic exploitation and structural marginalization on the founders' bodies and minds. These experiences were not limited to the mines.

Charlés's father left Serra Pelada to work for a large farmer as a "cat." "And what is a farmer's cat?" Charlés asked me, rhetorically. "A farmer's cat is responsible for an area of ten or maybe fifteen hectares of land, and he is responsible for assembling a crew of men that will deforest that area, burn it, plant crops, like corn, beans and so forth, and when those are harvested, plant pasture. We kept the harvest for ourselves, what they wanted was an area of closed forest transformed into an area of open pasture." Charlés's father and mother lived on the *fazendeiro*'s (large landowner) land, actively involved, if only as cogs, in the transformation of the Amazon from dense forest to cattle pasture.

Charlés and the rest of his brothers and sisters lived in Curionópolis with their grandmother while they attended school. Charlés remembered helping when he wasn't in school, and it was a tiring existence, going to the fazenda, clearing the land, burning vegetation, and planting crops, only to harvest and then plant pasture:

We would wake up at six and have breakfast, a little simple *cuscus*, and then pass the day in the *roça*.[2] My father, my uncles, my grandfather, all of them would work together. They would go and work together deforesting, and we would wait for it to dry, and then all help with the burning. My job would be to go and help collect the limbs that didn't burn the first time, and bring them into a pile, which we would then burn again.

And then we would plant, and I learned to plant in the process. We, my brothers and I, we would do everything: planting, harvesting, and milking cattle, all at seven or eight years old. But this was tiring, working for the fazendeiros, and our family was growing, and my parents were struggling to provide materials for us for school.

Charlés's mother, who by now had two new babies, moved back to Curionópolis to be with the rest of the family. However, the family's situation became only more difficult because their mother was unemployed. Like so many trying to make ends meet, Charlés's family became involved in the informal economy. His mother decided the family would produce and sell homemade popsicles. "I was probably eight years old at the time, and so I would leave for school at seven in the morning. I would be back at eleven, have a quick lunch, and then help my mom out selling popsicles."

As Charlés remembered, it was at this point, in the early 1990s, that a broad debate was emerging about getting access to land. The MST was new to the region, and a neighbor of his family was one of the first MST leaders in the state. As Charlés recalled it, "He [the neighbor] talked to my dad, and my dad wanted to earn a little piece of land, but to do so he needed to give up working for the fazendeiro, and he [Charlés's father] thought, 'How am I going to provide for my family? There's no way I can join the occupation.' And my family's neighbor said, 'Look, we're friends, I'm going to watch your shack in the occupation, and you can spend half the month in the occupation and half working for the fazendeiro to support your family.'" Such arrangements are relatively common in MST settlements even today, despite the fact that they are frowned upon. Family members will often reside at least part of the time in a nearby city, earning money to support the rest of the family that is encamped, during what is often a prolonged period of waiting that usually lasts between five and ten years. This was a very difficult process for various reasons. Partially it was challenging for Charlés's family because they had to survive for a month on their father's income from fifteen days. Charlés and his sister figured out that they could act as representatives for their father at the encampment's daily assemblies, where there was a roll call for which every household head—or their representative—needed to be present. Charlés's plan worked because at this time the encampment was located right on the margins of the city of Curionópolis in a place called Kofaparque, and so it was easy to walk there from Charlés's house. Charlés's father returned to working full-time, and he and his sister sold popsicles during the day, making sure to walk to the encampment by five o'clock in the evening when the leadership did the daily roll call. This was twelve-year-old Charlés's everyday routine.

On April 15, 1996, the encampment divided. One group moved on from Kofaparque to form a new encampment on a piece of land called Formosa, to which a city leader had granted temporary usage. A second contingent began marching toward the state's capitol of Belém to pressure the government to speed up the process of formally giving them the land. A third group remained at the encampment. Two days later, on April 17, nineteen of the MST activists who had left Kofaparque were killed by Brazilian paramilitaries at the S-curve, a sharp bend in highway PA-150—the massacre of Eldorado dos Carajás. Charlés and his parents felt fortunate that they had been among those who remained at the encampment.

The trajectory of Charlés's family is remarkable but completely ordinary among this group. Approximately 70 percent of respondents to a 330-person survey I administered during the research were from the Northeast (44 percent from the state of Maranhão). In addition to a similar geographic point of origin, approximately half of the pioneers had endured structural violence, working under desperate conditions in Serra Pelada's cavernous pit mine and then as sharecroppers transforming Amazônia's ecology and economy. Structural violence can take multiple institutional forms and involve the combination of direct violence, poverty, repression, and alienation. Frontiers, such as the southeastern Amazon, are often characterized by structural violence because these are the zones of expanding capitalism where riches are made and unmade and social histories erased (Tsing 2005). Prior to the founding of the settlement, Charlés's family and the settlement's other pioneers experienced explicit violent repression, psychological threats, forced labor conditions in the mines, and the extreme poverty of living as sharecroppers. Following the massacre, this violence continued but took the form of imposed development projects that ultimately crippled the community and destroyed its food sovereignty.

The injustices perpetrated by paramilitaries during the Eldorado dos Carajás massacre spurred the federal government to first create the 17 de Abril agrarian reform settlement and then several projects to benefit the survivors. The settlement's pioneers describe this as the era of *cala boca* (shut your mouth)— in other words, a time when they needed to accept what was offered to them without protest if they wished to survive in the settlement. Joatá, a pioneer who has long been at the forefront of the movement's politics in the settlement, suspected that these projects were explicitly designed to look great on paper but ultimately fail. He believed that the government used these ill-fated projects to permanently cripple the community and, hopefully, wipe out the movement. Joatá described the state's vision: " 'We'll set up that project, and we'll end up with a project report that looks really good, to present ourselves well to the world and the nation.' They were completely caught up in how they presented themselves as having benefited the families that had been affected by the massacre, that had been massacred, those that had been mutilated."

Under this agenda, the state inaugurated a massive series of interconnected development projects. First, it offered the settlement's association of producers a line of credit through the Special Credit Program for Agrarian Reform (Programa de Crédito Especial para Reforma Agrária, or PROCERA). With major financing through PROCERA, the state constructed a dairy, a *farinha* production facility, a rice processing plant, and a slaughterhouse for poultry and beef within the 17 de Abril settlement. The state's projects exemplified technologically oriented forms of intervention. Such ostensibly simple technical fixes—installing a manioc processing facility—are the hallmarks of a broader vision of development that is top-down and externally defined, negating individuals' and social groups' creativity, cultural traditions, and histories. The state's imposition of these projects was ignorant of local realities.

In 1997, uneven development characterized the municipality in general and the settlement in particular. Joatá contextualized this time and geography, enjoining me to remember that there was virtually no infrastructure to support these new facilities:

> This was an area that didn't have any roads, didn't have electricity, didn't have bridges, and they sent eight big trucks, a processing facility for producing manioc flour at a large scale, rice processing facility, a granary, and all of this was just implanted immediately.
>
> And so the leaders of the movement said, "Well, what are we going to do with this equipment, with no production that's up and running, with no capital to run the equipment or train people to run it, without energy, without roads, what are we going to do with this?"

Unsurprisingly, without resources, training, or infrastructure, without any agricultural products to actually process with the expensive equipment, these projects quickly failed. And with them went the settlement's potential for food sovereignty and that of the movement. The settlement's administrative council fell into insurmountable debt following the failure of these projects. What in 1998 was a loan of 2 million reais now amounts to more than 5 million.[3] Because the settlement's producer association has been unable to pay back the debt, they are prohibited from participating in similar large-scale group credit projects. Structural violence—the imposition of development on a topography of underdevelopment—forever damaged the settlement's capacity for food sovereignty. All that remains from these projects are festering relics of an alternative future. Scattered throughout the village and its outskirts are the concrete shells of these facilities, roofs long ago fallen in, trees growing upward toward the sky (fig. 2.1).[4] Through their spectacular failure, these projects shaped the spatial, social, and environmental formation of the community, constraining the realization of the MST's vision of food sovereignty and ultimately setting the scene for the struggle over its education programming.

In the aftermath of the massacre, the 17 de Abril's inhabitants experienced these development projects as an enduring legacy of structural violence. The imposition of technical projects, which were destined to fail due to lack of infrastructure and training opportunities, destroyed the economic potential of the community and the political capacity of the association. The state's external selection of development projects exemplifies the disregard for local agroecological traditions and knowledge systems that is characteristic of development as a broader political and economic project (Escobar 2010). While

Figure 2.1. Imaginary of development

many of the settlement's inhabitants had previously worked as sharecroppers, my survey results indicate that approximately half of the community's inhabitants have agroecological experience, including seed saving and intercropping. The cala boca project was not a singular force precluding alternative agroecological livelihoods. Various other group and individual credit projects came in quick succession, which played a major role in enshrining cattle ranching as the hegemonic form of land use. All of these projects were similar in that they projected a singular vision of development based around extensive cattle ranching and did not offer an avenue for the communities to utilize its agroecological knowledge or pursue alternative livelihoods. Structural violence, as this discussion shows, is an assemblage: the settlements' inhabitants endured violent repression, forced labor, and extreme state-sponsored poverty. The MST's agroecological vision of food sovereignty is not a given; once the struggle for land is won, the struggle on the land begins. In the 17 de Abril political economy, questions of the use of power and structural violence come together to shape the social and ecological landscape. These factors, key to political ecological analyses of social movement mobilization, resistance, and resource extraction (Robbins 2004), create an overdetermined context, shaping farmers' perceptions of viable livelihood strategies, which geographers term spatial imaginaries. I now turn to explore the characteristics of these imaginaries, their impact on land management decisions, and ultimately the landscape of formal education and informal agroecological learning.

The Persistent Shadow of Space

Spatial imaginaries are conceptions of space that shape social life. They might surround commonly held ideas about how landscapes should be spatially ordered (e.g., monoculture vs. integrated planting systems) or whether cooperative forms of production are seen as intuitive or archaic (Larner 1998; Golubchikov 2010). These are collective models, which are often grounded in historical understandings of past environments and prescriptive visions for future ones. Wendy Wolford (2004), working in Brazil's Northeast, found that the long history of sugarcane cultivation on former plantations, and in the minds and bodies of former sugarcane workers, partially explained the return of MST settlement residents to working sugarcane after experimenting with subsistence agriculture. Building upon Wolford's exploration of spatial imaginaries, I aim in this section to disentangle how long-standing patterns of land use, political-economic processes, and the politics of knowledge combine with previously describe forms of structural violence to shape MST pioneers' spatial imaginaries and ultimately constrain their food sovereignty and ability to actualize the MST's agroecological and education vision. My starting point is the spatial history of the landscape, by which I mean the large-scale spatial and temporal processes of land use and landscape change.

The pioneers of the 17 de Abril did not receive a pristine landscape onto which they could implant an alternative vision of society and agricultural production.[5] Rather, political-economic and social forces had long shaped the landscape of the newly created settlement. Prior to being expropriated by the National Institute of Colonization and Agrarian Reform (INCRA), the land consisted of five gigantic farms, whose names were Mucuripe, Ponta Grossa, Eldorado, Grota verde, and Macaxeira. These five farms composed what was termed the Fazenda Macaxeira complex. Following the massacre, INCRA conducted a survey to determine whether or not the Fazenda Macaxeira complex was "productive." This survey was necessary because Article 186 of the Brazilian constitution states that land that is not productive can be expropriated by the state. INCRA's technicians documented the ecology of the landscape as an open, submontane, broad-leaf rainforest, containing lianas in low-lying areas, a diversity of palm species, and an upper canopy dominated by Brazil nut trees (*Bertholletia excelsa*).[6] Stands of Brazil nut trees are signatures of long-term indigenous land management (Balée 1998). Although indigenous groups are not believed to have occupied the land in recent memory, settlers showed me stone grinding implements and arrowheads they had unearthed on the settlement. Given the contemporary proximity of indigenous territories (largely Kayapó) and the presence of these biotic and material artifacts, it is likely that the landscape has a much longer anthropogenic history.

For years, the landscape of the 17 de Abril confused me. During pilot research, I would often ask farmers while walking their land what the landscape had been like when they arrived. I couldn't make sense of the responses I got. A single farmer would often state that a plot of land was covered by forest but also degraded. How, I wondered, could land be simultaneously forested and degraded? Perplexed, I analyzed longitudinal remotely sensed data. Historic aerial photographs show that by the late 1960s the area of the Fazenda Macaxeira complex was an active frontier, with primary forest already well on its way to being turned into cattle pasture (fig. 2.2). If one removes the gray highlighting I've added to distinguish the deforested areas and digitally zooms in, a runway for airplanes is clearly visible. At this point, there were no roads. Those involved in transforming the landscape were not impoverished peasants but individuals with access to private airplanes. These results are significant because they problematize broader narratives that circulate in Brazilian society that rural peasants were to blame for deforestation. Rather, they show that the process of land conversion to cattle pasture commenced at least thirty years before the massacre of Eldorado dos Carajás, the watershed event that would lead to the creation of the settlement.

With this image as a spatial starting point, I sought to fill in the time series, documenting changes in the landscape between the late 1960s and 1997 when the MST got access to the land (fig. 2.3). When one compares images from 1986 to 1996, a clear trajectory of primary rain forest being converted to cattle pasture is visible. By the time of the settlement's founding, approximately 70 percent had already been deforested.

An analysis of these satellite images also demonstrates that this landscape change took particular forms that, like the airstrip, signal the presence of power and resources. Looking at the 1992 image, one notices straight, well-delineated

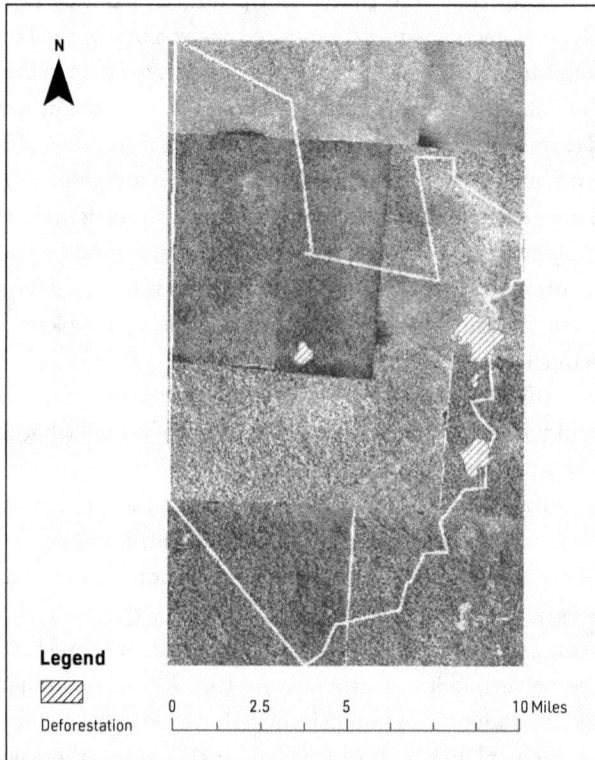

Figure 2.2. Historic aerial photomosaic of the 17 de Abril settlement

cuts through the forest. There is one linear swath that goes north to south, and another broader cut neatly distinguishes the top-left area of the settlement from the center. Linear features such as these are clear signatures of bulldozers and other mechanized forms of land conversion. If small-scale peasants had been responsible for converting the land, one would see a very different spatial pattern of land conversion.

The spatial history of the landscape—particularly the dominance of pasture—structured settlers' original agricultural decisions upon receiving land as well as their contemporary choices. For many readers, "pasture" probably signifies visions of rolling green hills composed of naturally occurring vegetation but in fact refers to a variety of types of grasses that are actively seeded and require active management. *Brachiaria mombaça* is the dominant type of

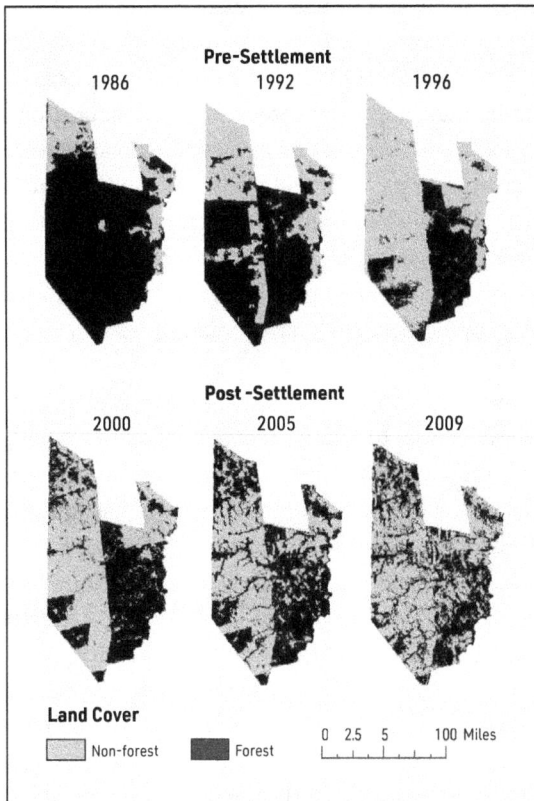

Figure 2.3. Land use and land cover change in the 17 de Abril settlement 1986–2009

pasture grass that fazendeiros have historically planted in this area. This species of grass is planted because it is adaptable to a wide range of climatic and soil conditions. However, *Brachiaria mombaça* demands intensive and regular application of nutrients, specifically phosphorous, which must be provided if the growth of pasture is to continue over the long term. One additional point is noteworthy about the grass: once it is established, it is remarkably difficult to get rid of because of the strength of its roots. It is therefore quite difficult for individuals to engage in subsistence agriculture if the land is already planted with pasture. Those successful in the remarkable labor required to remove pasture are left with soil that is physically compacted, due to the grazing of cattle; depleted of various minerals such as nitrogen, phosphorous, and potassium; and saturated with artificial fertilizers. To undo this degradation and return the soil to a fertile and uncompacted state requires massive, long-term inputs of labor, organic manure, and nutrients such as lime. The bar is thus remarkably high for those who wish to engage in agroecological production, or at least most people in the 17 de Abril have that conception. In actuality, novel agroecological methods emerging out of some of the very educational institutions I explore in this book—such as planting experimental varieties of beans on pasture land—can crowd out pasture while fixing nitrogen in the soil *and* providing food, all with relatively little expenditure and effort. So there is hope that pasture can be overcome, but to do so requires education on specific, relatively unfamiliar (because they are new) techniques of soil remediation about which virtually no one knows unless they have already been exposed to agroecological education.

Critical food systems, through teaching new agroecological techniques, has the emancipatory potential to redress histories of environmental degradation by mitigating soil compaction and the loss of soil fertility. However, education's potential is constrained by the ecological history of the landscape—a history that was politically and economically produced. Drawing upon the political ecology of education, a theoretical framework that brings together analyses of political economy and the politics of knowledge, highlights the very real challenges the settlement's residents face in mobilizing education for food sovereignty.

To fully understand how the spatial history of the landscape constrains food sovereignty, we must peel back further layers of causality to examine, first, political-economic processes that incentivized cattle ranching to the exclusion of other forms of land use and, second, the politics of agricultural knowledge, which are closely tied to agricultural credit programs. I now introduce agricultural extension and then analyze how it functions as a central arena in which the politics of knowledge and economy intersect, reinforcing settlement residents' spatial imaginaries of the landscape as designed for cattle ranching.

Agricultural extension lies at the intersection of the politics of knowledge and visions of agricultural modernization. Agricultural extension is traditionally seen as a process of educating farmers through the dissemination of new knowledge produced through scientific research (Scott 1971; Cash 2001). Yet extension is a central arena in which myriad power relations—between actors as varied as state agencies, extension agents, seed and fertilizer networks, peasants, and activists—are contested (Gray et al. 1997; Morgan and Murdoch 2000). Agricultural extension is a fertile area of inquiry for political ecologists interested in the ways in which education mediates relations to the environment: it combines the circulation of extensive funding streams with the promulgation of particular forms of agronomic knowledge that are intended to pattern land management.

Since its founding, the settlement's landscape has been continually shaped by a combination of financial incentives and technical forms of agronomic knowledge. Beginning at the same time as the cala boca project, credit projects began arriving that helped cement cattle ranching in the pioneers' spatial imaginaries. In 1998 the first extension team offered two PROCERA projects to the inhabitants. The first project provided a stipend for subsistence agriculture of 2,000 reais per family.[7] In 2000 many of the settlement's inhabitants signed up for another credit project known as PRONAF-A (National Program for Family Farming–A Version).[8] This project consisted of 6,500 reais for participating families and enabled the purchase of cattle and ranching infrastructure, such as corrals and fencing.[9] The PRONAF-A project reinforced the historical presence of cattle ranching in the settlement. As Arnoldo, the settlement's president, told me, "One project came, and then another, that only supported cattle. And so the type of land use didn't really change."

Extension is a key factor that drives what type of projects settlers can engage in. Each credit application must be authored and approved by an extension agent. As a result, individuals or cooperatives could access federal credit programs, like PRONAF, but only through the mediation of an extension agent.

Extension, as an act of knowledge dissemination, was essentially nonexistent in the settlement's early development projects. As Genival, an original settlement inhabitant who is now an extension agent, remembered, "These projects had an extension component, in that they were created by technicians. But that was the extent of it. These technicians weren't interested in helping the farmers." Rubbing his fingers together in a gesture to indicate cash, Genival concluded, "These extension agents were solely interested in the financial question, because the extension agents receive a percentage of whatever projects they create, and so what's going to earn you more as a technician: cattle or subsistence agriculture? Cattle, of course, and so the money goes straight into their pockets." Extension, rather than a means of imparting knowledge, functions to direct capital. The codification of cattle ranching as the hegemonic form of land management is unquestionably the result of a complex set of intersecting spatial, political, economic, and cultural processes. Political economy, in the form of agricultural credit, intersected with the politics of agronomic knowledge and the spatial history of land to structure settlement inhabitants' spatial imaginaries around ranching as the appropriate form of land usage.

Scaling out spatially and temporally, there are several important points to note about the trajectory of land conversion in the 17 de Abril. Figure 2.3 highlights changes in land use and land cover change between 1996 and 2009. Comparing longitudinal land cover changes from before the settlement was founded until 2009, it is clear that the settlement's inhabitants continued the already-existing process of land conversion from forest cover to cattle pasture, albeit at a smaller scale. However, there are other spatial trajectories embedded within a landscape. As political ecologists have long shown, remotely sensed data and particular forms of geospatial analysis can often obscure specific forms of land management, such as agroforestry, that occur at a small scale (Fairhead and Leach 1995; Velásquez Runk et al. 2010).

I had spent too much time with too many farmers to believe that there was a unilinear trajectory of land conversion from forest to pasture within the 17 de Abril. Farmers would often take me on walks around their lots in the roça, and invariably we would come to forested areas. Standing in a dense forest, characterized by multiple levels of vegetation and tall trees forming the upper canopy, I was stunned on my first few field visits to learn that the farmers had planted these forests (fig. 2.4). While the presence of cattle vis-à-vis pasture is hegemonic in the settlement, there are other landscapes that exist but are seen as marginal. I was even more surprised at the diversity of plants that were cultivated. From Brazil nut trees to *cacao* to *cupuaçu*, these were highly productive agroforests (fig. 2.5). Having collected GPS points within these forests, I went back to the remotely sensed data and explored other analyses.

Rather than rely on a binary land cover change assessment, I next employed a slightly more sophisticated analysis that enabled me to explore different directions of change. Figure 2.6 highlights the types of land cover change between 1996 and 2009 in the settlement. It illustrates where both primary

Figure 2.4. An invisible landscape?

Figure 2.5. Visualizing a productive landscape

forest cover and pasture remained unchanged as well as where forest was converted to pasture and pasture was converted to forest. Unquestionably, the dominant narrative is evident in these results: 30 percent of forest cover that existed in 1996 had been converted to pasture by 2014. Particularly important to note is that 47 percent of the settlement's area, which was originally pasture when the settlement was founded, remained cleared in 2009. This underscores the extent to which histories of land use structure contemporary land management practices..

However, there is another story embedded in the landscape and in this map. As my experiences told me, the story of 17 de Abril was not one exclusively of the codification of cattle ranching as hegemonic. There were other experiences. As depicted on the map, 9 percent of the land that was pasture at the time of the settlement's founding was forest cover in 2014. This can be seen particularly in the topmost left (and to some extent the right) quadrant of the settlement. This forest regeneration is largely taking place alongside the edge of streams.

Why is agroforestry so limited in 17 de Abril? Perhaps unsurprisingly, the cultural politics and economics of extension are a major factor. In 2002 the MST developed its own cooperative extension service to meet the needs of its agrarian reform settlements. This organization was known as COOMARSP and included MST state leaders on its coordinating council.[10] COOMARSP had a different vision of land use within the settlement. As Luis, a former COOMARSP extension agent, told me, "In the beginning, we had a vision of diversification. We sought to achieve this vision of diversification by creating PRONAF projects devoted to agroforestry: plantings of coffee, cupuaçu (*Theobroma grandiflorum*), and coconut."[11] COOMARSP was much more in line with the MST's national vision of diversified agriculture and opposed to the dominant model that was being extended through previous credit initiatives. "However," Luis continued, "in reality, approximately 70 percent of the projects that we created at that time were for cattle. And why is that? Because it's what works. Because you put cattle on the land, and they thrive. They don't have problems, they feed when they're hungry, go to the reservoir when they're thirsty." However, the problem with diversification also had a cultural basis in financial insecurity. As Luis explained, "All of these fruit or subsistence crops have a specific season; it's only during harvest season a farmer will make money. As opposed to this, cattle are a constant: they're a bank. If I need money, I can sell a calf in an hour and have money in my pocket." The prevalence of cattle ranching in the 17 de Abril is unquestionably not simply a narrative of state imposition. Rather, the settlement's resident transitioned to cattle ranching because it "made sense," given both the spatial history of the landscape and their ease of management.

The problems of financial insecurity associated with diversification were augmented by other constraints. One constraint was bureaucracy. COOMARSP technicians would order thousands of tree saplings, but they would arrive six months after the destined date, in the middle of the dry season. Without irrigation, the majority of these saplings died. Another constraint was the cultural tradition of swidden agriculture described previously. In the early 2000s many of the settlement's inhabitants were using fire to clear forest cover in order to plant subsistence crops. Frequently, these fires would get out of control, ravage a neighbor's land, and destroy subsistence crops and fruit tree groves.

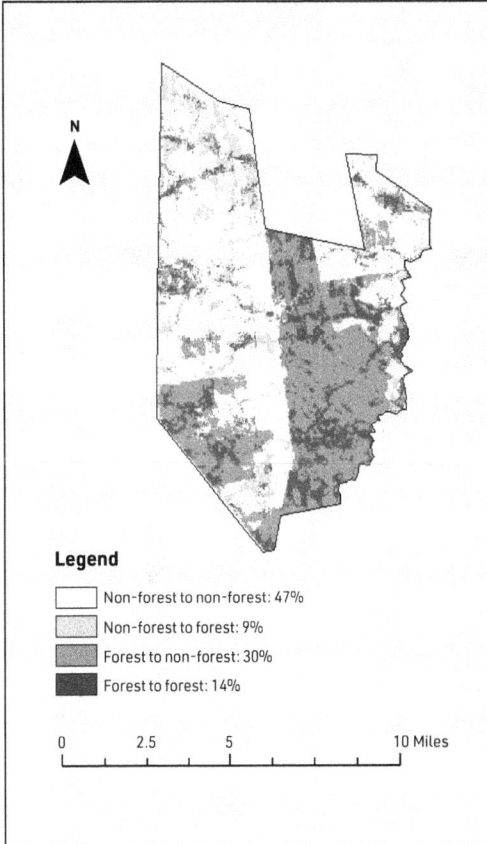

Figure 2.6. Trajectories of landscape change 1996–2009

The MST's financial decisions were a third factor leading to the failure of COOMARSP's agroforestry initiatives. The MST leaders directing COOMARSP used its vehicles to support MST land occupations instead of COOMARSP's intended extension work. Additionally, several times COOMARSP borrowed against its allocated funds in order to fund struggling MST land occupations. When this became public knowledge, INCRA was forced to change its policy regarding extension work. Following the disgrace of COOMARSP, INCRA liberated funding only after the completion of the project. Additionally, the extension projects, which were to last either three or four years, were reduced to one year.

Beyond these histories of failed extension initiatives, many of the 17 de Abril's inhabitants saw agricultural extension in a negative light because of familial politics. I first gained insight into the domestic struggles surrounding agricultural extension through a happenstance encounter that began in my backyard in August 2012 when Dona Maria reached over my rough-hewn wooden fence and asked, "Are you going to eat that?" The question was completely out of the blue. I looked up from my hammock to see her pointing to a cupuaçu that had fallen to the ground and realized that she was asking for it. I remembered going to Dona Maria and her husband's land several years ago and being amazed by their several hundred productive cupuaçu trees. I wondered why Dona Maria was requesting one from me.

Later on that afternoon, I sat with Dona Maria in front of her house in the setting sun. We chatted until Antonio, her husband, arrived home. I asked how everything was going on the farm, assuming that like most men he had been out tending cattle. "There's nothing happening out there," he said wiping the sweat from his forehead. But what about the cupuaçu, I asked, returning in my mind to the afternoon's encounter. "They're not doing anything, not producing at all," he answered, shaking his head. "None of them?" I asked, surprised. "*Nenhuma* [none]," he replied. "Do you have any idea what could be causing it?" I asked. "Nope." "Have you sought help from an extension agent?" I asked. He spat. "What would they know?" "Have you ever worked with an extension agent before?" I asked, surprised that this was his impression of agricultural extension. "We sure have," Dona Maria interjected. "We participated in one of the early projects. We had an extension agent come out who decided that we should work with fish, money started flowing from the bank, and a crew came out, dug a ditch, filled it with water and dumped five thousand fish in. Turns out they hadn't done a soil analysis, and before we knew it, the water ran out, and the fish died, and we ended up *sujo* [literally dirty, or "in debt"; fig. 2.7]. So yeah, we've worked with an extension agent before."

Figure 2.7. Seu Antonio and Dona Maria's fish pond

Cultural politics shape extension agents' patterns of engagement with the community. Agricultural extension contracts currently last for just one year—a short span of time that makes it difficult to develop sustained projects or meaningful relationships with one's clients. As Adriana, an extension agent working in 17 de Abril, told me, "We're not able to form a close link with the farmers. These one-year contracts strongly affect the provision of technical assistance, because you begin to develop a relationship, to become closer to the community, you begin to feel like you're part of a family, and you begin to organize a project, to start it, but never finish. The contract simply ends." Micropolitical negotiations are necessary for an extension company to continue working in the settlement. Adriana explained, "In order for us to return the next year, to have a contract to continue, we rely on the social movements. We really depend on them. In particular, we depend on the president of the Association, who has so much power. Soooooo much power. . . . The president of the association can go directly to INCRA and personally request that INCRA issue a new solicitation to a particular company." These politics of interpersonal relations determine whether or not extension agents can stay in the settlement and whether extension projects get completed.

Extension agents have the potential to be drivers of the agroecological transition in the 17 de Abril settlement. Adriana, who has extensive training in agroecology, hoped she could help shift the settlement's monoculture away from milk production. However, her efforts were constrained by a larger issue facing the transition to agroecology: people had become so conditioned by the spatial history of the region and by credit projects that they were largely uninterested in diversifying. Adriana was actively trying to encourage people to adopt agroecology: "We try to give them various options, talking about the benefits of diversifying. If the farmer takes a portion of his land and really diversifies it in terms of having cattle, sheep, bees, pigs, an orchard, and subsistence crops, then he could get much more economically out of the land, but also would be contributing positively to the environmental question in terms of needing less pasture, not compacting the soil as much." I asked Adriana if many of the farmers are interested in diversifying. "Very few," she responded. "Really few." When I asked why, she explained,

> Because since the settlement's creation, the projects have been set up for ranching. The farmers don't see any income coming from actual agriculture, and they see technical extension as something that was never present. And so the farmers don't believe in agricultural extension any more. They stayed with cattle, because there was so much pasture, and they see the cattle as giving a better income. They're not interested in creating a project in order to have agriculture.
>
> The farmers don't believe in agricultural extension in general, or in projects, or in the companies, or even in the settlement's association. They want money in their hands. For us to develop a project, regardless of in which settlement, whether it is in the 17, or in any settlement in the region, it's difficult, really difficult, because it's the same situation across the board.

People's spatial imaginaries conditioned them to see cattle ranching as the only viable form of agriculture. Adriana's description of the farmers' distrust was itself in considerable theoretical tension with her interest in moving the community beyond milk production toward agroecology. Perhaps because of the absence of these strong relationships with farmers, she was unable to develop an understanding of what they actually wanted in terms of a project. Without a sustained dialogue with community members, Adriana's commitment to a shift toward agroecological production rather ironically became another form of imposition.

The history of agricultural extension—not just in the 17 de Abril settlement, or even just in Brazil, but throughout the world—has long been associated with the imposition of particular spatial imaginaries of development. What I've tried to tease apart in this section are the tight feedback loops that exist between the spatialized history of environmental and social exploitation that structure the landscape and the subsequent imposition of visions of development from outside. The landscape's historical usage for cattle ranching, when combined with histories of credit devoted to cattle ranching and poor trust of extension agents, have conditioned the present agrarian landscape. These spatialized histories and cultural politics illuminate how agroecology itself can be seen as a form of cultural invasion. They are also imperative to understand the forces transforming food ways and constraining food sovereignty.

Buying Food Sovereignty?

The experience of living in the 17 de Abril settlement provided deep insight into how dependent the community had become on external markets for its food supply. I had this realization each time I waited for the shared pickup truck at the gas station in Eldorado dos Carajás. Pump 3 was the meeting place from which the local public transport left at ten o'clock in the morning to return to the 17 de Abril's central square, having left the settlement at seven that morning. The perimeter of the truck's bed had been converted to benches, and ten of us sat with bags of recent purchases in hand. We began to slowly ply the dirt roads of the city, stopping to pick up agricultural implements, construction materials, and appliances that people have already purchased on their trip to this small city. The driver got out of the truck, took a ticket from Sandra, a passenger seated across from me, and went inside the store, returning with a fifty-kilo bag of rice, which he tied to the roof alongside the lumber. "How much was it?" Vancivagne, a wizened pioneer of the settlement, asked. "A hundred reais," ($42 in 2009) answered Sandra. Whistling, Vancivagne asked Sandra if she thought this was expensive. She remarked that it was not, painting a broader picture that situated the perceived cost of rice in the context of the processes of agrarian change that had brought us to this market. "Look, these days, people are increasingly leaving for the cities; my children, your children, your grandchildren, everyone wants to live in the city. And it's gotten so expensive. It costs too much to produce food. When your kids leave for the city, you need to hire day laborers, and the cost of labor is too expensive. It's really expensive. When you think about how much it costs to produce rice, and then about how much it generally costs

in the stores, well, it's no surprise that no one wants to produce any more."
Vancivagne simply shook his head as we headed to our next stop and then
back up the bumpy road to the settlement. Sandra's analysis highlighted the
complex ways that processes of demographic and agrarian change intersect
to constrain food sovereignty within the 17 de Abril. Why produce food when
there is so little labor to assist in production and it is cheaper to buy it from
the store?

Pulling into the village's central square, we all descended from the truck.
As I headed toward home, I was surprised when I passed a wooden garage
door that I'd never seen open before. I stopped and looked in, finding the dirt
floor littered in a fine layer of amber husks. From the door to the center of the
room they accumulated in increasing density, rising into a cone that sat below
a giant green machine. José, who was working the machine, looked up as I
stuck my head in. I expressed my surprise at having never seen this door open
or this type of machine before. "It processes rice," José told me, and sighed,
"Nowadays there are really few people planting rice, really very few. Maybe
fifteen or twenty people. My machine is off most of the time; maybe one day a
month I'll crank it up and process five sacks. But it's just a little. I won't process
much anymore, rice is over." I asked José what it was like earlier in the settlement's history.

> I used to work a lot with this machine, and I earned a lot of money. It was
> a good job, cleaning and processing rice. I've had this machine since the
> beginning; and at that time, everyone was planting crops, and everyone
> had rice, and so I would be out here from six a.m. until six in the evening.
> We were selling rice and eating rice, I would buy rice from the farmers,
> process it, and have bags to the ceiling, which I would then sell to those in
> the community who weren't planting rice. But then rice ended. Everyone
> started becoming involved with cattle, rather than crops.

José went back to tinkering with the machine, and I headed off up the street.
José is a dying breed: the settlement used to have at least five other small-
scale rice processors. Pioneers described these days with nostalgia—a time
when there were bags of rice piled to the ceiling. But then rice died out.
Nowadays, for most, getting access to this nonnegotiable staple of everyday
Brazilian fare required a journey to the city of Eldorado dos Carajás to return,
like Sandra did, with a fifty-kilo sack of rice.

Dropping off my bag of vegetables in the refrigerator, I hopped on my bike
and headed across the settlement's dusty streets to the house of Genilson. With

his wide-brimmed straw hat, thread-bare MST T-shirt, and machete tucked into his belt, Genilson was the archetypical image of an MST farmer. Genilson, like so many of the settlement's founders, was originally from the neighboring state of Maranhão. He grew up farming, but his family never had their own land. Instead, they worked as sharecroppers, paying their rent through their harvest. Genilson's story shares virtually all of the defining characteristics of Charlés's: he worked first in mining and then clearing land on fazendas. Living in Curionópolis, he signed the ledger and joined the MST not out of an ideological commitment to social transformation but because he wanted a piece of land and a life of dignity.

"What did you envision doing with the land in the beginning?" I asked Genilson. Leaning forward, he touched my knee, and told me, "When you're in an encampment, the movement is always emphasizing getting a piece of land, planting crops, having a few cattle to generate a little income to sustain the family, and your own harvest to provide food on the table." Genilson's perspective underscored that for the MST food sovereignty and having cattle are not mutually exclusive; what the MST opposes is a singular focus on ranching. "And what happened? Did that work out?" I asked. "Well, we participated in a variety of projects to do permanent forms of cultivation, but they didn't take." Genilson was referring to the agroforestry projects associated with COOMARSP, which failed due to neighbors' fires and the delayed arrival of the saplings. "The only thing that really worked here was cattle. It was more risky to try to make a go of it with subsistence agriculture on our land. And it just made more sense to leave the land as pasture. Put cattle on it, and leave the grass for the cattle. You get twenty, thirty, forty cattle, you've got a decent living, you've got enough to support your family." Genilson's perspective supported that of Genival, the extension agent profiled earlier, who highlighted that cattle are a sure bet, even a form of financial insurance, serving as a bank.

As Genilson described, the spatial history of the landscape played a major role in shaping agricultural choices. When we arrived, "maybe 25 percent or so of the settlement was forest at the time, but many lots, like mine, were 100 percent pasture." Genilson's assessment buttressed the analyses of the previous maps of land use and land cover change as well as the narratives of pioneers like Arnoldo and Genival, which taken together illustrated why it was simply impractical to engage in subsistence agriculture for many settlers who received land that was already pasture. "So what did you do, given that the land you received was all pasture?" I asked. "I tried planting crops a bit, mostly on a neighbor's lot, where there was forest that could be knocked down and planted." The tradition of swidden agriculture is incredibly prominent within the settlement. For those who were brought up in an agricultural context in the neighboring state of Maranhão, it is what they learned working with their parents. As Samuel, a young activist who was interested in producing agro-ecologically but had been brought up within a traditional system of production, told me, "[Our parents], they lived through their past experiences, the experiences of their generation, their objective was to bring a new vision of agriculture to Amazônia. But all they knew was that in order to have roça you need to burn and keep moving. Cut the forest, burn, plant, harvest. . . . Cut the forest, burn, plant, harvest. My father learned from his father and so on. That's all they knew." *Botando fogo* (setting fire) was the form of land use that they were hired to do as sharecroppers. It was a form of land use that mapped onto a spatial imaginary; one in which forest was perceived as valuable because it was a potentiality—a form of land use that could be converted.

For Genilson, the relationships between ecological dynamics and systems of production propelled changes in people's food ways, food security, and food sovereignty. Leaning forward again, he told me, "Nowadays, people here consume mostly imported products and I'll tell you why. When we first came here, there was a lot of forest around, so everyone had their own harvest." Genilson emphasized the ecological conditions that enabled food sovereignty. Although much of the settlement was already deforested, there was still enough forest cover left for people to convert to swidden agriculture. The ecological conditions ensured food sovereignty, for a short period. "However, over time, this forest cover was exploited, and since other areas, like mine, had already been degraded and used for cattle pasture, things got harder for us." As the pioneers converted land, there became fewer and fewer remaining pieces of forest that could be transformed. "This made people consume more imported products. Today, what we produce is a lot less than it was before. Most everything we consume is from somewhere else. Rice comes from somewhere else, beans come from somewhere else. Almost none of what we consume comes from here." Genilson provided examples to highlight how far the community has moved from its agrarian roots. "When we used to have our routine, more of our agricultural traditions, everybody had food at home. Nowadays there are no more farm chickens (*galinha caipira*), and that's because the chicken is fed with corn that comes from somewhere else, probably modified. Even the eggs consumed come from somewhere else . . . this is the reality of this place." Farmyard chickens are seen as a food quintessentially associated with life in the campo. Many people still have them—in fact, they made their way into my house each morning—but Genilson was suggesting that they are not true galinha caipira because they're fed on imported corn, which is probably genetically modified.

The larger issue undergirding his critique of farm chickens was that the community had lost its food sovereignty, its ability to produce corn and use a portion to feed its chickens.

> People come from outside and say, "Since you all are from the campo, you produce things," but the truth is that we struggle every day to survive around here. It hurts to say that now we consume things that comes from other places, even if we are from the campo.
>
> The other day there was a car driving around the village selling squash in plastic bags. . . . Do you understand me? (pauses, adding emphasis): *We're in the country, and someone is selling squash here that comes from the road* [road used colloquially to refer to the nearby city of Eldorado dos Carajás]. It would be nice if *we could take our products to sell on the road*, but this is the reality.
>
> It has changed a lot from what it was before to what it is nowadays. For example, the things that used to be imported were things that came from industry, things that couldn't be cultivated easily here, like sugar and things like that. Even bread we would make ourselves. The difference is huge.

Foodways, or the cultural, social, and economic practices related to how food is produced and consumed, are highly dynamic, situated at the intersection of culture, traditions, and history. For Genilson, changes in foodways were coterminous with the loss of food sovereignty: whether it was the absence of culturally perceived true galinha caipira or a truck selling squash from the road in the 17 de Abril settlement, it was clear that "the difference is huge."

What then does the future hold? Is there potential to realize the MST's agroecological ideals in the 17 de Abril? Perhaps, but it won't be easy. Genilson was unequivocal in this respect. "To go back to what once was is next to impossible. It's very sad to say this, but that's the truth. Perhaps there's some form of mechanized agriculture that would work, but I think it would be hard; it's difficult to go back to what we had before." From Genilson's perspective, the community used to be more food sovereign; it used to more closely approximate an agrarian ideal, whereby individuals produced their own food and had no need to make the trip to Eldorado dos Carajás to buy food. This was a time when the linkages between ecology, livelihoods, food security, and food sovereignty were tight. However, the past never approximated the MST's agroecological vision. People may have been more food sovereign, but only because they were living on borrowed ecological time, engaging in swidden agriculture and harvesting bumper crops from the ephemeral nutrients of the recently burned forest. Even so, as Genilson went on to describe, there have been too many changes to return to this imaginary of the past.

> There are only a few people who produce food. That's just how it works. The money is in the milk production. So, we are able to survive, but not doing what we originally did on the farm; to go back to that is very hard.
>
> And there is nobody that's really doing that. There is always work for people. Some people work on other people's land, some sell their lots to someone else in the settlement, other people have the lots but they can't work on them because of a personal crisis. No. Everyone here has a way of living. Everyone is stable. It used to be everyone working on the farm, everybody, but it's not like that anymore. It's gone.
>
> So, we survive here, but we consume things from the outside for the most part. And our biggest production, milk, goes away—sold to people outside. We buy a little pack of it, for three reais. This is how it is. So you understand?

Genilson's analysis underscored broader processes of agrarian change. The community has no food sovereignty, no real control over its own food system; even milk, its primary product, is in short demand in the settlement. On so many mornings I walked to the house of one of the few community members who sold locally produced milk only to find that within a few minutes it had all sold out. The community had agriculturally and economically transitioned: Genilson believed that no one was really farming anymore and that there was greater financial security. But that security has been costly, resulting in the loss of culturally salient foodways and food sovereignty.

Genilson connected the shift away from food sovereignty to the challenges facing the advance of agroecology. Genilson told me that many people have small gardens, but invariably pests destroy the plants. People often resort to chemicals to try to save their crops. However, if farmers tried agroecological techniques, such as planting peppers surrounded by spicier peppers, "I can guarantee that the flies won't go even close to the garden. But that's too much work for them." Genilson's ending point—that agroecological methods are too difficult—intersected with various arguments he had put forth: pulling out the pasture to plant subsistence crops would have been impossible in the earlier years because of the labor required; cattle made sense as a major form of production because they are less work; buying imported foods simply made sense given the ecological constraints and economic costs of labor. Advancing agroecology was a dubious prospect. For historical, political-economic, and cultural reasons, it was just too much work. But that was the work that educators saw as necessary in order to actualize the movement's broader vision of food sovereignty. In chapter 3 we will turn to the potential role that education can play in transforming the agrarian landscape and the internal struggle among educators in realizing this vision.

Conclusion

Isabel asked the provocative question in chapter 1: "Why don't we have agricultural production?" This question has plagued many more besides Isabel. As Genilson described in this chapter, the settlement is far from food sovereign. This is perceived as an absence, as a loss, and for Genilson is epitomized by a truck trolling the streets, selling squash in plastic bags, and by the lack of farmyard chickens. Throughout this chapter I've explored the factors leading to the loss of food sovereignty in the 17 de Abril. Settlers' embodied histories of marginalization combined with the spatial history of land management, the politics of knowledge, and financial incentives to structure the hegemony of cattle ranching.

The Amazon has long functioned as a promised land for disparate groups. "Eldorado" might persist in the cultural imaginary as a famed city of gold, but it is real in the minds, bodies, and histories of those in southeastern Pará. Thousands of migrants came to the region in search of a golden promised land, but what they found in the mines of Serra dos Carajás was an almost unbearably arduous reality. From the mines, many migrants moved on to work in the region's large farms, reinforcing degrading forms of land management and inequitable labor relations from their earlier lives. For those in such a position of extreme marginalization, the idea of "land for those who will work it" was a clarion call, a new "promised land." Although most who joined the MST in Curionópolis did not share a political ideology, they did share a history of marginalization, and ultimately this was what brought them together around the 17 de Abril settlement.

This was not simply a history of marginalization but one that was reproduced through state policies and projects after people got access to land. The state, quick to "whitewash" over the massacre, redressed the explicit violence of the massacre with the structural violence of development. A series of interconnected development projects were implanted on the landscape; however, this was a landscape already characterized by uneven development. Without functioning infrastructure, these projects failed, and as the settlement's residents believe, they were always intended to do so. Their failure was crippling for the settlement's producer association, casting it into perpetual debt. The movement became *sujo* (dirty) in the eyes of not only the bank but also the broader community, where many people began to see it as a failing vehicle for development.

The survivors of the massacre of Eldorado dos Carajás did obtain the promised land, but the history of exploitation was already etched into the landscape. Throughout this chapter I've detailed the complex interchange between the social production of space and the spatial production of the social. The promised land the marginalized received had been long deforested and compacted, cleared by bulldozers and used for cattle ranching; this was not a natural process, but rather a historical one facilitated by government subsidies, public policies, and geopolitical imperatives. These social forces structured the spatiality of the landscape: bulldozers transformed the rainforest to cattle pasture, producing a particular vision of productive land use. I've also highlighted the flip side of this relationship, showing that space plays a major role in defining social life. The intertwined spatiality and history of the landscape—the hoof print of cattle ranching—structured the perceived land management options of the pioneers. Except in areas where forest could be converted, subsistence agriculture was perceived as a nonoption. Yet it is not only space that structures social life. Rather, as exemplified by the perspective of Genival, a pioneer who is now an extension agent, agricultural credit incentives configured both agricultural extension and cattle ranching. Extension agents earn more money by signing off on projects for cattle, and ranching is a less risky form of land management; knowledge centered around diversification took a backseat to that relevant to a ranching context. The spatial imaginaries of the settlement's pioneers were structured around cattle ranching.

This chapter has painted a rather dismal view of agriculture in 17 de Abril. If one's vision is of agroecological forms of production and food sovereignty, that is, if one holds the imaginary of the MST, then those days are quite possibly long gone. That's at least what Genilson, a staunch MST supporter, believed. To go back would be impossible. There are innumerable reasons that one cannot go back; lack of extant forest cover to convert, cultural malaise surrounding extension and credit, the hegemony of cattle in the spatial imaginaries, and the landscape itself. Perhaps one can never go back, in part, because that reality never really existed. Swidden agriculture, although it was productive for some, was never the MST's agroecological imaginary. If the community was food sovereign, it was on borrowed ecological time, relying on forest to convert, and not ecologically, economically, or socially sustainable.

This book, however, is not about the possibility or impossibility of going back but rather about going forward. While cattle ranching may be hegemonic, there are alternative forms of production that are embryonic in the community. Critical food systems education might bring these into broader proliferation and perhaps even into their own hegemony, but to do so will unquestionably be a struggle. A conflict over the meaning of land, in this setting, is also a conflict over the purpose and function of education.

CHAPTER 3

Space Wasn't Easy

"Space wasn't easy. No, space wasn't easy," Lucinede informed me. "When one struggle ends, another begins." As a teacher and an activist committed to the emancipatory educational and political vision of Brazil's Landless Workers' Movement (MST), Lucinede has long played an integral role in the community's struggle to build a quality school within the MST's 17 de Abril settlement in southeastern Pará. She has been a teacher in this settlement for nearly twenty years and by the time of our conversation in June 2015 had amassed a textured understanding of the long-term struggle over space. This chapter revolves around Lucinede's multifaceted analysis. In describing space as arduous, Lucinede was referring both to the community's long-term struggle to build a new school but also to the subsequent contestation over space that now rages within the recently built school.

At the core of Lucinede's statement is one of the central ideas of human geography: space is a social product (Lefebvre 1991). Space is a complex social construction, constituted by the intersection of social values, political-economic forces, and political ideologies. Branford and Rocha (2002: 109) beautifully illustrate this concept by describing a school within an MST settlement: "On the walls inside a big white house on top of a hill hang some of the letters of the alphabet, the MST alphabet: A for *acampamento* (camp), M for *marcha* (march), R for *reforma agraria* (agrarian reform), S for *seca* (drought), T for *terra* (Land), U for uniao (union), V for *vitoria* (victory). That this house is now a school is in itself a victory. Until a few years ago it was the house of the boss, the sugar planter. . . . Now all this land . . . belongs to the workers themselves." This passage conveys how social groups produce particular spaces for specific reasons. MST teachers imbue this space with political symbols and ideology to convey these values to MST students.

In this chapter, I analyze how teachers and administrators understand the spatial meaning of the municipal school in the 17 de Abril settlement.

Answering this question is pivotal to understanding the political ecology of education in the 17 de Abril because the school's space is highly contested and the struggle over it determines whether or not the MST's critical food systems pedagogy gets implemented. Over seven years of working in the 17 de Abril, I saw this contest play out in tightly coupled material and ideological forms.

When I first began conducting pilot research in the 17 de Abril in 2009, the school was adjacent to the village's central square, consisting of classrooms separated by flimsy rough-hewn wooden walls and a cafeteria under a thatched roof (fig. 3.1). When I returned in 2010 the old school had been leveled and a new one completed. From either side of a covered walkway, individual class-rooms stood, built from cinder blocks and with polished cement floors. At that time I was struck by the visual absence of the MST and its political symbols in the new school in comparison with the old one: there were no MST flags, no revolutionary quotes, and no movement posters. In 2012, when I returned for a year of fieldwork, the school had once again metamorphosed, taking on the appearance of a more radical space. MST posters now graced the walls of the administrative wing. A large spray-paint stencil of Che Guevara adorned one exterior wall (fig. 3.2).

Figure 3.1. The wooden school circa 2000

Figure 3.2. Face of the movement

In 2013 many of these revolutionary vestiges had seemingly vanished; in 2015 they had somehow reappeared. These symbols of the movement had not simply appeared and disappeared but had been actively removed and just as actively replaced. Each of these actions was intentional and carried out by particular individuals for specific purposes. When educators and administrators who support the MST govern the school, its political presence is visible on the walls. When there is a change in leadership and those who do not support the movement take the helm, its presence is removed. As these brief examples illustrate, this municipal school is not a homogenous space of movement pedagogy; rather, many of its educators are estranged from the MST and engage in quotidian forms of resistance to erase the movement's presence. Symbolic transformations in the school are closely associated with struggles over the meaning of its space.

Resistance takes a diversity of forms (Hollander and Einwohner 2004). At its most basic, resistance is an oppositional activity or attitude. It is traditionally understood as an action carried out for progressive purposes by an oppressed group against another that has more power. However, this is not always the case, as evidenced by the example of structurally powerful white groups in the United States that resist racial integration associated with school redistricting (Bartels and Donato 2009). The history of the 17 de Abril's school is intertwined with two broad patterns of resistance. First, MST members have engaged in various explicit acts of resistance against the state, closing down roads, railroads, and government offices to pressure the government to build the school. These actions are similar to those of other social movements whose activists tactically occupy space (McAdam and Snow 1997; Nicholls 2007; Halvorsen 2015). Second, educators and administrators in the settlement's school who are estranged from the MST engage in what I understand to be "everyday resistance" (Scott 1987). These individuals resist the efforts of other educators and administrators who seek to maintain the MST's ideology and pedagogy within the school. These educators negate the MST's presence within the school through quotidian actions, such as taking down MST posters and not showing up at meetings where political objectives are discussed. Understanding how such actions structure the political ecology of education requires a careful analysis of how the school functions as a "site of resistance" (Chin and Mittleman 1999).

In this chapter I combine theories of "third space" (Bhaba 1994; Soja 1996) and "heterotopia" (Foucault 2008) to understand this conflict in the 17 de Abril's school over the meaning of space. Bhaba (1994) sees third space as a site of ambiguity where dualisms are dissolved through perpetual movement between forms. For Soja (1996), inspired by Henri Lefebvre, third space is radical because it is constructed by marginalized groups and defined by openness and creativity. These conceptions of third space share many similarities with Foucault's (2008) conception of heterotopias, which are hybrid spaces that call into question the conventional meanings and practices associated with that space. These are "countersites" because they are different from the rest of a society's spaces. Although they are oppositional, heterotopias still contain elements or images of more dominant spaces within them. As Foucault describes them, heterotopias are "capable of juxtaposing in a single real place several spaces, several sites that are in themselves incompatible" (2008: 25). The above introductory example of the 17 de Abril's school presents the ambiguity and contestation of this space. As evidenced by the continuous removal and replacement of the movement's symbols, this is neither a homogenous space of movement ideology and pedagogy nor one of mainstream education. Rather, it is characterized by the continuous oscillation of forms and the conflicting juxtaposition within a singular site of several different conceptions of space (Bhaba 1994; Soja 1996; Foucault 2008). By integrating these two theories of heterotopias and third space into the political ecology of education framework, I seek to answer the following questions: How do processes of resistance—in their myriad forms—intersect with the production of educational space? How is the MST's vision of education—known as Educação do Campo—spatial at its core and defined in opposition to the spatial logics of other visions of education?

The chapter is divided into three sections. First, I explore the community's decade-long struggle to build the present school in the 17 de Abril. This enduring campaign became one of the primary manifestations of collective action in the settlement. In the second section, I explore what space means in an educational context and why the "face of space" (cara do espaço) is so important within the MST movement. The third section explores the struggle over space *within* the school. Taken together, these three sections show that political struggles over the production and meaning of space are central to the implementation of counter-hegemonic visions of education.

The Struggle to Build the Settlement's School

The history of the creation of the 17 de Abril's present school was one of prolonged resistance. Once the settlement was created, the pioneers began building a wooden school in the village's central square. This functioned as the main building of the school for eleven years (1998–2009). However, the wooden school was always a stopgap measure. As Lucinede recalled, "From the beginning, as soon as the wooden school was constructed, we began mobilizing to build the next one." The wooden school was woefully inadequate for several reasons. It provided basic education to approximately three hundred students but went up to only the fourth series (approximately third grade in the US system). In addition, the settlement did not have a high school program, and older students would commute daily along the precarious dirt road to the city of Eldorado dos Carajás, returning home at midnight. This was never the community's vision for education, Lucinede remembered. "We always wanted a good school, because we knew that other settlements have them. We never wanted our children to study outside of the settlement, in the city, we wanted our children to be here." Bussing students to the city of Eldorado dos Carajás to attend an urban school was more than a logistical nightmare but also carried intensely negative symbolism. Sending students out of the settlement simultaneously validated a dominant narrative in Brazilian society that rural spaces are not sites of quality education and cast doubt on the MST's vision of Educação do Campo, which seeks to provide an alternative education to students in their own rural locales.

The community knew that they would need to begin a new struggle against the state for educational facilities to serve the growing number of students and their educational needs. In 2002, after four years, the wooden school expanded to offer a high school program; however, while this was an advantage in that older students no longer needed to commute daily, there were now more students in the already tight space and no more infrastructure to attend to them. As enrollment grew, the community collectively rallied around the school as a shared object of mobilization. This involved a grassroots process of dialogue, which the movement calls the *trabalho de base*, and consists of developing a common vision and plan for action. As Lucinede described it, "We were always engaged in a discussion about what would this school look like. We would get the education collective together: teachers, parents, students, the leadership of the movement. We worked to put together a plan for this school: how is it that we can create this school? We had this discussion again and again until we were able to reach a consensus, and put together a proposal to the state." Creating this shared vision was about more than determining how many classrooms would be necessary to attend to the growing student body; it was a dialogue about the purpose of education and its linkages to the movement's objectives. As Lucinede reflected on the broader meaning of education within the movement, "Without education, we're not going to obtain our objectives. We need people to have critical consciousness, people that can debate, people that can understand issues. And we're only going to get this through education." While the school's physical edifice was the primary demand, the collective's broader objective was to have a space where students could become politically educated and develop a shared identity with the movement. The struggle for the school was one over educational sovereignty, which is a community's right to challenge enshrined systems of educational inequality and develop its own education systems (Moll and Ruiz 2005). Educational sovereignty can, in certain contexts, advance food sovereignty by providing grassroots movements the pedagogical autonomy to help their members develop agroecological skills, critical analyses of agrarian change, and experiences with cooperative forms of organization. Educational sovereignty is a process of constituting agrarian citizenship (Wittman 2010). Through Educação do Campo, the MST seeks to actualize its members' rights as citizens to schools and curricula that valorize cultural traditions, agrarian livelihoods, and ecologies.

Unsurprisingly, ongoing social mobilization is necessary to develop educational sovereignty. The state simply ignored the community's proposal for a new school complex consisting of elementary, middle, and high schools. "And so we began with mobilizations, protests in the city, protests on the side of the highway to denounce to broader society that, in reality, we don't have a school. That children are being forced to study in a place that's simply not appropriate." Lucinede went on to paint a vivid picture of how the community symbolically transformed space to achieve its vision: "We took the whole school to Quatro [4, the number of the kilometer road marker on the highway that marks the settlement's entrance and is colloquially used to describe its location]. We went with chairs, with desks, with blackboards, with everything. We set up four classrooms in the middle of the highway. The same students in the same classes with the same professors. The students were working with their textbooks just as they would normally." The image is vivid: a highway shut down from either side. The asphalt reconfigured into four classrooms, each with rows of wooden school desks. Students dutifully paying attention to a teacher, who works at a portable blackboard. The struggle for the school was becoming a central form of struggle on the land.

The MST's transformation of the road into a classroom exemplifies what Tilly (2000: 137) terms the symbolic geography of contentious politics. The symbolic geography of social movements includes the "use of emblematic monuments, locales, or buildings in dramatization of demands, [and a] struggle for control of crucial public spaces in validation of claims to political power. Lucinede and the broader education collective decided to occupy this particular space because of its symbolic value, as "locations carry meanings, and those meanings can telegraph the message that the movement wants to convey" (Hammond 2013: 501). I read the meaning of the MST's highway occupation as a symbolic critique of the geographic disparity in education: Students should not need to go to the *rua* (road, used colloquially to refer to the city of Eldorado dos Carajás) for education. The symbolic geography of the MST's transformation of the road into a school classroom highlights that rural spaces require specific forms of education, which are different than those of urban spaces.

The occupation worked, or so it seemed at first. But those hopes were short-lived. As Lucinede recalled, "Following the occupation of the road, the government resolved to sit with us to discuss, to find out our priorities. They made these promises for construction; they promised this material, but those materials never arrived, and so we began to conduct other protests." On various occasions in 2006 and 2007, hundreds of MST members occupied the state secretariat of the National Institute of Colonization and Agrarian Reform (INCRA) in Marabá for months at a time as well as the rail line that takes extracted raw minerals from Vale's Serra dos Carjás mine. These protests were not restricted to the *assentados* from the 17 de Abril; rather, MST members from encampments and settlements throughout southeastern Pará came together in protest. The leaders of the various MST communities would put forth a broad list of demands to the state; some would be general and relevant to all communities, such as releasing agricultural credit; others would be more specific, such as the new school for the 17 de Abril.

Many I spoke with discussed this as a period when there was a zeitgeist of belonging in the 17 de Abril; people truly and actively felt part of the movement. Raunir, a twenty-year-old MST activist from the 17 de Abril who had been a student of Lucinede's, described the broader feeling of these collective moments:

When we occupied the railway, the whole world participated: cars brought people there, and those that couldn't stay there—as people stayed for more or less a month there—those who couldn't stay a month there, that had to tend to the cattle, or their crops, they returned and more people came that could go and took their place. In a certain way, everyone participated. The whole world participated.

When people are interested, they participate in all of the movement's actions. For example, look at the occupations of INCRA. That was a time in which the base really participated: that was so that the community could get the school we have now.

What Raunir described—a time when the "whole world" (by which he means the whole community) mobilized together in pursuit of a common objective—stands out in people's minds because it is a sharp contrast to the everyday political complacency that came to define the settlement after its creation and still characterizes it today. Political participation naturally ebbs and flows as part of a cycle within social movements (Katzenstein 1998; Suh 2011). Recognizing that space structures social life helps illuminate the geographic factors shaping political participation within the MST; in an encampment—a liminal and ephemeral geographic space—MST members have higher political participation because they have fewer constraints on their time in terms of agricultural responsibilities and are motivated by the immediate desire for land. When that struggle *for* land is successful and a settlement—a legally recognized and more permanent geographic space—is created, the struggle *on* the land begins. MST members must engage in ongoing resistance to pressure the state for resources such as health care, education, and agricultural credit, and they get burned out. Mobilizing the base to engage in this long-term process of social change is itself an ongoing struggle as individuals become increasingly complacent and demographic changes bring new individuals into the settlement who never experienced the initial struggle for land. However, political engagement gets reignited at watershed moments like the school in the road occupation because these moments symbolize a shared struggle over resources and meaning. As Raunir described, when there is a cause that brings the community together—such as the struggle for the school—the whole world ends up participating. Announcements are made on the *voz* (the voice; the community radio system that blares from speakers atop a tower in the central square). People go door to door. The struggle for a quality school in the campo was a shared goal that brought the community together. These diverse occupations for the school became a central way that the settlement's members acted collectively, participating politically in the movement. As Lucinede told me, "When people occupy the highway with children, with their parents, when people saw this they realized that this was a project the community wanted a lot. We were struggling for a school, but it wasn't just the collective of educators, it wasn't just the leadership from the movement, it was the community that wanted it, it was the community as well that had the desire to have a space, a space that was good to study, so that one's children could study." With the grassroots mobilized, people utilized the tactics they knew. The occupation of space forms part of the vocabulary of the movement, the lexicon through which its members understand how to enact social change. MST members occupy diverse spaces, ranging from highways to the offices of INCRA, because it is what defines them as a group and their collective struggle. Occupying space as a tactic for achieving social change is a practical manifestation of a shared identity.

Transforming space, whether it involves the occupation of a fazenda or the demand for social services, requires sacrifice and commitment. As Lucinede described, "Space wasn't easy. No, space wasn't easy. It wasn't easy for us. We had to struggle a lot: Calling parents to participate in the protests, calling the children." Through ongoing mobilization, which involved creating a school in the middle of a highway, occupying INCRA for several months, occupying the railway line for more than a month, the community was ultimately successful. "It was a dream that took ten years to realize. Some people in the settlement thought it would never happen, because it took a long time. It's incredible, because to have a school in the campo, this was a really big victory for us." The struggle for the 17 de Abril's school required the community to become politically mobilized once again. This time the victory was not over getting access to land but rather for the resources to actualize the community's shared vision of a quality school in the campo.

Lucinede concluded our interview by reminding me that a common saying in the MST is "a struggle ends, but another always begins." With one last example, she described how struggle recapitulates itself in the lives of MST members: "People succeeded in the struggle in order to get the physical space that we have today, but we have a physical space in which some of the technology doesn't work. For example, we have an information technology area with computers, but there is no internet. And we have a chemistry laboratory, but without supplies. We have a cafeteria, but the chairs and tables are too tall for the small children. So, we have a building, we have a space, but we still have certain limitations within this space." This last example is pivotal for understanding at a broad level the relationships between social mobilization and the struggle over space. Spaces are not simply created at a single point in time but rather constantly reshaped, and this process requires ongoing struggle. The community of the 17 de Abril was successful in pressuring the state to build the school, but it is still materially ill equipped for the community's needs. To actualize the community's vision of a quality school is an ongoing process requiring continuous mobilization. Given how difficult it is to mobilize the community, it is unclear whether the educators, parents, and students will be able to self-organize and continue the struggle for the school's needed resources. What is clear is that the ongoing struggle over the school has transformed into a different struggle—one over what educational space means. Once the school was built, its edifice became the center of a debate surrounding the linkages between space, culture, and political participation. In the next section I move from Lucinede's account of the struggle for the school to an extended vignette from the school that I use to tease apart the difference between rural education and educação do campo and how these dual spatial and pedagogical distinctions are central to the political formation of students' agrarian identities.

Educação do Campo versus Rural Education: The Struggle over the Production of Space

Although I have long been attentive to the politics of education within the 17 de Abril, it was only in July 2015—six years after beginning to work in the settlement—that I first gained insight into the significant differences between Educação do Campo and rural education. I came to this realization by observing an evening political meeting at the school, which Lucinede had invited me to attend. The first thing I noted when I arrived at the school was that students and teachers had recently worked together to whitewash its façade. With a blank slate, they had painted murals that symbolize Educação do Campo: In one panel a cartoon boy skipped across a field beneath a verdant Brazil nut tree, heading toward a curving road that leads up to a school. The phrase "Educação do Campo" framed the panel. Next in the line of murals, another cartoon child—who stood next to a flagpole holding the MST's unmistakable red flag—watered flowers. The last scene depicted a child pointing at a quote from Brazilian critical pedagogue Paulo Freire: "To teach is not to transfer knowledge but to create the possibilities for the production or construction of knowledge" (fig. 3.3).

Students and educators have worked together to transform what was until recently a blank cinder block wall. As educators put it, the "face" of the school (*a cara da escola*) now projected a clear picture: this is an *escola do campo*; its identity is linked to a specific political project. This vision—of Educação do Campo—is multifaceted: it is simultaneously political, epistemological, agricultural, and spatial. It is a model of education that is diametrically opposed to

Figure 3.3. The political face of the school

the traditional education system. The wall projects a vision of the school as a third space (Soja 1996). Landless activists have created this site as one of difference; it is a subaltern space that is disparate from traditional schools. The mural on the wall is a symbolic geographic "othering" of this space, used to highlight this political and epistemological identity.

However, this conception of space is contested; the majority of educators within the school undoubtedly do not accept it, and those sentiments are prevalent among the community at large. As I explained at the start of this chapter, individuals either remove or reintroduce movement symbols in public spaces as part of a back-and-forth process of quotidian resistance taking place among the community. For Foucault, heterotopias call into question hegemonic discourses and practices. The school's newly painted façade is one such declaration, marking the school as a site of alternative knowledge production and dialogic pedagogy in opposition to the conventional educational model. Space, as Lucinede described earlier, "is never simple." Rather, as Foucault (2008: 181) argues, heterotopias juxtapose within a single place several "incompatible emplacements." Because these are "mutually repellent spaces" (Lefebvre 1991: 366), actualizing the MST's vision of Educação do Campo within the school involves resistance. Proclaiming the school an escola do campo and actualizing educação do campo in practice are two very different things. Whereas a group of politically active educators and students can relatively easily paint a mural, actually enacting educação do campo will require a much more difficult process of social mobilization within the school. I now continue with this vignette to illustrate these overlapping politics that unfolded during the meeting at the school.

At seven thirty in the evening it was cool outside. The sun had just set, which provided a welcome reprieve from the day's heat. Inside the school's administration building, however, it was a much different story. The air conditioners were not working, and the classroom where our meeting was to take place was hot and humid. I joined Sebastião, the school's principal, who was arranging the students' chairs into a circle. Sebastião only recently became the principal; previously he had been a teacher in the school and an evangelical pastor. In the several years I had known Sebastião, I had never associated him with the movement; he had always been someone the settlement's politically active inhabitants described as *bem afastada* (far removed) from the movement. I was curious as to his presence that night, given that this was to be a discussion of a recent conference of MST educators.

Soon, other individuals started streaming in and finding seats. First Lucinede entered, followed shortly thereafter by Zé, the school's physical education instructor. Although I had thought this was going to be a meeting primarily of educators, I was surprised to see that Nino joined us; Nino had no formal relation to the school but was actively involved in local MST politics. Nino wore clothing that I associated with an archetypical peasant farmer; he always had on a wide straw-brim hat and a machete tucked through the belt of his heavily patched pants. Following Nino, the settlement's political leaders, Gemeio and Martín, arrived. Gemeio and Martín had long alternated serving as the president of the settlement's administrative body, and Martín had now entered municipal politics, winning an election to be city councilman in Eldorado dos Carajás. While neither were educators, everyone recognized that they were at *na frente* (the front) of the settlement's political debates and their presence signified the importance of our meeting to the MST. By seven fifty, as we sat in the school desks and waited for the meeting to start, people became fidgety. One person and then another started grumbling that the meeting was already twenty minutes behind schedule. Martín, the city councilman, started remarking that we should all leave; Gemeio indicated that we need to stay, reminding us, "This meeting is important." Martín responded, without sarcasm, "Every meeting is important." I learned early on in my research that Martín's sentiments were correct: meetings like these are key sites for political debate. They are spaces where individuals debate ideological positions and try to bring the settlement's everyday politics in line with the movement's ideals.

The purpose of the meeting was to hear a report from the educators who participated in the recent three-day conference of agrarian reform educators at the MST's Palmares II settlement, located outside the nearby city of Paraupebas. The conference was organized and led by the MST state leaders and was intended to broaden a debate about the place of educação do campo in the schools and provide training for teachers who might not be familiar with the movement's educational philosophy and pedagogical practices. Sebastião, the principal, stood up and began to provide the formal report, noting the presence of the various educators from the 17 de Abril settlement who had participated, including Lucinede, Zé, and Luz (who had by now shown up). As Sebastião described, the event was the first MST-organized training in which many educators who were not closely associated with the movement had participated. Sebastião told us that, for example, he had never before been to an event like this. The fact that many educators, including the principal, had never been to one of these teacher trainings signaled how uneven the MST's vision of educação do campo was within the school. Rather than a homogenous space of movement pedagogy and ideology, the school was a heterotopia, comprising disparate visions of education.

Orating as he commonly did as an evangelical preacher, Sebastião pontificated that one of the primary lessons from the conference was that "our school, the schools in the settlements, are not urban schools but rural schools. These are schools that exist in the campo, and not in the urban centers." As educational scholars argue, Brazil's urban schools have long simultaneously emphasized the value of urban lifestyles while positioning rural landscapes and livelihoods as archaic and in need of development (Plank 1996). Urban schools are based in a pedagogy that is distinct from the realities of rural youth. But even more so, Sebastião told us, "We don't want to be simply a rural school, but rather, an example of educação do campo." What Sebastião emphasized, however, was that the difference between being a rural school and an escola do campo was just as significant as that between being an urban and rural school. Previously, I had largely internally translated the geographic descriptors *rural* and *do campo* as synonymous. But that night I learned that they are not; whereas the *zona rural* can be a fazendeiro's land, the *campo* is something qualitatively different. It is a place produced by, and closely tied to, the *camponês*. The descriptors that Sebastião and those in the movement used to describe schools, and their geographic and pedagogical context, were at once spatial and explicitly interwoven with questions of identity. These mark the 17 de Abril's school as a heterotopic third space because they signal the school as a site of resistance to the mainstream education system and its rural schools. The school is produced by and reciprocally reinforces the identity of a subaltern group.

As I discovered, the distinctions between an escola rural and an escola do campo are not only spatial but also explicitly geographical, cultural, and political. Lucinede leaned forward and reminded us that there is a general perspective that rural schools are unimportant; in a mocking tone, she told us, "Oh they [rural schools] are just these little schools wayyyyyy out there, and anyone can be a teacher at a rural school. The kids need to learn things to leave the campo and go to the city. Look, rural education is a type of education where people don't really need to study to live in the campo, they don't need to learn the things from the campo, because it's a poor place, because it's a place without life. So these are not schools that valorize the campo." Here Lucinede was describing how schools in rural areas are often seen as conduits of depeasantization, supporting the increasingly global exodus of outmigration of rural inhabitants to urban centers (Araghi 1995; Byres 1996; Akram-Lodhi and Kay 2012). Ordinary schools, whether urban or rural, devalue the agrarian traditions, livelihoods, and landscapes of the campo; they differentially valorize urban spaces and culture, encouraging youth to abandon their agrarian identities and landscapes. This negation, Lucinede went on to tell us, is the starting point for the MST's alternative educational vision. "And Educação do Campo comes in exactly with this: we need to valorize the work that's done in the campo, the people of the campo, the educator of the campo. These things need to be valorized. And we know that the campo needs to be valorized, in the schools, with the subjects; because we say that subjects of the campo have a history; the subject of the campo has a culture, have their own way of producing." In describing these individuals as *sujeitos do campo*, she emphasized a unique subjectivity—one that is a historical product of particular relations to the landscape. Educação do Campo begins from the supposition that the agrarian identity of these subjects is valuable and that education needs to valorize, rather than negate, these identities and livelihoods. "So in this sense, we [the educators] have been discussing this, to say to those in the city: look, we're from the campo, we have our own value, we are subjects, we constructed a history, and the school has to be a part of this. We can't teach our students that they need to study here just about the things from the cities, so that when they graduate they can go to the city." Lucinede describes here the important identity work that takes place as part of Educação do Campo. The identity of the sujeito do campo is explicitly historical; it is carved out of the imagination and memorization of tradition. For Foucault, heterotopias are temporal as well as spatial—they "accumulate time" by facilitating the consolidation and embodiment of tradition. The 17 de Abril's school is a heterotopia because it is oppositional in relation to those of the conventional education system, seeking to preserve and promulgate the identity of being camponês. Lucinede concluded by noting that although this discussion was one of the central elements of the educators' conference, it was nothing new—at least to those educators aligned with the movement. "As you all know, our school has been engaged in a massive and very long struggle about whether to be an escola do campo, or an *escola da cidade*, that is an urban school. And we would like it to remain an escola do campo." Although she did not expand upon it at that moment, I would soon learn that by describing this as a "very long struggle," Lucinede was foreshadowing the heterotopic politics that are at the center of the question also reflected in its ever-changing façade: whether or not the school would remain MST-oriented.

Luz, a twenty-three-year-old language teacher in the school who has long *andava com o movimento* (participated in, or literally walked with, the movement), picked up where Lucinede left off. She completed an undergraduate degree in journalism through a project in the northeastern state of Céara sponsored by the National Program for Education in Agrarian Reform (PRONERA) and now helps organize youth within the settlement, serving as a mentor in the youth activist group known as the Evolução Juventude Camponesa (EJC).

Luz highlighted a pivotal tension surrounding the school's spatial and political nature. Although MST educators want the school to be grounded in educação do campo, "the truth is that our school from the outside, it's not seen as an escola do campo." Rather, "it's seen as an urban school. It's seen as an urban school both in the sense of its physical structure, as well as the manner in which we work." Luz went on to compare the 17 de Abril's school with that in the Palmares II settlement, where the conference was held. Although the exterior wall surrounding the 17 de Abril's school had newly painted educação do campo murals, the entirety of the interior of the school had a more urban feel. It was an institutional space largely characterized by conventional municipal education posters and apolitical student artwork. It lacked the symbolic artifacts that suggest an association with the campo, much less with an agrarian social movement. On the other hand, each wall of the Palmares school was covered with murals from the movement, quotes from famous revolutionaries were in each classroom, and the movement's signature flag hung from the eaves (fig. 3.4). Luz here signaled that the 17 de Abril's school was neither physically nor ideologically tied only to the MST. Although educators and everyday community members sympathetic to the MST would like it to be a space for political education, in reality that vision was not shared. Rather, the school was heterotopic, defined by the overlap between the movement's politicized pedagogy and that of the traditional education system..

Figure 3.4. Palmares II school

However, Luz wasn't only comparing the material space of the 17 de Abril's school with that of Palmares but also critically reflecting on the pedagogy that distinguishes an escola do campo.

> At the meeting [in Palmares] it was emphasized that what we are is not an urban school, and not a rural school, but rather a school of educação do campo. And what does that mean? It means that an escola do campo is different. And why is it different? It means that when the people from the Secretary of Education arrive and say, "You're going to work with this [preset curriculum]," then we say, "No, we're going to adapt it, because our reality is different. Our reality is different than that of the city." So the material that arrives that we're supposed to work with, we need to adapt it because our reality is different. We need to work with materials that are directed towards the movement; the city doesn't need to do this.

Luz's argument connected the spatiality of politics, ecology, and education: the reality of the campo is different. For the MST these are culturally vibrant territories defined by political identities and diverse agroecological systems, which together exist in counterpoint to the depeopled, mechanized, and monocultural landscapes of the fazendeiros. For MST educators, traditional curricula make invisible peoples, politics, and ecologies. The third space of a school grounded in Educação do campo makes them all visible and valuable.

Sebastião, seeking to get control of the conversation, took Luz's point and expanded upon it. "The second main element of the conference was the question of what the school is doing to support the struggle. Education is a process of struggle, it's a process of training; it's a process of preserving the culture of the rural area." Clearly not done, Luz jumped back in, developing Sebastião's point further:

> This question of what the school does to support the struggle is closely tied to the broader question of whether we're a rural school, urban school, or an escola do campo. The reason it's important is because a school of the campo needs to be based in the daily reality of its students, and the history of the community, and the history of this community is one of struggle.
>
> Take for example the question of the anniversary of the 17 de Abril. The day of Abril 17th is a holiday for us, but it's not for the urban schools. Part of being an escola do campo is adapting the curriculum to include these things, so we're differentiated. If the school turns into an urban school, we're going to lose this. In addition to the actual 17th of April, we

wouldn't have the entire week of the 17th of Abril, which is one of the major times that we used to teach about the movement.

The school is a central site for the formation of students' political identities. Educação do campo is about more than the institutional freedom to declare the day of April 17 as a school holiday but rather is a call by teachers, for teachers, to actively organize events that deal with movement themes, such as gender equality, agrarian reform, and agroecology. As Luz described it, through these pedagogies "we are differentiated" from a traditional school. History is key to the demarcation of an escola do campo and its nature as a heterotopia. Nearly all educators I spoke with mentioned the history of the massacre of Eldorado dos Carajás as the prime manifestation of how the school employs educação do campo. As an example, on display in the school auditorium is a history class project containing the biographies of the nineteen MST activists killed during the massacre. For Foucault (2008), one of the markers of a heterotopia is that they alternate between "accumulating time" and making it ephemeral, or as he describes it "absolutely temporal." Similarly, the school's educação do campo pedagogies that focus on the massacre contribute to the codification of history, but the fact that these pedagogies are circumscribed to what Foucault describes as a "narrow slice of time" in April means that these are highly ephemeral moments. In order to further actualize educação do campo on a more continual basis, the meeting's participants believed that these pedagogies must be tightly interwoven with questions of history, memory, and identity.

At that point João Pedro took the floor to offer his perspective. João Pedro was a short light-skinned man with the build of a boxer. I mention his skin color here because it marked him as a relatively recent migrant to the community. Whereas nearly all of the settlement's pioneers were from either the Amazon or Brazil's Northeast, most with mixed Afro-Brazilian descent, more recent migrants have hailed from the country's largely lighter-skinned South. João Pedro came from Brazil's South to the Amazon because land was cheap and good for cattle. Although he did not participate in the original encampments, João Pedro had become closely affiliated with the settlement's political sphere and movement politics. João Pedro sat to the right of Martín, the city councilman, and it is exclusively in this pairing that I had encountered him.

João Pedro cut into Sebastião's comment: "One of the major problems is that the youth won't wear the 'shirt of the movement.' They don't understand their identity, they don't understand the history, they're losing the shirt, and this begins at home." João Pedro's commentary was paradoxical, given that he himself was a recent migrant and that he did not participate in the struggle for land; yet his analysis was spot-on. Whereas earlier youth would have grown up within the struggle, these days things were different. Many of the students now were the children of recent migrants, like João Pedro himself, and had little linkage to the movement. Their parents bought land rather than encamping and therefore would not have received the political training associated with participating in an encampment. These migrants wouldn't know the movement's anthems, what its flag symbolized, or how the MST envisioned social and agroecological transformation. Rather, many of these new migrants found the movement distasteful; they, like broader Brazilian media and political discourses, often suggested that the movement was composed of thieves and vagabonds. As João Pedro pointed out, familial political orientations structure students' engagement with the school. "Many parents won't let their children participate in the movement's events." Here, João Pedro's analysis tracks that of Foucault, who argued that a heterotopia is defined by its relation to "all other sites"; the problems of advancing Educação do Campo within the school are a microcosm of the broader family-level politics in the settlement.

The question of how to address these challenges dominated discussions at the recent education conference, which Sebastião had been reporting on.[1] These were not new debates but rather similar to what Lucinede described earlier as a "very long struggle." Luz began by picking up where João Pedro left off with the question of identity: "The transformation of society, it's a process that advances every day. Here, for example, this settlement there is already a sub-prefeito [subprefect]. In a sense, it is already a small city within the larger city [of Eldorado dos Carajás]. It's a village that's lost its sense of being part of the rural area in the vision of people, at least in some people. This process brings many people from outside, these children when they grow up . . . and this new generation doesn't understand very well this history."[2] Luz used the question of identity to introduce a proposal for constructing a memorial to the massacre; this memorial would be located in the center of the settlement's main square and would help to keep the movement visible within the community. Luz advocated,

> For us to continue with our history alive, we need to make a memorial, and have it done in a manner so that those who grow up here, those that come from outside can have access to this knowledge.
>
> We [the educators] began to discuss this idea of the memorial, because . . . there are many people that ask "why do we have the land today"; they've bought the land ten years before, they've have passed

through the process [of the development of the settlement], but they say "I'm not Sem Terra."

I consider myself Sem Terra because I've helped to construct this identity. I've helped to construct this process; I participated extensively in the meetings. I learned A LOT through the activities that we did, like the marches, with the training workshops, the seminars, the congresses.

The question of the memorial had been a long-standing debate within the community. The memorial would recognize the ultimate sacrifice of the nineteen MST members who were massacred on April 17, 1996, in Eldorado dos Carajás. Proponents of the memorial, like Luz, argued that it would help newcomers understand a bit of the history of the community—how it was born directly from a process of struggle. It would help youth develop an identity of Sem Terra, even among those who hadn't survived the massacre. Luz moved on to connect this proposal directly to the school and broader processes of agrarian change:

This question of history, of memory and identity, needs to be worked with extensively. In addition to not producing food anymore, there are many that have sold their land. And [as a result] many have bought land. These are people that don't know the history of the movement. So we have to start from the history of assentados who were here originally, and those of us that make up the teachers at the school; we all have to work with this question of identity, of belonging. Explaining, developing a methodology, for working with this in the school, for working with the youth, with the young children, and also with the adults [who attend nighttime classes].

Because the school itself [presently] doesn't have anything to do with agrarian reform. Look over there at the wall. Just a little flag [of the movement]. But at the entrance there should be sayings of the movement, "Lutar, construir a reforma agraria popular!" [Struggle, build popular agrarian reform!].

Our school is being transformed into an urban school. Because it no longer has that *mística* [cultural performances] of the movement, we don't have that anymore. And even at the S-curve, the youth don't go. Why don't the youth go? Because their parents don't let the youth go. Why don't the parents let the youth go? Because they don't understand the importance of participating in the youth collective at the S-curve a week before April 17. So the parents don't let their children participate, because the question of the family isn't dealt with. And those that have recently arrived and bought land, they don't understand our history, they don't understand the struggle that we've passed through. They know a little bit in general, but not the essence, what was at the roots.

In Luz's analysis, advancing educação do campo required thinking critically about political identity and its linkages to place. For the school to be a countersite, it needed to work directly with the question of memory and landscape to build a feeling among students that they are part of both a movement and a community that was born out of a very real struggle over land. Drawing upon Foucault, this memory work is tied to the broad familiar politics in the settlement: for many recent migrants and their children, this settlement is nothing more than cheap land. That several signs declare this land to be associated with the MST is largely irrelevant (fig. 3.5), an inconvenient truth many would likely forget given the media- and politics-driven depiction of MST members as thieves. It is in this context that educação do campo is epistemologically, politically, and materially relevant; the school is at a crossroads, and perhaps has been since its construction. This is its nature as a heterotopia; the school

Figure 3.5. Sign of the movement above the settlement's headquarters

is a countersite defined by the discordance between disparate visions of space that are in contradiction..

Education and the Politics of Place in Everyday Resistance

In this last section of the chapter I turn to focus on how everyday micropolitics shape the struggle around the status of the school. Having my eyes opened to these micropolitics at the evening meeting at the school, I stopped by Lucinede's house one late afternoon the next week to discuss the MST's recent teacher training event that we had been debating at the evening meeting. I reflected to Lucinede that I had been surprised to learn that the majority of teachers working in the school at that time had never been to an MST training before. "It's because they are new," she told me. Only three, Lucinede and two others, had been working in the school since the beginning. Providing context, she explained, "Most of the new teachers are the children of the assentados. They completed high school in the city of Eldorado." This was significant for Lucinede because "they began at a time when the MST had already begun to distance itself somewhat from the training [of teachers in the settlement]; they didn't participate in the organization of education in the same way as the other earlier teachers." The movement's state leaders had trained Lucinede and many other educators politically aligned with the MST in the early years of the settlement. This formation remains relevant to the ongoing struggle of actualizing the movement's vision of educação do campo within the school because of the micropolitical struggles between educators. As Lucinede explained, the politics of the teachers themselves would ultimately determine whether or not the MST's pedagogy could be implemented:

> We have a series of problems in the school. Even within a settlement of the movement we have significant difficulty implementing the pedagogy of the movement. . . .
>
> I've suggested at various times in various meetings that what we have to change is the mentality of the educators who are here within the settlement. Teachers used to be trained by the movement, and understand the importance of debate within the school. These days frequently, you invite the teachers to come to a discussion and they don't come.

The political participation of educators mirrors that of the larger settlement. Neither the school nor the settlement is a homogenous space of movement activism. The fact that all educators in this MST settlement do not actively support the movement's educational vision might be surprising given the community's political victories in attaining the school, yet these types of struggles define heterotopias. On another occasion, Edison, another teacher who had participated in many MST training events, offered me a deeper analysis of the micropolitics within the school: "It's really quite complicated, this relation between the school and the movement. The school tries to work by following the organizational principles of the movement. But the problem is that not everyone who works in the school belongs to the movement. It's one thing to live in an MST settlement; it's another to belong to the organization. These two things are quite different, and it's difficult to reconcile these two aspects." What Edison termed "the problem" is the complacency that sets in over time among the assentados. As Raunir, the young MST activist profiled earlier in the discussion of the occupation of the railway, told me when asked about the ebb and flow of political participation, "Everyone's got their television, their house, their motorcycle. They have enough food, and can go and hang out with their cell phone in the central square. What need do they have for the movement?"

Lucinede and Edison's perspectives draw attention to the political nature of teaching. First, the act of educating is political because—depending upon one's intent—it either transmits or omits particular ideals supported by the movement. Lucinede and Edison "walk with the movement" (*anda com o movimento*) and participate politically on a daily basis by communicating the movement's ideology to other teachers and students. By contrast, other educators either actively denigrate or simply do not acknowledge the importance of the movement by simply dragging their feet. Their daily resistance to the MST's efforts to advance a counter-hegemony within the school takes the form of not showing up at teachers' meetings where political projects were being discussed and not encouraging their students to participate in movement events.

Lucinede went on to describe how being an educator committed to the movement was at variance with the interests of the majority of educators in the school.

> Working with the movement is something that demands a significant focus: more availability on behalf of the people, in terms of being available to come to the school to discuss things, to become involved in activities. What we [MST educators] have found is that people [other teachers] don't want to be more available; they don't want to be present at the school more than is required in their little contract.
>
> But in the pedagogy of the movement it's more than this. The person

needs to really be able to make time available to plan and organize, to propose activities, to involve the community in these discussions, and these discussions go forward veryyyyyy slowly within the community. You have to find methodologies that bring the community to the school, and we've not been able to achieve this because this requires time, it requires resources.

Particularly important, from Lucinede's perspective, is educators' own political commitment to the MST's vision. If there is going to be a lasting "face of the movement" at the school (including posters and slogans, curricular content and applied student research projects), it needs to arise from the educators' own political commitments. This requires an extraordinary level of sustained energy and commitment for individuals who are generally underpaid and overworked in the first place.

For some, the challenge of advancing the movement's vision within the school has intersecting spatial and cultural dimensions. As Edison explained,

There are a number of teachers that disagree with the MST's principles, and because they disagree with these principles it becomes difficult to direct this process [of integrating MST principles into the school]. For example, a teacher arrives, and he's from São Paulo, but he grew up in Goiana, and he grew up with a completely different reality than ours. And he arrives and wants to work with the principles that he brought from there.

I'm not saying that the principles that he brought are wrong, and those that we have are right. We have an ideology, and so we want to preserve our ideology, and work with the grassroots, in the manner in which we think is correct. But it's really quite complicated.

Edison's perspective provided nuance to an analysis of the school as a heterotopia. It is not only that multiple sites come into conflict within the school but rather that some of these sites are geographically and culturally distinct. As Edison pointed out, teachers' region of origin and the social reality they were raised in can structure whether or not they will defend the MST and its pedagogical principles. As educators who do not identify with the peasantry come to teach in the movement's school, class politics shape pedagogy. All of the teachers give lessons in the same physical space—the school—but how they understand the history of that place, its transformation, and their current role in it is structured by their backgrounds.

This was certainly the case for Luana, a biology teacher who works in several schools, spending three months in each of five communities on a rotational basis. At one class I observed, Luana showed students pictures of the larval stages of bee development using a digital projector. One student asked, "How in the world can we see it that close?" Luana informed the student that they would use magnifying glasses, which they should all have. "Magnifying glass?" the student remarked. "Where are we going to get money for a magnifying glass?" Luana responded with a tasteless play on words: "*Sem Terra*, I swear, it should be *Sem Nada* [those that have nothing]." This comment was an insult to the students and the movement as a whole, and it underscored how far removed Luana was from the realities of her students in the settlement. One's class position is not simply an identity but a set of relations to other identities. Luana's class background—self-identifying not as part of the peasantry but rather as an individual from an urban reality—is an identity of difference. Being of a different class and place shapes her relation to her students and other educators who understand themselves as peasants—a social class defined by its relation to rural space.

These contentious class politics need to be seen in the context of broader national sentiments about the MST. The movement has long been maligned in the Brazilian media—a highly concentrated communications empire tied to agribusiness and the landed elite (Hammond 2004). Its framing of the movement as violent vagabonds has helped shape public consciousness and the stigma MST members face. One experiences this prejudice frequently when taking public minivans that connect the urban centers; on various occasions, when our minivan passed an agrarian reform encampment or settlement, I would overhear a passenger criticize the area's residents as "lazy," "thieves," or "good for nothing." When rural students enter urban schools, their rural habits, dress, ways of speaking, and traditions mark them as different. Increasingly, the broader national sentiment toward the MST has moved beyond prejudice to outright condemnation. Following what many scholars describe as a coup that deposed President Dilma Rousseff in 2015, the political landscape has shifted from the left to the far right. While the interim government of Rousseff's successor, Michel Temer, was hostile to the MST, that of current president Jair Bolsonaro has elevated the tensions to a much higher level, having declared a veritable war on the movement. The politics of space and class that inform Luana's positionality in the classroom, and her relation to her students, are shaped by these broader processes of structural marginalization perpetuated by the state and media. As I discuss in the epilogue, while the impact of these politics on the movement and its vision for education are incredibly dire, they are also producing conditions of hope.

Conclusions

Space is never easy but rather won through struggle. In this chapter I've highlighted how diverse processes of resistance, ranging from the explicit occupation of the highway to the everyday micropolitical maneuvering among educators, come together to socially produce educational spaces. The production of space is not a one-time moment but rather a string of intertwined struggles. While occupation forms part of the MST's spatial language of resistance, it inflects its usage in particular contexts. One way to understand the MST's occupation of space from a social movement studies perspective is as a moment of rupture. MST members' spectacular occupation of spaces, ranging from roads and railways to governmental offices, such as those of INCRA, exemplifies these rupturing moments. Yet while these moments of explicit resistance might have been responsible for attaining the political and economic resources needed to build the 17 de Abril's school, resistance itself has transformed. The struggle *in* the school takes the form of everyday resistance. Perhaps surprisingly, educators themselves resist the MST's vision. They engage in what James Scott (1987) refers to as foot-dragging, for instance by not showing up to MST educators' debates. Looking at the *cara*—at the face—of the 17 de Abril school, we see a continuum of explicit and everyday forms of resistance and how they change over time and space.

The MST's vision of social transformation is in peril. As João Pedro noted, many do not wear the shirt of the movement. Educators can play a pivotal role as activists in this context. They can directly support the MST's long-term struggle by trying to shape the identities of a new generation of youth, many of whom are newcomers to the settlement and feel no affinity to the movement. To form these youth into activists, the educators are attempting to engage in identity work, creating class projects that rescue the history of the massacre, and building a memorial within the settlement's central square. This is a pedagogical process of rescuing, and creating a collective memory of struggle, which will ultimately connect students to the history of the struggle for land. Yet the politics of place constrain these efforts. For educators, such as Luana, who feel no attachment to the movement, education is not part of a political project; rather, it is a means of trying to help move backward students into a more developed space—the city.

Education is undoubtedly a spatial arena of social struggle. Different visions of education—urban education, rural education, educação do campo—are more than geographically explicit in their nomenclature. Rather, they index a set of overlapping cultural, political, and agricultural axes of difference. As opposed to a rural school, where peasant culture and forms of agricultural production are seen as backward and urban society and mechanized monocultures are seen as signs of development, educação do campo explicitly valorizes peasant traditions and agroecological practices. The social production of the school's spatiality, whether it is rural, urban, or escola do campo, is tightly intertwined with its vision of the land. As a heterotopia, the school is a contradictory space where these different meanings of space come into conflict. Thus, for MST educators, the struggle over the school is a central form of the struggle *on* the land. The school and what meaning the spatiality of the school takes play a central role in determining whether or not the MST is able to actualize its political and agroecological vision.

CHAPTER 4

To Stay, or to Leave?

A cloud of dust crested the hill, causing us to stop in our tracks. Entering the village on a badly rutted dirt road was a luxury long-distance bus. Fabío, my research assistant, had lived here for the last seventeen years, since the settlement was created. I asked whether he had ever seen a luxury bus here. "Not until recently," he said, spitting on the ground, with a sour expression as though he had just tasted acid.

The bus's side was marked with only two words, Vale Amazônia. As it coasted to a stop at our feet, the cloud of dust engulfed us. The door slid open, mixing the refrigerated air of the bus's interior with the chalky, red air of rural Amazônia. Exiting from this surreal mixture in front of the political headquarters of the settlement in to the cool evening was an even more bizarre sight: ten or fifteen workers, small day bags in hand, blue uniforms on, coming home after working in the mines all day. They dispersed as the bus turned around and beat its way back against the rutted road.

As we walked down the dirt street, Fabío bemoaned, "We're losing all our *militantes* to Vale." "Vale," as it is colloquially known, refers to the mining extraction corporation Vale do Rio Doce, a major player in the environmental devastation of Amazônia. It operates the Carajás mine, the largest iron ore mine in the world. Vale and its buses are pulling young activists away from the movement by offering lucrative jobs at the mine. As Fabío told me, "Clesío was chosen to participate in the MST's agronomy program, but is apparently going to work for Vale instead. Maneu is already gone."[1] I read Fabío's tone as indicating a mix of resignation and defeat. Yet while many within the movement are critical of Vale, it has unequivocally developed a presence in the community.

Whatever the community's founders envisioned life after settlement to be, it was almost certainly not this: going to work for a major mining corporation. However, on the numerous occasions I asked people in casual conversation about Vale's presence, I almost invariably received the same response: "It's a good thing." Most people I spoke with did not see it as a contradiction. Those who did—like my research assistant—were those most active in the MST. The disparity between Fabío's and the broader community's view of Vale speaks to competing cultural visions of development within the community. Most members of the settlement saw Vale as positive. It provided sorely needed opportunity, a chance for youth to gain income and potentially be able to remain living in the settlement, traveling out in the company-provided transport to work during the day. That *I* was critical of activists going to work for Vale brought into focus my positionality as a researcher politically aligned with the movement but removed from the difficult everyday struggle of trying to make a living on this rather barren land.

The 17 de Abril settlement is at a crossroads—quite literally between different visions of development. There are two main roads in town, one that leads in and out of the settlement toward Eldorado, the nearest city, and another that leads to the roça. From the first direction Vale's buses come and go, taking the settlement's inhabitants to labor in the mines, far afield from their rural land. From the second direction others—such as Fabío—are digging in—figuratively, setting deep roots in the community and literally cultivating biologically diverse agroecosystems in the roça. At the crossroads is the settlement itself; while some parts of the village are increasingly abandoned, for many the settlement remains the manifestation of a dream—a quiet and safe rural space won through struggle—and a space that is part of a broader project of transformation.

Situated at this crossroads, the settlement epitomizes the agrarian question: what will happen to the peasantry? This is a century-long academic debate but also a question that many in the settlement—especially the youth—are asking themselves: *ficar ou sair?* [to stay or to leave?]. Will these young adults move off the land, become capitalist farmers, or reinvent themselves through alternative forms of production and exchange? These two options—to stay or to leave—are, respectively, synonymous with depeasantization and repeasantization. Depeasantization involves the emigration of peasants away from rural areas and livelihoods to urban centers, resulting in the dissolution of peasant identities and production systems. Repeasantization, by contrast, consists of individuals (both peasants and those who have not historically identified as farmers) becoming "more peasant like" (Van der Ploeg 2008) by adapting agroecological practices and cooperative production systems. Both the youth's question "to stay or to leave" and much of the academic literature on depeasantization and repeasantization are framed around a binary: one is either leaving the countryside or putting down roots. However, reality is rarely if ever so neatly dichotomous. Rather, as I show in this chapter, residents of the 17 de

Abril are suturing together disparate livelihood strategies, going off the farm for work in order to remain on the farm for life. In doing so, they challenge academic conceptions of the peasantry and its dynamic relation to the land.

Definitions of "the peasant" and "the peasantry" have long been subjects of debate among academics, grassroots movements, and international political bodies (Edelman 2013). Eric Wolf's (1969) classic typology, for example, distinguished peasants based upon their focus on subsistence production, limited engagement with cash crops, and communities closed to outsiders. Yet in recent years earlier views of the peasantry are being radically reconsidered in the context of debates surrounding food sovereignty (Bernstein 2014; McMichael 2014). On one side of the debate scholars argue that peasants are multitudinous and widely present throughout the world. La Vía Campesina, for example, claims to represent more than two hundred million peasants, small and midsize farmers, landless peoples, fisherfolk, and farmworkers from 164 organizations in seventy-three countries. Agrarian scholar Henry Bernstein is perhaps the most vocal oppositional voice (2004, 2015), arguing that in the contemporary globalized world there are essentially no peasants. What we need to be careful about, Bernstein (2015: 1044) argues, is asking "who farms, in what conditions, and in what ways." Peasants, when seen from this side of the debate, are defined by being able to reproduce themselves based on their own subsistence production. However, Bernstein argues, the commodification of subsistence agriculture has turned smallholder farmers into petty-commodity producers, and class differentiation is responsible for creating a hierarchy of differential access to power and capital. Family labor, once the staple of agrarian societies, is increasingly itself commoditized, and farmers are frequently supplementing their income through wage labor. Rather than a bucolic agrarian imaginary perhaps associated with the writings of Wendell Berry, what Bernstein (2015: 1044) sees is the "relentless microcapitalism of the countryside."

Yet peasants are neither a timeless nor a homogenous entity but rather, as anthropologist Sidney Mintz (1973: 93) argues, "always and everywhere typified themselves by internal differentiation along many lines." The recent work of Jan Douwe Van der Ploeg (2008, 2012) is perhaps most important to my conceptualization of the peasantry. For Van der Ploeg, "peasant farming" consists of crop diversification that provides a balanced livelihood, cooperative systems of production that enable nonmarket forms of exchange, and the struggle for autonomy from the market through the creation of on-farm-produced inputs and saved seeds. Rather than defining peasants as exclusively engaged in on-farm agricultural production, Van der Ploeg argues that *pluriactivity*, or generating subsidiary income through off-farm labor, is one of the quintessential mechanisms of repeasantization. Pluriactivity takes diverse forms: from the international migration of family members who send remittances to farmers who work in urban areas during the day and tend their land, animals, and crops during whatever moments they can carve out. Pluriactivity does create a dependency on wage labor (à la Bernstein), but it can help facilitate greater autonomy from the creditors and create agency as farmers gain more self-control over the flow of resources. Valorizing, rather than denigrating, pluriactivity helps reframe an analysis of ficar ou sair (to stay or leave). As the farmers' voices I lift up in this chapter will subsequently highlight, the future of the peasantry is not dichotomous; rather, agrarian livelihoods are inherently hybrid, constituted by diverse spatial relations and dynamic forms of exchange.

Whereas many distinguish peasants from famers (Wolf 1969), I follow the example of grassroots movements, such as La Vía Campesina, that use the term interchangeably in their own framing.[2] As Nettie Wiebe, an activist within La Vía Campesina and past president of the National Farmers Union of Canada, describes, "If you actually look at what 'peasant' means, it means 'people of the land.' Are we Canadian farmers 'people of the land'? Well, yes, of course. . . . We too are peasants, and it's the land and our relationship to the land and food production that distinguishes us" (Edelman 2013: 10). In this chapter I focus on what Wiebe describes as paramount: the relation between the social group and the land. At the center of my discussion is the relative difference between pasture and roça. For camponês in the 17 de Abril, having land generally means an area of roça, or a space to engage in subsistence farming, agroforestry, and limited cattle production. For those in the 17 de Abril who aspire to be *mini-latifundíario* (a play on words meaning small-large landowners), having land means having pasture, or an extensive space consisting of only grass (i.e., no natural or anthropogenic forest cover) that can be used to raise large numbers of cattle. As I will show throughout this chapter, these different meanings and functions of land are tied up with questions of identity and critical food systems education in the 17 de Abril.

In this chapter I analyze the potential for critical food systems education to intervene in the agrarian question. In the first section I profile Clesío, whose political identity has transformed in recent years to such an extent that he now sees the movement, agriculture, and life in the settlement as dead ends. Clesío's case highlights the linkages between shifting political identities and depeasantization, which is an ever-present reality in the settlement. In the second section I explore the process of repeasantization through two contrasting perspectives. Alan believes that through agroecological practices he can help guarantee the persistence of peasant identity and his family's tenancy on the land. Raymond, by contrast, works for Vale yet uses his salary from the job to further develop his diverse agroecological land management system. Taken together, these two individuals show how repeasantization reconnects smallholders to the land through ecological agriculture (Van der Ploeg 2008), even if they are engaged, like Raymond, in what most people would consider nonpeasant employment. In the third section I analyze how educators from the school mobilize to intervene in these twin processes of de/repeasantization, attempting to reclaim an abandoned harvest festival as a way to assert new agroecological identities and landscapes. I now turn to twenty-one-year-old Clesío, who finds himself caught between the movement and reality. His life story exemplifies the factors leading to the increasing disappearance of the peasantry.

Life Here Is *Parada*

Clesío looked to me the picture of a disgruntled young adult. Sitting atop a table in front of the settlement's main butcher shop, he wore stylish ripped jeans and bleached blond hair and was listening to music on his cell phone, glaring with a faraway, broody look across the central square. Over seven years I witnessed Clesío maturing from a fourteen-year-old teenager to a young adult of twenty-one. Although Clesío told me that he had been part of the community since the beginning, having been born in 1995, there was something about him that felt disconnected from this place. This tension I perceived in Clesío between belonging and disengagement was a thread throughout our conversation, and it spoke to the broader tension between depeasantization and repeasantization.

Clesío's way of describing his relation to the settlement, having been here "since the beginning," was a matter of pride—and I found individuals frequently emphasized it in recounting their oral history. Although Clesío was only one year old when the massacre took place, remembering nothing as his mother ran with him in her arms in search of safety, he started his history at that point. The movement shaped Clesío's early life. He was a *Sem Terrinha* (little landless one), a member of the children's MST group that participates in marches and meetings. When asked about the most important experiences in his life, Clesío told me that one of the most *marcante* (literally marking, or structuring) moments was the MST's national march in 2006, when he joined thousands of others on a four-day journey by foot from Marabá to the state capital of Belém. Despite the importance of these experiences in his life, Clesío narrated his relation to the MST in the past tense. He described how "until a little while ago, I was a militant of the MST. But owing to certain personal problems, I've distanced myself from the movement. At the same time, however, I'm trying to bring myself closer again to a certain extent." When I first was conducting pilot research in 2009, Clesío was just starting to become politically active as an organizer within the movement.

In 2009 Clesío was one of a throng of youth who had started coming to the meetings of the EJC (Evolução Juventude Camponesa)—the rural youth activist group affiliated with the MST. By the time I returned in 2010, Clesío had become even more actively involved in movement organizing, helping to facilitate meetings in encampments and settlements throughout the region. In 2012 Clesío helped organize the pedagogical encampment—one of the region's signature MST events—where youth gathered at the S-curve memorial in the week leading up to April 17.[3] Clesío listened there to speakers on agroecology, agrarian transformations in Amazônia, and class conflict, taking the microphone and asking probing questions during the discussion sections. Following Vergara-Camus (2009), the process of becoming a peasant, or claiming this identity, is more a political project than an abstract economic condition. Moments of political education, such as organizing experiences and the pedagogical encampment, are part of a process of repeasantization because they help a group come into being as a political class, united by a shared collective history of struggle against social marginalization.

Clesío's relation to the movement began to change that year, after the pedagogical encampment ended. He got into a fight with his mother over his participation in the movement, and she kicked him out. "Look, it [life within the movement] is really difficult," he recalls her telling him. "You're going to encounter various difficulties if you enter the movement." Clesío's mother was concerned that as her son became more and more politically active he would join one of the MST's encampments in search of his own land. If this happened, she had told him, "First, you're not going to have anyone to support you. If you get sick, you'll have to go and find someone who is available to take you to a hospital, because there won't be any medical facilities there. You won't have any money. So, you won't be able to buy medicine that you might need, because you won't be working. So, for one reason or another, you're going to end up having to leave the movement." Like many teenagers, Clesío, however, acutely desired his independence. He didn't want to rely on his mother, especially when she was unsupportive of his dreams. That week he made her fears a reality, leaving the 17 de Abril settlement for Frei Henri, an MST encampment about an hour away. Clesío built his own shelter and became involved in the daily struggles of the encampment. These struggles were incredibly difficult. Clesío learned a hard reality there: his mother was right. Life within the movement was not necessarily sustainable. "The unfortunate truth is it's just not possible to support oneself only through the movement. If you are living in an MST encampment, then you receive your *cesta básica* [basic box; staples such as oil, rice, flour, and beans provided from time to time by the government to those encamped]. But you don't get anything else. You don't have money to buy new clothes, or shoes. What I experienced is that in Frei Henri, to a certain extent, people just have to be content with what they have. They get their cesta básica, and they just remain there. *Parada*." Stationary, stopped, dead, dull—these are some of the meanings of parada. Clesío's use of it to describe the social milieu in Frei Henri is telling; it signifies the cessation of normal, everyday life, the entrenchment of desperation, and a total lack of hope. It highlights what everyday life *can* feel like in the encampment—a state of constant, and precarious, waiting. Living in flimsy shelters made out of plastic tarps. Slaking the heat of the Amazon midday sun with hot water from a stagnant creek. No job prospects. Hiding out during the day, as armed militia—hired by a local fazendeiro—fired on those in the encampment from behind earthen barricades. And throughout this time, no indication that land would be expropriated by the state at any point in the near future. In some nearby encampments that I visited, such as Peruana, MST members have been encamped for a decade or more—ten years spent in a perpetual state of waiting. As Clesío surmised, "This isn't good for anybody. You have to find means of developing, because otherwise you're just parada."

Clesío had thought he could build a life in the movement, but in the encampment at Frei Henri Clesío realized it just was not possible. "I thought for a while I would stay in Frei Henri, but there are no means. So, unfortunately, you end up needing to leave the MST if you want something. Within the movement, there's no place to work. There's no place for you to earn your own money to maintain yourself. You need to be able to provide for yourself so that you have the things that you need to feed yourself, to dress yourself. If you don't have any auxiliary support from outside the encampment, then you need to leave." Clesío ultimately proved his mother right: he left the encampment and the movement, moving to the nearby city of Paraupebas in search of wage work.

Clesío's disenchantment with the movement is in many ways tied to a broader social perspective on agriculture. Clesío went on to describe how the community at a broad scale regards agriculture—by which I mean the planting and harvesting of fruits and vegetables—as doomed. Settlement residents view working with cattle as quite distinct from agriculture in terms of its perceived social viability. "In the 17 de Abril, there are incredibly few people, whether they are young or old, who are interested in the life of a farmer. They're simply not interested, and why is that? Because they see that their parents lived a life that was very difficult, and they don't want that same difficult life; they want to move forward. They see that when their parents entered into the movement, they entered into a degree of complacency with what they had." Clesío described this state of complacency as a *mesmice*—a state of constancy that is similar to being parada. Asked what mesmice feels like, Clesío told me that it is "this sense that you'll always continue on in the same condition, forever." And it's not a simple and enjoyable lifestyle of sameness but, for Clesío, one of physical and emotional duress:

> If you want to have the life of a farmer, a life in agriculture, you need to be prepared to struggle substantially. Because, it's not easy. There's always the period of drought. Many things inevitably die. It's a life of constant struggle. The life of a farmer is a mesmice because you're always going to be planting, selling, and whatever you achieve in this life of a farmer, you're going to have to replant once again. To feed yourself, you'll sadly have to get it from the roça. And of what you are able to get from the roça and sell, very little you're going to be able to earn to buy new things, because you're going to need to invest in the roça. Because if you don't invest in the roça, then you won't be getting anything. *Nossa* [oh man; he sighs], I think it would be very difficult to have the life of a farmer. From my point of view, for me, it wouldn't work.

Despite the settlement's agrarian roots, and the movement's agroecological ideals people like Clesío (and he is not the only one) see no future in either the movement or the movement's agricultural vision of vegetable and fruit production. As Clesío described it, the cultural landscape is ripe for depeasantization: "There is no future here for the youth. Many have already left, and surely many will continue to do so."

Clesío did not necessarily hold the opinion that the death of either the movement or the peasantry was inevitable. "The pedagogical encampment is great, but it by itself doesn't keep the movement alive. We need more *jornadas* [journeys or thematic movement campaigns], more struggle, and more actions by the movement. Because just the pedagogical encampment by itself doesn't provide sustenance for the movement." It is this pedagogical encampment, this space of alternative knowledge production, of political formation, and movement networking, that is indeed *the* face of the movement for many youth. But it is not sufficient to breathe sustaining life back into the movement. The pedagogical encampment is similar to a seed; it's a central starting point that provides a kernel of nourishment, but it needs further sustenance. Without that broader horizon of action, the movement will wither. Education can play an important role in solidifying the movement and its members' permanency on the land, but these moments of political formation need to be scaled up.

Clesío's relation to the movement, the settlement, and the land itself is complex. On one level he loves the settlement; like virtually all residents of the community I spoke with, he really appreciates the tranquility and relaxed pace of life there. He also identifies with the movement and believes that it's only through struggle that they will improve their lives. But his disenchantment with the movement and the lack of job opportunities in the settlement, coupled with the difficulty of agricultural labor, spelled the end of his future there.

> I won't say that I don't identify as Sem Terra, because there's always a root, a root of Sem Terra; that root of the movement, it's genetic. I do identify as a Sem Terra, but unfortunately, I need to leave to find work in other places. To live here, you need to transform yourself into a mini-latifundíario. You need to be able to acquire five, six, seven plots of land in order to have enough cattle. Because agriculture doesn't work; there's no return, there's no benefits. If someday I have a son or daughter, I wouldn't want them to group up in this way, in this settlement. For the last ten years it's been simply parada.

Clesío's view was that one is always Sem Terra—an identity that is stable over time and space. However, being Sem Terra, being a part of the movement, being engaged in agriculture, was not sustainable. What was sustainable was what was hegemonic: extensive cattle ranching. To be successful one needs to move away from being a peasant and toward being a fazendeiro—the livelihood that his parents struggled against. Yet for those settlement residents who believed in the MST's transformative potential, there were alternative futures. For Clesío the community was parada, but as he told me, "There are other visions. The population of the 17 de Abril, we could work for ourselves. But we need stimulus. Just like any other community in any other place, we need stimulus. There could be a center for artisanal craft production, or a milk processing facility, people could be working for themselves. But there just needs to be stimulus, and there needs to be training. It's like a child learning to walk. You need to offer the child something to encourage them as they're learning to walk." Clesío's concluding sentiments bring us back to the original hope for the 17 de Abril—for it to be a food-sovereign space, a space for both value-added production and the production of raw materials, where settlement residents work collectively. This is the vision of not only many residents but also the MST at a larger scale. It is the vision of food sovereignty, of being in control of one's food system, of not exporting raw materials so that another entity captures the value-added production. But it's simply a vision—one that will likely not be actualized—without two things: financial support, in the form of credit, to get a processing facility off the ground and training both on the technical side of facilities operation and on the logistical side in terms of cooperative business management. The opportunities and constraints of political economy and its intersection with education are once again at the root of agrarian change.

What Clesío highlights is that the agrarian question is at its core about sustainability. Life within the movement simply is not sustainable; that is, political participation cannot go on indefinitely without material sustenance. Yet for Clesío life within the settlement is not sustainable either; that is, one must become a mini-latifundíario in order to produce at the scale necessary to maintain a family. The sustainability of movement politics (i.e., the long-term viability of the MST) and that of the environment (as increasingly the landscape is defined by highly compacted and degraded cattle pasture) are intertwined. A pivotal element of Clesío's analysis is that education can make a direct intervention in these questions of political and environmental sustainability: education, as exemplified by the pedagogical encampment, can help codify an emerging political identity (supporting the political sustainability of the MST), and training opportunities can help develop new agroecological cooperatives that could keep people on the land. But for Clesío there needs to be material support. As Clesío concluded, "You need to offer the child something to encourage them as they're learning to walk." Clesío's last comment underscores that the political economy of education—in the form of agricultural credit provided in tandem with technical training—remains a major hurdle for the permanence of the peasantry. But if many people like Clesío are giving up, who is staying?

Creating Diversified Connections

"Raymond of the fruit," as he is playfully known in the settlement, exemplifies the complicated face of repeasantization. At just over five feet tall and with short cropped hair, Raymond peeked his head through the opening in his cinder block home that functions as a window. His thirty-three-year-old life is one of movement, and he is rarely still. It took me several weeks just to find him at his house for brief chat. He was in the village only in the evenings and on Sunday afternoons. Sitting in his home next to a horizontal freezer that he uses to hold cupuaçu fruit pulp that he harvests from his trees and sells in town, he explained that every morning he leaves by six o'clock to travel an hour and a half to Vale's mines, where he directs traffic, returning to the settlement by six in the evening. On the weekend he is on his rural land, working toward his dream of opening a small fruit business. It is his off-farm labor, working at the mines, that provides him the income he can invest in agroforestry.

Raymond is able to remain on the land due to what Van der Ploeg (2008) refers to as pluriactivity, reciprocal interrelations between his agroecological production and off-farm labor. He has planted several thousand trees on his land, all of which are economically valuable fruit trees, including açaí (*Euterpe oleracea*), cacao (*Theobroma cacao*, known as the source of cocoa beans), cupuaçu (*Theobroma grandiflorum*), and graviola (*Annona muricata*, also known as soursop). Raymond has also invested in apiculture and is raising a few cattle. All of this, he told me, is paying off; the cupuaçu in the freezer in particular is providing quite a good income. Although some scholars see off-farm labor like Raymond's work in the mines as proof of the death of the peasantry and grassroots visions of food sovereignty (Bernstein 2014), for others pluriactivity is one of the constitutive factors of the peasantry and a characteristic of repeasantization (Van der Ploeg 2008). Raymond agreed: it's the ability to go off the settlement that is enabling him to remain on the settlement, working the land agroecologically.

Raymond's fledgling agroforestry initiative speaks to a new vision of the peasantry—and their contemporary aspirations. Raymond's family, like so many of the settlement's original inhabitants, moved from the state of Maranhão, where they were sharecroppers, to Pará in 1982. "We lived, never having land of our own. And I grew up, alongside my mother, planting rice, corn, manioc, and giving a portion of what we harvested to the landowner." By 1994, after approximately a decade, Raymond's parents had been able to earn enough money selling their remaining produce that they were able to purchase a small piece of land near Marabá, becoming landowners for the first time in their lives. But they always had a desire, a desire for a piece of land that was just slightly bigger and would be more capable of providing for their family. Raymond's mother went to Curionópolis, signed her name in the ledger, and moved into the MST's encampment. She was present at, and survived, the 1996 massacre in Eldorado das Carajás. Following the massacre she was awarded land from the National Institute of Colonization and Agrarian Reform (INCRA), and the family moved to its new plot. On the "promised land" they continued life much as they had been living, planting roça and raising a few cattle.

Like many of the settlement's inhabitants, such as Clesío, Raymond has always had the desire for something a little better—more opportunities for study, a little additional income. He wanted a life that was not exclusively of the roça. Since the mid-2000s, Raymond has operated a small bakery. One day when he was visiting friends in the nearby the city of Tucúma, he met people who were engaged in growing cacao and other types of agroforestry, such as cupuaçu and *pimento de reina*. When he returned to the settlement he came with a car trunk full of saplings—açaí, cupuaçu, and cacao.

When I asked why he brought home this load, Raymond answered by first providing context, disentangling the constraints that the settlement's farmers face. Land, he explained, is seen as one of the primary limitations. The land plots originally awarded MST members by the government are simply too small to use for cattle ranching, unless one can manage to assemble a larger plot by buying the surrounding plots, as Clesío said one would have to do. The problem of the land's carrying capacity is exacerbated by the fact that families are growing in size and number, and as children grow up, marry, and have families of their own, the land isn't sufficient to support multiple families through ranching.

There are a few ways that residents grapple with these dual pressures of environmental constraints and demographic change. The first is by purchasing more land. Acquiring more lots enables the scaling up of cattle production. This is a major trend in the settlement, with some owning upward of ten conjoined lots. This reconcentration of land is directly at odds with the MST's vision and broader political project of decentralizing landownership. It is what Clesío described earlier as becoming a mini-fazendeiro and is depicted in the oft-heard saying around town, "These days, everyone wants to be a fazendeiro." This reconcentration of land is indeed increasingly a reality as individuals choose to stop farming subsistence crops and others gain the economic resources that enable them to consolidate. This is the process of differentiation—individuals changing their relative class position by acquiring more financial capital, land, and social capital (Bernstein 2014). It's a transition that many folks were resigned to—brushing their hands back and forth as if wiping dust off them, they would indicate it was a process outside of their control.

Another option for dealing with the tension between small land plots and growing families is to diversify, as Raymond has done. Diversification can be thought of as the spatial and material reversal of consolidation. As opposed to scaling out and acquiring more land, one scales in and increases the diversity of production, remaining on the one plot of land. As opposed to a spatially extensive cattle ranching operation, which requires large expanses of space to meet the subsistence needs of a family, this is a spatially intensive form of production where there are multiple layers of interconnected production. Raymond told me, "On this little piece of land, everything's working out: I've developed a small area for raising bees, raising cattle, I'm investing in the production of açaí, cupuaçu, cacao, acerola, cajo, all these things—so as to create an income that's a little bit better. Because it's impossible to survive on cattle alone. So I take the approach of trying to invest a little bit every day, a few more transplants of açaí, of cacao, of cupuaçu, which over time will provide a fuller income." Raymond was proud not only of his ability to increase his income on a single plot of land but equally of his contribution to the "environmental question," as he put it. "The manner in which I am investing in the land, planting transplants and so on, I think this is really contributing to the environment. Because these days, it's difficult to work using fire, and we don't have the financial ability to use large machines. So I think this is a really great thing, that at the same time that you're receiving a better income, you're also contributing to the environment." Many critiques of peasant studies are that they reify populist notions of noble peasants who have timeless sustainable traditions (cf. Bernstein 2014). Raymond is certainly not some mythical ecologically beneficent peasant, however. He grew up, like most in the community, practicing swidden agriculture—or what in popular parlance is known as slash-and-burn. This agriculture made immanent sense for the settlement's pioneers. Areas of forest needed to be cleared, and doing so provided fertile soil and in turn food. However, ecologically speaking, that is not possible any longer. The forest is simply not there, nor could people like Raymond afford heavy machinery for larger-scale monocropping. Agroecological land management just makes sense, not because of an imaginary innate peasant nature but because of the pragmatics of spatial and economic constraint: scarce land and few resources to acquire inputs.

When land is scarce or at least insufficient to meet the needs of the family—particularly the expanding family—peasants are confronted with a few options. Will they move off the land in search of wage labor? Will they become capitalist farmers? Or will they become more peasantlike? The first option—to leave—most often takes the form of a youth exodus. They head to nearby cities, or, as in Clesío's case, they try to enter the movement for themselves in order to get a piece of land of their own. The second option—to acquire more land and become a fazendeiro—is available only to those with some cash reserves in the first place. The third option—to diversify, producing more products on a smaller piece of land, as Raymond did—can function as a form of repeasantization because it differentiates one's income base.

Framed through these three options, the agrarian question is simultaneously a question of ecological and social reproduction. It is both ecological and social because the spatial constraints of land access, when coupled with the environmental degradation wrought by overgrazing, mean that one cannot sustain the family if one cannot sustain the land. And, on the flip side, it is both ecological and social because to sustain the expanding family on the land means sustaining the land, developing integrated systems of agroecological production that provide diversified incomes and do not overtax the land. Raymond might not fit the mental imaginary of a peasant because he works in Vale's mines, yet he encapsulates Van der Ploeg's conception of the "new peasantry." Similarly, Alan, whom I now turn to, will probably not fit most people's mental picture of Sem Terra, but his vision is one directly in line with the movement.

Being Sem Terra

In the years I have known him, Alan has never participated in an MST event nor worn its shirt or hat. Yet he unequivocally identifies as Sem Terra. As we loaded a fifty-pound bag of cupuaçu on his motorcycle one day, he told me, "Identity for us is everything; it's how my father earned the land, it's where we raise our children, it's how we're able to give continuity to this life we've created; it's how *here*—in the rural area—we're always trying to enable our children to be able to move ahead a bit." For Alan, identity is a question about what it means to be Sem Terra, but not in the simplistic sense that many activists and academics assume, where being Sem Terra is synonymous with one's degree of participation in the movement—with wearing red, pumping one's fist in the air, and occupying INCRA. Rather, for Alan, being Sem Terra is in a broader sense about one's historical relation to the land vis-à-vis the struggle—as he indicated, it's about how his father won the land and how he wants to give continuity to that struggle.

Alan did not grow up being deeply involved in the movement. As he recalled, "I never really walked with the movement, because I was always too young. It was always my father who participated if there was an occupation of INCRA or the railways. I accompanied it a little bit within the settlement—participating in meetings—specifically meetings for youth, but never really walked with the movement." Alan's usage of the word *andava* (to have walked) is significant here because it is tied to his understanding of participating in the MST as being a life of movement. Walking back into his cupuaçu agroforestry area, Alan reflected that as he was growing up, he saw what his brother Vancivaldo's life was like, as someone who had been much more explicitly involved in MST politics than he, Alan, had been. By the time he was sixteen, Vancivaldo was a member of various state-level MST collectives. Vancivaldo's political participation paid off, and he was rewarded, quite literally, selected by the MST's state leadership for a scholarship to study in a social movement medical school in Cuba. Vancivaldo's life was—and remains—one of extensive movement; even before he left for medical school, he was constantly traveling to various workshops, meetings, and demonstrations. And this was not what Alan wanted. Leaning against one of his cupuaçu trees, Alan asked me, "If to be *in the movement* means to *be always in movement* itself [*pra ser parte do movimento significa estar sempre em movimento mesmo*], then how would I tend to the land?"

Alan's thorny question warrants critical reflection on the relationship between political participation and agrarian change: Alan did not want to join the movement in an active sense because it would mean being away from the land. This is perhaps one of the many contradictions of life within the movement's higher echelons; the life of the movement is indeed *one of movement*, and by definition not of sustained interaction in place. If we think about how the MST at a national level frames its objectives—namely activists engaging in the long-term process of social transformation from within the settlement itself—then it becomes clear that the process of building a new society within the shell of the old is difficult to materialize if one is active in the movement, shuttling between movement activities, and by default not embedded in the daily processes and relations of settlement life.[4] And this is the irony, perhaps, that for the movement's vision of activist-farmers to materialize, those at the vanguard must choose only one half of this identity—to focus on being an activist, as Vancivaldo did, or a farmer, as his older brother Alan did. To be both, all the time, is virtually impossible.

For Alan, identity is also a question of familial relations. It's about whether one is able to maintain a consolidated family farm where the children help out, learning while working the land. It's about the future of those children too: whether or not they will be able to work the land, providing for their own families as they grow older, or whether they will need to move off the farm.

One answer to this family question involves agroecological diversification. It requires figuring out ways to derive more sustenance from the land and to involve the family more fully in its production and reproduction.

Agroecology is indeed complex, and to learn its techniques requires training. This agroecological learning—where individuals develop new knowledge or skills in agroecology—is integral to diversifying land usage and passing on an agrarian identity. Over the last year Alan has begun working with Solomão, an agricultural extension agent based in the settlement. Solomão has encouraged Alan to become involved with rotational grazing. Alan showed me that he has been setting up picketed areas on his land and is cycling cattle through them, which he tells me reduces the cattle's impact on the land. For Alan, simple agroecological methods, such as rotational grazing, enable the pasture to regenerate while not necessitating more land. These agroecological methods are at the core of spatially intensifying one's connection to the land. As he went on to tell me, they were also crucial in ensuring the viability of his livelihood and the future of his family. "With this work of rotational grazing—where we can raise more cattle—this is one of the ways that we're able to keep our children here. Because with the land we have which isn't being used, it's possible for us to raise our family as well, to derive the sustenance for our family as well." Here Alan was speculating that the intensification permitted by practices like rotational grazing will allow his son, when he grows up, to earn a livelihood on the same piece land as well. "This in reality, this is the challenge for family farming: to bring together the whole family on that piece of land; so that we can raise cattle, but not just cattle, but so that there is enough water to raise fish, to be able to plant. So, it's about being able to harness culture [agroecological traditions] to be able to remain on the land with all of the family. This is good for us all. It's about an identity, because it's about developing this project." The agroecological system that Alan is creating is characterized by diverse cropping systems integrated in spatially complex configurations; this is an approach to farming that is closely connected with questions of identity and the agrarian question itself. It is no surprise, then, that this is the form of agriculture around which the MST has rallied.

Concluding our walk around his cupuaçu area, we sat in the shade of some mango trees beside the house. Taking long, finely pointed scissors, Alan began the tedious process of cutting from the cupuaçu seed the fleshy mucilage that he will sell. After a few minutes I took a break from cracking open cupuaçu shells (my job, as I don't have the precision to cut the cupuaçu) and returned to what I'd realized is the most elemental question—the one we'd somehow avoided talking about throughout our walk. "Do you identify as a camponês [peasant], and . . . ," I wondered out loud in a trailing fashion, "what does that even mean anymore?" Putting down his scissors, Alan nodded his head: "Sure, I identify as a camponês. I guess in the sense of being a rural producer. I was born in the middle of it, my father and mother bringing me up working roça. I like the campo, I like to fish, and I like to be out in the roça and everything. If you know how to do it—with proper management—you can earn a decent income. I identify as camponês because ever since I was born, I was in this environment." For Alan, identity is clearly tied to place, but it is also framed by its relation to broader agrarian concerns:

> It is through these activities that we are able to feed everyone, even the rich in the cities. Corn, manioc, beans—all these things are going to the city. Now, [the production of] these things are decreasing, because no one wants to plant roça anymore. Everybody wants to move to the city, everybody wants to work in industries, no one wants to stay. And so the rural area is ending up being depopulated.
>
> The government sees this, and is looking to develop courses, ways of keeping the students in the rural areas. And I think this is necessary, because these days, all of the children of the assentados are just going away.
>
> From my time, when I was a student here, the only people that are still here are myself and Edinete [his wife]. Out of a cohort of twenty-five students in my high school class, there are just two of us. Everyone else has left. And Edinete doesn't really work with roça.
>
> But not me, I like it, I see it as really necessary, both for those of us that identify, and for the rest of society, who is consuming, who needs to be able to buy these foods. For me, to be camponês means to live in harmony with nature; you live within a rural area, and you're able to have various types of production. You're able to take from the soil your suste-nance. This is living in harmony.

The interconnections between food sovereignty, identity, and the political economy of education are at the forefront of Alan's narrative. Depeasantization is transforming the campo: nearly every student in Alan's high school cohort has left the settlement. Alan is the only one who remains actually working the land (Edinete works with the settlement's health clinic). Alongside this broad demographic transition are accompanying transitions in food sovereignty and foodways. As individuals move to urban areas or remain in the settlement and abandon farming, they lose control over their food system and become reliant upon the limited variety and volatile prices of commercial foodstuffs in the settlement's tiny *comércios* (local markets). That year, for example, I observed the cost of beans (*feijão do sul*) in local markets double in price (from approximately eight to seventeen reais per two-kilogram bag); this price volatility was a subject of wide conversation. The shift from being a producer to a consumer, for Alan, marked a transformation in identity: "From the moment you're buying products that you know contain transgenics [GMOs], from that moment on you're not living in harmony." Not being in harmony with nature, Alan equated earlier with the dissolution of the camponês identity. But it need not be this way. Education in the form of new courses, Alan noted above, is necessary if youth are going to remain in rural areas and not abandon the campo for urban centers.

Up until this point I have portrayed two visions of rural change in this chapter. Depeasantization is undoubtedly occurring as the settlement's youth, disillusioned with agriculture and the possibilities of life with the movement itself, head to urban centers. However, repeasantization is also occurring as individuals diversify; they are creating the material conditions of production that enable themselves and their children to remain on the land. As Alan intonated, formal education may play a role in mediating these processes of agrarian change. In the final section of this chapter I turn to explore how education might contribute to repeasantization. This third section begins with, and revolves around, transformations in the highly symbolic anniversary of the settlement.

Agrarian Change and the Politics of the Possible

I gained deeper insight into how education interfaces with the politics of agrarian change during the settlement's anniversary celebration in November 2012. That morning I groaned as the settlement's radio began crackling at five thirty. Samío, the man in charge of the community radio system, cannot be starting this early, I thought. However, it was the unmistakable first notes of the MST's anthem that caused me to sit straight up in bed. Although I'd lived here for seventeen months, it was the first time I'd ever heard the MST anthem played on the community radio in the 17 de Abril settlement.

I was surprised as the song ended and began again. I reached the central square, watching what would appear to be another normal morning unfold, if not for the fact that the anthem finished and then began yet again. After the fourth repetition I heard a voice break the radical monotony, but it was not Samío's. Rather it was Gemeio, the settlement's president. In his speech on the community radio, Gemeio extolled the importance of the settlement's anniversary in the historical context of regional agrarian reform. Three other MST leaders from the settlement followed Gemeio and gave speeches on the importance of the movement.

As if on cue a vehicle lurched into the central square. It was a flatbed truck carrying sets of giant speakers bolted together. A man with a cowboy hat stood on a stage that rested atop the speakers. He did a sound check and proceeded in what was clearly a professional rodeo announcer's voice: "Wellllllllllcome Amazonian horsemen from all neighboring cities. Wellllllllllcome to Amazônia's biggest rural horse parade!" As his call bellowed out, from all six intersecting streets men, women, and youth on horses began to stream out into the central square (fig. 4.1)..

Douglas was orchestrating the horse parade. He was a large-scale dairy producer and in this role had become one of the settlement's most powerful individuals. While directing the riders he told me, "My dream is for this event to be on the scale of the big cattle expositions. Complete with lasso events, and a real rodeo." Douglas handed out flags to several horse riders: a state of Pará flag, a Brazilian flag, and one from the MST. Aside from this morning's radio

Figure 4.1. Cattle culture in movement

Figure 4.2. The lone symbol of the movement

announcements, it would be the only sign of the MST on this settlement's seventeenth birthday (fig. 4.2). Absent were the MST flags, banners, T-shirts, and hats. Also absent were the members of the MST's state leadership and activists from other encampments or settlements. Sometimes absences are more telling than presences..

Changes in the settlement's anniversary celebration epitomize the tension between depeasantization and repeasantization. This anniversary used to be a harvest festival, marking the importance of various subsistence crops. However, as detailed in chapter 2, a number of factors, ranging from credit incentives to urban migration and the failure of agricultural projects and cooperatives, have resulted in the large-scale transition away from agriculture and toward milk production. As a result, what used to be a harvest festival is now a rodeo. The hegemony of cattle culture is in no way synonymous with depeasantization directly. As many would argue, without the income from dairy they wouldn't be able to remain living on the land, and would have long ago moved to nearby urban centers. However, what Jeffery Hoelle (2014) refers to as "cattle culture," ranging from the *cauboi* (cowboy) dress to *sertaneja* music and milk production, has come to replace the movement's agroecological vision—at least in large part. Despite the dominance of cattle culture at this event, there are still some indications of the settlement's agrarian roots. José Batista was one vestige.

On the settlement's anniversary, José Batista stood in front of a cart decorated with hanging fresh mangoes, papayas, squash, and various other agricultural products (figs. 4.3 and 4.4). On the cart's edge sat a homemade water wheel, fed by a tank in the back of the cart. "People hardly remember these," José Batista admonished, "but they should. I'm here to remind them, to represent the settlement, to represent the small family farmers and the various products they produce." José's reminder was of the traditional agroecological experimentation that characterizes the community's agrarian history. In some senses, José Batista was an image of the past. Walking inside the settlement's headquarters, I saw a series of photos on a bulletin board to the side of door. One photograph was of a man grinning widely as he harvests rice. In another photo a group sat processing a bumper crop of corn (fig. 4.5). The last photo, which was taken directly in front of the door where I now stood, showed a settlement resident giving the thumbs-up sign while proudly displaying a variety of fruits and vegetables he produced. According to the last photo's date, it was taken five years ago today, when the settlement's anniversary took the form of a harvest festival. Looking out the door and at José Batista standing

Figure 4.3. Vestiges of an agrarian past, or of a food-sovereign future?

next to his cart, my eyes felt like they were in parallax, trying to bring together a disjunctive reality into singular focus. Was José Batista an icon of the past? Or perhaps of the future?.

Educators politically aligned with the MST see this anniversary celebration, and José Batista, as "a potentiality to be rescued." I'd previously seen these educators marshal Batista's image at a presentation about agroecology at the settlement's school. With an image of Batista projected on the wall, one teacher described to an auditorium of students how the settlement comprised not solely cattle ranching but rather diverse experiences of agroecological production. José Batista exemplified that agroecological vision. More recently, I'd heard various murmurings from these MST educators that they were developing a project to reclaim the symbolic and material underpinnings of this event, which had once been a harvest festival.

One afternoon I biked across the settlement to speak with Zé, an MST-aligned educator from the settlement's school whom I had recently heard talking about rescuing the harvest festival. I wanted to know from Zé how he and other educators saw the relationship between the *calvagada* and the harvest festival as well as what role education might play in mediating their connection. Upon entering his shaded porch, Zé invited me to sit down for a *cafezinho*. I remarked at the beautiful quilted floor mat that sat in front of the doorway. With a wave of his hand Zé motioned his daughter inside, who promptly returned with one in a plastic bag, which she set at my feet as a gift. "Traditional culture," Zé told me. "My wife makes them." Placing his jelly jar of coffee down, Zé reflected, "The calvagada is part of rural culture. But the calvagada points back to the culture of the fazendeiros, it points back to practices of raising cattle at a large scale. And this isn't our vision. Our vision [that of the MST] is agricultural production. And the calvagada isn't about agricultural production; it's a demonstration—a visualization of who has pasture. The calvagada is a demonstration of difference; when you see a calvagada you think of fazendeiros, of fazendas." As Zé described it, the calvagada is literally how space is visualized, how difference is symbolically performed, how power is manifest, and how hegemony is maintained through cultural production. It's an event that performs a normative sense of identity, an identity of becoming. As Douglas had told me at the calvagada, his dream is for the event to be renowned at a regional level.

Yet the politics of the visible constrains what Guthman (2008) refers to as the politics of the possible, the repertoire of political change individuals think of as actual possibilities. The ultravisibility of cauboi culture makes invisible the small farmers and their agroecological production. It makes it appear that the 17 de Abril has transitioned in its entirety to dairy and that the only form

Figure 4.4. Representing all of the producers in the 17 de Abril

Figure 4.5. Imagining a productive past (Courtesy of Luis Lima)

of production that is *possible* is cattle based. While the omnipresence of cattle culture seems to denote that the failure of the MST's agroecological vision is a foregone conclusion, educators use the example of José Batista to impress upon students that this is a cultural mirage: the near omnipresence of cattle is simply obscuring other forms of culture. As Zé explained, "When you see another type of culture—in relation to agriculture—you see the farmer *in* the produce. If you see pumpkin, watermelon, rice, beans, corn, if you see these types of produce, you can visualize the farmer. You don't see a fazenda, which is what you see when you see a calvagada. It's a question of the visualization of culture." For Zé, the importance of the festival is about visualizing what many in the MST would call a "matrix of production"—a social-agricultural system. The type of production embodies social relations and ideology. The festival is so significant in this because it symbolically indexes the settlement's political, agricultural, and cultural identity. The hegemony of cattle production portends depeasantization—associated with the increasing consolidation of land in the community and the disavowal of the movement's agrarian ideals. Visualizing corn, beans, and squash at the festival, by contrast, highlights a different social reality—a vision of the world that ideologically, materially, and culturally tracks the MST's agrarian ideals. As José Batista's cart and sign symbolize and he himself literally declared, he is representing the small farmers. His presence is a form of agroecological resistance. For Zé and other educators, "rescuing the harvest festival," having it replace the calvagada, would be a symbolically powerful form of resistance.

Yet Zé went on to tell me that rescuing the harvest festival was about more than symbolic politics; it was also about giving people a concrete incentive to produce so that they will have something to show on the day of the festival.

> The importance of the harvest festival is about motivating productivity; the fact is this festival is not just about having a harvest festival, but the broader objective is that the farmers, the producers, they'll return to producing, to producing something for the harvest festival. Because today, if we were to have a harvest festival today, few people would have any produce to put forward. Because here in the 17 de Abril, everyone is basically focused on cattle, and on milk, so the importance of recovering the event is so that people will show on this day that the 17 is producing. So it's that the producers really are producing, for that day.

Zé visualized the recovery of the harvest festival as a way to help reorient the broader matrix of production and the settlement's agrarian identity.

Zé and other educators see the school as playing a pivotal role in rescuing the harvest festival. When I asked Zé about where education in general, and the school in particular, fit into this picture, he began by telling me about the MST's educator conference that took place at the nearby Palmares settlement and was profiled in chapter 3.

> This conference was very good because it went over the history, and opened our eyes, encouraging us to valorize the culture that we have, and to intensify what we're doing in the school. Because we don't do it [valorize the MST's agrarian culture] in a manner that's continuous, like all the time. Rather, it's one day here and another day there. The workshops and so on [at Palmares], these opened our eyes, they showed us that we have to do something, we can't remain stalled. They taught us techniques, various things that we need to put into practice. If not, then the history is going to be lost. So I'm going to work with Lucinede on reviving the harvest festival, emphasizing this history.

Zé went on to tell me that the school's role in reinforcing agrarian traditions is broader than simply the harvest festival.

> We have a school garden, and we'd like to increase our usage of the garden, increase the students' exposure to it. We've got an apiary now, and the students will participate in running it. We want to create a mandala [an agroecological plot consisting of concentric garden beds filled with companion planting that are irrigated by a pond at the center of the circle doubling as a fish production area] because we have all of the space behind the school down to the river. So the school is going to have more initiatives like this in relation to these diverse forms of production, to do this transition from the present, past, to the future.

For Zé, discussing the harvest festival in the school, building a school garden, involving the students in the management of an apiary were not apolitical projects. Rather, these were part of a broader process of rescuing the MST's political identity. As he went on, moving seamlessly from the discussion of food systems education to political education,

> The school needs to work to recuperate the memory, because our students, our children, are coming from diverse places, and don't necessarily have contact with our culture, with our values, with our identity.

The school needs to put it into practice and valorize it, for example we need to start singing the hymn of the MST, talking about the flag of the MST, asking questions [to the students] about why [do we have] the flag, what is the symbolism of it? Why does the flag have a woman, a machete, and so forth? What are the meaning of these symbols? Why when we sing the anthem do we use the left hand and not the right? So these symbols, these values, need to be discussed in the school, with the children in particular.

As Zé and I talked, it increasingly seemed like our conversation was revolving around education and the agrarian question: What would become of the settlement? Would youth like Clesío continue to become disillusioned with agriculture and political participation, leaving the community for an urban imaginary? Or would youth be encouraged to diversify, to value their rural culture and livelihoods? I asked Zé what I felt was the elephant-in-the-room question: how does education play a role in the question of ficar ou sair? He responded,

The youth want to be able to sustain their lives. Before, the youth were incentivized to do a technical course through the movement around agroecology, around culture; for example, we had a course that took place in São Luis [city in the state of Maranhão], including some students from here, and today they're working as technicians in the settlements.[5] By having these opportunities, the youth would be getting trained on the outside in order to work here in the settlement.

From the moment you open the window for these youths, to get trained and be able to come back, the settlement grows a little bit each time. Now, when you don't have the opportunities, the youth leave for Marabá, Paraupebas, and so on, and who knows whether or not they'll return.

As Zé pieced it together, education can serve as either a depeasantizing or repeasantizing force. Without educational opportunities crafted through the movement, courses that value local landscapes and forms of production, students will leave the settlement and perhaps never return. Education, whether it's at the local school helping students learn about the movement and diverse forms of production or professional training courses aimed at imparting technical knowledge, can help bring another reality into existence. For Zé, education can play a role in rescuing the movement's vision of agricultural production, political identity, and, as a symbol of all this transformation, the harvest festival too.

Conclusion

The question of ficar ou sair (to stay or to leave) is at the heart of the so-called agrarian question: what will happen to the future of the peasantry? Through this chapter I've explored how questions of political identity, agroecology, and education mediate the twin processes of depeasantization and repeasantization and in turn the agrarian question. The settlement is at a crossroads between these disparate visions of development: leaving for the promise of an urban imaginary or remaining and trying to actualize an agrarian one.

The MST's vision is of repeasantization. The movement seeks to create a political identity of agrarian connection among many who have never had access to land. Yet as Clesío and Alan highlighted, that project is constrained by the politics of sustainability. Being simultaneously active in the movement and maintaining one's commitment to being a farmer are not sustainable. Life within the encampment and the settlement is seen as parada—stopped. The movement, for many, is seen as a failure because it has not produced sufficient benefits, material resources, and opportunities. Depeasantization is unquestionably taking place, as youth stream out the settlement in search of jobs in nearby urban centers.

Leaving the settlement is not necessarily synonymous with depeasantization. As Raymond highlights, it is through pluriactivity (Van der Ploeg 2008), through leaving each morning to work in the mines of Vale, that he is able to achieve his, and the MST's, vision of agroecological production. For Alan as well, space must be carefully negotiated. Given the small lot sizes, it's simply not possible to produce at the scale needed to maintain one's family if one relies on cattle production. But if one diversifies, creating spatially complex and reciprocally integrated agroecological systems, then the constraints of space can be reimagined. Alan believes that food sovereignty—diversifying and remaining in control over one's production—can provide a future for his family and preserve his identity as a camponês.

Educational processes, ranging along the continuum of pedagogical formality, play an important role in this repeasantizing process: Alan highlighted the importance of technical training. Clesío underscored the value of political education gained through the pedagogical encampment. Zé drew our attention to the capacity of the school, as a formal education space, to shape students' agroecological practices and political subjectivities.

The settlement's anniversary symbolizes the complex crossroads that characterize the community. An event that was long a celebration of political struggle and agroecological production has become a horse parade. This is common sense, as cattle culture has become increasingly hegemonic and the movement's agrarian vision is for many an anachronism. But it's not only the community's agrarian roots that are withering; its political ones are in dire straits as well. For the settlement's MST-affiliated educators, it is through critical forms of food systems education—through pedagogies that rescue peasant identities, memories of struggle, and agroecological practices—that the future of the movement and the settlement can be rewritten.

Interlude

The rural countryside is at a crossroads. Social movements have carved out new territories, beginning a process of decolonizing the historically inequitable system of land concentration. However, as we saw in chapter 4, these new territories are somewhat fragile and are under attack both literally by armed gunmen as well as by the economic pull of capital and visions of modernization. The struggle over territory is not simply material but also ideological. For peasants to engage in agroecological production, it is not enough to simply break down the fences surrounding land; rather, the fences surrounding the production of knowledge must also be dismantled.

Throughout part II I explore the ways in which education is deeply imbricated in the question of whether or not, and how, the peasantry will remain on the land. MST educators see the traditional education system as interconnected with processes of depeasantization. Rural schools promulgate ideas of peasant livelihoods and identities as archaic. Youth are also increasingly sent to schools in nearby urban centers. Many within the MST see conventional education as breaking the bonds between generations and enshrining a new commonsense view of agriculture as backward. The traditional education system in this context is functioning as a form of social reproduction; it is reproducing the dominant ideologies, usages of space, and land management.

However, education can also serve as an alternative form of social reproduction. Grassroots social movements, such as the MST, are actively working to bring new systems of education into existence. Educação do campo is one such vision. As opposed to rural education, which prepares rural youth for lives in urban centers, educação do campo offers an alternative visualization of how space and society can be interconnected. Rather than depeasantization, education can help contribute to a process of repeasantization. Through helping youth learn about agroecology, critical food systems education can advance new ways of engaging with the landscape as well as codifying insurgent agrarian identities.

For education to serve as an alternative form of social reproduction, it must be decolonized. Decolonization is both a physical and epistemological process through which subaltern groups construct insurgent forms of knowledge and embed these within the broader structures of society. Decolonization is both physical and epistemological, because territory is both material and ideological. The landscape is tightly interconnected with particular forms of knowledge. The Green Revolution and its ideology of agricultural modernization have played a formative role in shaping educational institutions, systems of agricultural credit, and agricultural land management practices. Decolonizing education calls upon youth to rethink taken-for-granted assumptions of agrarian development, including what constitutes productive and backward agriculture. Part of decolonization is reinhabitation, of building new relations to the land that are sustaining culturally, of coming to exist and engage with the landscape in novel ways. Critical forms of food systems education offer this potential: to help students deconstruct the historical violence that landscapes and peoples have endured and to redress that through agroecological practices. Decolonization is a dialectical process whereby not only the land but simultaneously education and the self are transformed through reciprocal processes. What emerges are new visions of the world, which hold the potential to transform the terrain of ideologies.

This next section takes its name from the writings of Antonio Gramsci, who saw ideologies as historically situated forms of domination that must be combatted as part of a process of political struggle. To liberate the governed from the governing, to cast aside enshrined common sense, to destroy hegemony and create another new vision of the world, it is crucial for individuals to become conscious of their social position and of the tasks needed to collectively mobilize and transform society. This is a struggle of the battle of ideas. It is a struggle that happens on the terrain of ideologies, which is a superstructure upon which social groups become conscious of their own existence, strength, and process of becoming. My goal within the next few chapters is to shed light on how questions surrounding the nature of space intersect with the politics, economics, and ecologies of education to shape this terrain of ideology. There are three broad ways in which space is intricately involved in the contest over education and the struggle over insurgent ideologies.

First, questions of hegemony are inherently scalar. That which is hegemonic at a local scale is a function of its ubiquity at scales that are higher up. For example, there was consensus within the community about not only how açaí should be prepared and consumed but what it meant symbolically. Açaí should be blended with equal parts sugar and served with tapioca balls; this local approach was what Gramsci would describe as "common sense" (as I found out by making the egregious faux pas of not adding sugar one afternoon). Açaí was to be consumed in the afternoon, following work as a respite from the heat. But increasingly, as Jane Fajans writes in *Brazilian Food: Race, Class, and Identity in Regional Cuisines* (2012), this regional approach is informed by cultural meanings attributed to the fruit by those in the Global North and elites in Rio de Janeiro and elsewhere who see it as an energy drink. Similarly, what Jeffery Hoelle (2014) refers to as cauboi culture, consisting of specific forms of dress, music, and home furnishings, is dominant within the 17 de Abril settlement because it is hegemonic within the region. Cultural practices, such as foodways and land management techniques, can undoubtedly have local meaning and inflections but are just as assuredly shaped by regional, national, and global processes. That which is "common sense" is hegemonic because of scale. Hegemony has an innate capacity to obfuscate. Emergent alternatives, whether they are forms of social organization, agricultural practices, or educational institutions, are invisible when seen against a broader landscape of common sense and domination. One misses the proverbial trees for the forest. How do these trees come into view? By viewing their interconnections they become recognized as a forest in their own right. Throughout part II I explore the interrelations between formal educational institutions and nonformal pedagogical spaces. Paying attention to the interconnections between these spaces highlights that a scalar shift is happening. Educação do campo, while unquestionably an emergent alternative system of education, is becoming scaled up. This process of scalar change does not happen naturally. Rather, transformative change is accomplished through forging linkages with allies in diverse state institutions.

Second, the concept of the frontier is frequently employed to describe southeastern Pará. Within many narratives, the term *frontier* is used to refer to the dynamic agrarian land structure and processes of demographic transition whereby individuals shift in relation to changing land availability (Hennessy 1978; Foweraker 1981; Schmink and Wood 1991). In other contexts the phrase is used to describe the processes of environmental exploitation associated with deforestation and the expansion of agroindustry. For example, the Brazilian news has long focused on the arc of deforestation and the expanding soy and palm oil frontier in the eastern Amazon. Tied to these conceptualizations is the usage of the concept to denote conflict. Southeastern Pará is a frontier because it is characterized by a land war; the frontier in this context is synonymous with agrarian violence. What these three conceptualizations touch on is the materiality of the frontier and its violent conflicts over physical resources. This is an imaginary of the frontier as material territory. Yet there is another, and co-occurring, form of territory, which Brazilian agrarian geographer Bernardo Mançano Fernandes (2009) describes as "immaterial." Immaterial territory is the landscape of ideas and helps structure the material form territory takes. In Fernandes's conception, material and ideological territories are interconnected. For example, agroecological knowledge about planting informs the spacing of plants and what form intercropping takes; knowledge shapes the landscape. Drawing upon Fernandes, southeastern Pará is not simply a material frontier but an ideological one. When seen through this lens, the frontier is a struggle over both material resources but also the production of forms of knowledge that structure access to, control over, and usage of those resources. The terrain of ideologies captures the dual nature of this struggle over immaterial and material resources. In part II I explore a novel conceptualization—that of the knowledge frontier. Southeastern Pará has been long been peripheral to centers of established knowledge production. The state has increasingly sought to establish its ideological presence in the region by developing new educational institutions. Yet as part of their efforts to transform the social and ecological dynamics of the frontier, social movements have sought to transform these educational institutions. Movements, such as the MST, are promulgating subaltern forms of knowledge and emancipatory pedagogies. As part of a terrain of ideologies, educational institutions come to compose a knowledge frontier, whereby there is a struggle to advance counter-hegemonic knowledge practices and visions of society within state educational institutions. I focus on two educational institutions in part II that are both dialectical products of processes of frontier expansion. They highlight how transformations in material and immaterial territory are intrinsically related.

Third, social movements are extensively engaged with questions of place. A key assumption of modernity is that knowledge has no geographic context; formal knowledge is seen as produced in a geopolitical vacuum, an ethereal space devoid of spatial politics. As we will see in part II, political-economic processes of agricultural modernization associated with the Green Revolution have created forms of agronomic education that inculcate singular visions of productivity, imaginaries that are produced in disparate contexts than the cultural and geographic realities of the Amazon. Educação do Campo is diametrically opposed to this spatial erasure. Through novel forms of pedagogy, which help students understand the interrelations between hegemonic and counter-hegemonic systems of production, educação do campo helps students form geographic understandings of place as explicitly relational, as a network of interconnected struggles. Creating this critical territorial consciousness is a process of unlearning, where students challenge commonsense ideas and become conscious of their own agency on the terrain of ideologies. Unlearning is a process of decolonization. Spaces with histories of explicit violence are reconfigured from geographies of repression to those of hope; this process of decolonization is driven by nonformal learning, which deconstructs common-sense ideologies of agriculture as "backward" and promulgates new conceptions of the world based in food sovereignty.

Part II

Terrain of Ideologies

CHAPTER 5

Communities of Praxis

Diana and Sandra began slowly, using sticks to etch an image into the soft clay. Sitting beneath a tree, I craned my neck to make out the figure. Diana, a teacher from the 17 de Abril settlement, wore a white T-shirt with an ostensible quote from Cuban revolutionary Che Guevara on the back: "Being young and not a revolutionary is a genetic contradiction."[1] I watch in silence as Diana grabbed a handful of white sand, allowing a thick stream of grains to fall from her fingers and fill the gouged line in the clay. While Diana filled in all of the shapes' defining lines, Sandra took a bag of corn and began sprinkling kernels throughout (fig. 5.1).

Figure 5.1. Reimagining Amazônia

As I stood on a nearby chair to take a photo of the approximately ten-meter image, it became clear what they were drawing: Amazônia. This was a map of the region's agroecological education initiatives, Diana told me. She was helping facilitate the construction of this morning's mística. Mística are cultural performances within the movement that integrate arts such as sculpture, theater, poetry, and dance; MST members frequently use them as ways of opening or closing important discussions (Issa 2007; Barcello 2012). The white lines demarcated the nine nations whose borders encompass Amazônia. The corn symbolized both the similarity and the broad distribution of agroecological education experiences of resistance throughout the region. Diana and Sandra's map of Amazônia, and this morning's mística, symbolized how critical food systems education is being scaled up to a regional level.

"Scaling up" critical food systems education means taking emergent examples at the local level and implementing them at higher geographic levels, such as the region or nation (Ferguson et al. 2019). This is scaling hierarchically (Brenner 2005: 9). But scaling critical food systems education also takes place horizontally, as social movements create pedagogical interconnections between disparate struggles that build a broader movement, which transgresses geopolitical boundaries (Leitner 2004: 237).

With Diana, I was at La Vía Campesina's Agroecological Institute of Latin America–Amazônia (IALA) for the concluding section of a university graduate certificate program on Educação do Campo, Agroecology, and the Agrarian Question in Amazônia. MST leaders and professors organized this concluding seminar as an opportunity to strategize the development of this institute as a Pan-Amazonian center for radical agroecological training. Approximately fifty MST leaders and educational activists had traveled from the Pan-Amazonian region to discuss how IALA can achieve its mission to be a space for agroecological convergence. Bringing together these educators from throughout the diverse states and countries that compose Amazônia is a process of both hierarchical and horizontal scaling; IALA—a local experience—was serving as a space to articulate a larger regional vision of critical food systems education (hierarchically scaled), and it was doing so by creating linkages between diverse movements and interlocutors (horizontally scaled).

Diana and Sandra began to construct the focal point of the mística. They started by writing the words *Educação do Campo* in white sand, then encircling them with palm fronds. They placed a hoe and a basket of fruit and vegetables to one side. Other symbols were laid in the center: a large traditional flat wicker basket had a photo affixed to it. It was an image of protest, youth marching down the highway carrying a banner reading "The Forest Cries" ("A Floresta

Chora"). A small booklet on the political platform of Colombia's National Agrarian Coordination (Coordinador Nacional Agrario) sat to one side and, to the other, a publication these students had produced on agroecology in Amazônia (fig. 5.2).

As I tried to mentally connect these disparate symbols into some sort of narrative, one of the students gingerly stepped into the middle of the map and with an acoustic guitar began singing "Free America," a movement song about transnational solidarity among Latin American nations against imperialism.[2]

Soon, about forty individuals arrived, forming a line around the perimeter of the tent. Diana took a ball of twine and began passing it down the line, each person wrapping the twine around her hand and passing it on. When the ball had made its way around the circle, the music stopped. Hector, an activist from Ecuador and a student in the certificate program, walked into the middle of the image, carrying La Vía Campesina's green flag. He slowly turned around and around, displaying the flag while giving a brief speech on the theme of internationalism. Just as the exploitation of the Amazon is taking place at an international scale, Hector reminded the students that all peasants are one people. The time is right, Hector emphasized, for all Latin American peasants to unite hands, to strengthen the individual struggles within each country.

Figure 5.2. Educação do Campo místíca

As Hector became silent, others entered one at a time—first an activist from Colombia, then one from Ecuador, followed by a Brazilian from the western Amazonian state of Rondônia; between each speaker, the chorus of "Free America" was sung once (fig. 5.3). The underlying message, expressed through the symbolic geography of the mística that Diana and Sandra had created as a pedagogical space, was this: Amazônia is united in its diverse agroecological struggles. The symbolism of this mística could not have been more clear: the map, the ball of twine linking the activists' hands, the Educação do Campo cornucopia, the activists' messages about internationalism interspersed within a song about regional solidarity. Here at IALA we were scaling up critical food systems education by creating a space of convergence, bringing together activists and educators from the disparate corners of Amazônia. Educação do Campo is an alternative vision of education, one just emerging. For the MST, and other social movements that make up the broader national Educação do Campo movement, it is a long-term goal to have this new vision of education become common sense, for it to become hegemonic..

But to make this happen, Educação do Campo must be increasingly scaled up. We see this beginning to materialize in the increasingly regional character of Educação do Campo, as epitomized by the Regional Forum of Educação do Campo, to which we will subsequently return. Here at IALA, a space of convergence has been forged to both hierarchically and horizontally scale an alternative vision of food systems education. Forms of pedagogy that are being developed at IALA here in Paraupebas will be disseminated throughout Amazônia by a horizontal network strengthened in this very space. What were once isolated experiences and institutions are increasingly interconnected.

In this chapter I argue that communities of praxis are responsible for the scaling of critical food systems education. My conception of a *community of praxis* builds directly upon sociocultural educational theories of situated learning that describe the importance of "communities of practice" (Lave and Wenger 1991; Wenger 1998). Communities of practice are collective learning communities characterized in part by a shared interest, craft, or profession. These groups revolve around collective activities and discussions through which members share information and learn from each other. Individuals who belong to a community of practice are practitioners, and their sharing of experiences, stories, tools, and strategies contributes to the ways they address shared problems.

The educators that I describe in this chapter constitute a community of praxis. What differentiates these concepts is the perceived endpoint. While practice can be political, it is not so necessarily. Groups of artisans, bricklayers,

Figure 5.3. Songs of solidarity

and electricians can all be considered communities of practice, but their objectives are not by definition political. Praxis, by contrast, is explicitly political. For Brazilian pedagogue Paulo Freire, praxis consists of a dyadic relationship between reflection and action, which is directed at transforming social structures (Freire 1973). Praxis generates critical consciousness—among both oppressed peoples and their allies—of the structural forces constituting their social position and their ability to work toward liberation. Praxis is a process of becoming. What defines the relationships between these individuals—as a community of praxis—is the commitment that these individuals as individuals *and* together as a collective have toward transformative social, ecological, economic, and political change. Praxis is a concrete action taken to transform the world.

Through an analysis of five interconnected sites of agroecological knowledge production, I make the argument that a community of praxis is responsible for scaling up critical food systems education in southeastern Pará. These include a nonformal agricultural training center, a vocational high school, a public university, La Vía Campesina's agroecological training center, and a recurring regional conference surrounding educação do campo.[3] To understand why and how this community of praxis has scaled up critical food systems education, it is necessary to look at changes in the broader educational landscape over time.

Planting the Seed for Agroecological Education

An exploration of this community of praxis requires that we go back in time to the mid-1970s, a period of rapid demographic, ecological, and educational change in the Amazon. Many people, such as Jean Luc, remembered this time as a period of upheaval but also new beginnings. Jean Luc is a wizened seventy-five-year-old white man with long silver hair cascading down his back. He is a French national as well as an agronomist, educator, and activist who has worked in southeastern Pará for the last forty years. Jean Luc's face has been aged by the sun, and when he smiles his characteristic ear-to-ear smile, he shows only a handful of remaining teeth, evidencing that his life in the campo is not much different from those of the peasants with whom he works. I ask Jean Luc to tell me about the broader history of educação do campo in the region. He began at that watershed time in the 1970s, telling me, "I was born *as* a Brazilian with the arrival of the campesinato in this region." What Jean Luc meant is that as a Frenchman he first came to Brazil, and to the Amazon, at the exact same time as the peasantry was migrating into the region.

Jean Luc was different from both the poor migrants coming from the impoverished and drought-stricken Northeast and the wealthy large landowners from Brazil's South who were incentivized by the Brazilian government to open up the region to cattle ranching. He was born into a family of small-scale farmers and grew up working as part of a farmer cooperative in France. Jean Luc's identity was thus closely tied to peasant farming in France, just as it now is in Brazil. Waving his hand toward a family farmer's small field of manioc, he emphasized with pauses for effect, "I am a peasant farmer. I am the son of peasant farmers. . . . I am the grandson of peasant farmers. . . . I am the great-grandson of peasant farmers." Besides being a peasant farmer, Jean Luc had a university background in agronomy and is passionate about agricultural education.

It was not a mere coincidence that Jean Luc came here at the time of the great migration to the Amazon. Rather, his life-changing voyage to the Amazon was directly predicated on the journey of those thousands of northeastern migrants. Two Catholic priests who were working in the southeastern Amazon with these farmers as part of their missionary work visited Jean Luc's farm in France in the early 1970s and encouraged him to go to Brazil. These priests were looking for someone with a background in agriculture who could help these new migrant farmers with the agricultural challenges they were facing in trying to get established in the region. In 1975, Jean Luc arrived in the city of Marabá in the southeastern Amazon, the gateway to the Transamazon region and its colonization settlements where he was going to be working.

Since his arrival in the Amazon, Jean Luc has been at the front lines of supporting the peasantry and its struggles for social, environmental, and economic justice. Within a year of his arrival in the region, Jean Luc helped form the first office of the Pastoral Land Commission (Commisão Pastoral da Terra, or CPT) in the region. The CPT, associated with the Brazilian Catholic Church, is committed to ending the violence of landowners against the rural poor by supporting the creation of rural unions and teaching agroecological techniques.[4] For a decade, Jean Luc helped coordinate the CPT. Then, in 1988, he left the organization to help form an institution, which would change the face of agroecological education in the region.

The organization was essentially a partnership between researchers from the Federal University of Pará, rural unionist organizers like Jean Luc, and Brazilian and international agricultural research organizations.[5] Its vision was for peasant farmers, technicians, and researchers to collectively advance a new model of both agroecological education and production, in hopes of strengthening farmers' livelihoods.[6] They also created a formal school for the children of small-scale farmers, which was directly associated with the nonformal training center. This was the first institution in the southeastern Amazon that focused on educating farmers' children.[7] Educators and activists I spoke with shared a singular perspective: this center and its school were pivotal springboards for building the regional Educação do Campo movement, which remains vibrant today. It was where a cohort of other educators would become trained and emerge as a community of praxis. It was also a space that developed pedagogical methods and began a dialogue about developing agroecological education opportunities at the regional level. In the mid-1990s these discussions about developing alternative forms of education dovetailed with coalescing national-level debates about the need for an alternative model of education—debates that came to a head in 1996 after the Eldorado dos Carajás massacre.

Jean Luc and various other educators I spoke with were unequivocal about the significance of the fateful day April 17, 1996. The Eldorado dos Carajás massacre was a pivotal moment that transformed the face of agroecological education in the region and even the nation. Following Tarlau (2015), the massacre created a political opportunity in Brazil. Political opportunities are spaces in which social movements are able to advance their demands, following a change in political administrations or amid highly politicized events (Tarrow 1998). After the massacre there was intense international media attention focused on the Brazilian government. The MST seized this opportunity and in April 1997—a year after the massacre—organized a national march for agrarian reform on the capital of Brasília, with more than a hundred thousand people participating. This march helped pressure President Cardoso to address the movement's demands for land reform, and indeed land reform picked up great speed within Cardoso's first few years: 260,000 families obtained access to eight million hectares of land—nearly double what had been allocated within the last decade (Tarlau 2015: 1162). With this political climate the MST began to foment a national debate concerning education. According to MST education sector activist Edgar Kolling, the movement's demands for education took a *carona* (slang for hitching a ride) because they were able to get slipped in with the demands and discussion about broader agrarian reform (Tarlau 2015: 1162). Several months following the National March for Agrarian Reform, the MST organized the first National Meeting of Educators in Areas of Agrarian Reform (ENERA), out of which was born the movement for Educação do Campo. Also out of this meeting came a demand for a federal program that would provide opportunities for education in agrarian reform settlements and encampments. That program, which was ratified in 1998, became known as PRONERA—the National Program for Education in Agrarian Reform. The national policy of PRONERA played a major role in structuring emerging educação do campo opportunities in the region. It helped fund courses at the Federal University of Pará (UFPA), the Federal Institute of Education, Science, and Technology of Pará–Rural Campus of Marabá, as well as the family farming school.

Although I've drawn extensively upon our interview from the car ride, Jean Luc was only one of the people who was involved in this highly collective process of political mobilization. As part of a broader group of individuals, Jean Luc helped bring into existence a regional movement for critical food systems education. Before turning to the other voices involved in this community of praxis, I want to highlight several key lessons we can take from his narrative to better understand how opportunities for critical food systems education became scaled up. First, the nonformal education center, which was created to meet the demands of small-scale farmers, was the originating point for the regional Educação do Campo movement because it served as the first central space for agroecological training. Second, this regional movement was able to begin scaling up because of the political opportunity created by the massacre. This scaling up was both vertical and horizontal. It took the form of isolated institutions, such as the one Jean Luc helped create, becoming integrated into a national-level network. Third, the creation of a funding program for alternative education provided the resources to expand the curricular offerings beyond this single institution and create new educational opportunities throughout the region. Taken together, these three points illuminate an important theoretical point: the regional proliferation of critical food systems education developed from the intersection of social grievances, political opportunity, and political economy. The political ecology of education was a product of collective desire and a highly organized set of linked campaigns, not merely a happy coincidence.

In the following section I explore how this constellation of agroecological education spaces emerges out of a community of committed activist educators, which I term a community of praxis. I interweave the narratives of Wagner and Denise, who are close colleagues of Jean Luc and intimately connected with the nonformal agricultural education center. Through their narratives I explore how this community of praxis has helped to scale up critical food systems education.

Communities of Praxis

Wagner and Denise both described themselves as products of the regional agroecology movement; they explained how their *formação* (training) took place alongside their participation in the broader movement—they were trained or quite literally *formed* by it. But Wagner and Denise were not just products of the movement but also active progenitors of it. They were part of the broader community of individuals who, through dialogue, social mobilization, and institutional advocacy, have formed the regional agroecological Educação do Campo movement. They appear here together because their relationship to one another helps us understand what constitutes a community of praxis. Movement between urban and rural spaces defined the early lives of Wagner and Denise, as it did many of the individuals I came to know.

Wagner declared that he is a "child of Marabá," meaning that unlike many of the region's inhabitants who migrated from the Northeast or South, he was born here. Wagner had always lived in the metropolitan area, but as he told me, "I've always had a very strong relation to the rural area; it's a space that has always captured my attention since I was a child." His family lived directly next to the nonformal training center and were neighbors to Jean Luc. As a child Wagner ended up spending much of his childhood playing at the nonformal training center while Jean Luc, as an adult, helped to develop this institution.

Wagner's childhood and adolescence were significantly marked by these experiences. He grew up knowing the researchers and activists working at the center and played with the children of the researchers who were stationed there, becoming an extended member of many researchers' families.

Denise was, by contrast, an immigrant to the region, like the majority of the population of southeastern Pará. She was from the interior of Bahia, the Sertão—that dry rangeland in Brazil's Northeast that has served as one of the major feeder populations for resettlement in the Amazon over the years. Denise was like Wagner in that although originally from an urban area, she felt drawn to the roça early in life. "I was the granddaughter of a farmer, from the Sertão, and I grew up in a rural life. It was a village we lived in—a small city really—of eleven thousand people, but I always had the relation to the rural area, always going to the roça. Principally during the cultural times of year, during the harvest, making the tamales; living and studying in the city, but spending the weekends in the roça. So I had a very strong relation to the roça." While Wagner's early childhood was defined by the rhythm of time playing at the nonformal training center, Denise's was also shaped by education—albeit in a different way. As Denise described it, "I came to Pará out of the desire to study." Like many nonnative Paraense, she had family already living in Pará; her sisters were here working as teachers. Two months after Denise arrived in southeastern Pará, the massacre of Eldorado dos Carajás took place. After the massacre she participated in an aid mission that brought food and supplies to the survivors. In 1997, the year after the massacre, Denise began on an educational path that would make her an intimate ally of the movement and its broader educational project.

Strong linkages to the region's agroecological education centers mark both Wagner and Denise's life histories. As Wagner got older he remained closely linked to the center and farming school. He completed a high school program, which had a focus on agricultural extension, and then went on to do an internship at the center. Denise also became involved with the center; she worked as a research assistant for a French scholar who affiliated with the research institution, conducting ethnographic research in both MST and extractivist settlements throughout southeastern Pará.[8] She would spend weeks on these settlements, interviewing farmers about their life histories: how they came to Pará, how they struggled for land, and what they were doing to try to conserve it. Denise remembered, "It was at this time that I really became close to the movement and its struggle for land." When Denise was not in the settlements doing fieldwork, she was in the city reading the works of seminal agrarian scholars of Brazilian Amazônia, such as Jean Hebete and Octavio Velho.

She remembered her life at this time as simple and focused: studying agrarian social theory and doing fieldwork. It was through this *rotina*, this routine of embedded study, that Denise came to understand at a deep level the struggle for land.

Wagner and Denise's lives were characterized by a gradual progression toward increased involvement in the community. They began with what Lave and Wenger term "legitimate peripheral participation," whereby newcomers become experienced members of a community by first participating in peripheral activities, such as an internship, and as they gain expertise they become increasingly central to the community.

Wagner and Denise both benefited directly from the education financing that emerged after the massacre. Wagner received a scholarship through PRONERA and matriculated into an undergraduate program in agrarian sciences at the UFPA. Similarly, Denise received a scholarship through PRONERA that employed her an instructor, training teachers to conduct basic literacy education in the settlements. She reenrolled in the program in 2002, continuing as a coordinator in MST and extractivist settlement for a national literacy program.[9] Wagner and Denise then subsequently received PRONERA fellowships to help coordinate the first cohort of the high school program that was taking place at the family farming school, and they lived there for three years while directing this program. They worked with cohorts of students from MST, extractivist, and Federation of Agricultural Workers (FETAGRI) settlements who were training to become agricultural extension agents. When combined with their degree programs at the university (also funded by PRONERA), these coordinating experiences gave them the time to develop alongside the community and later take important roles in the development of regional education institutions.

It was only through multiple periods of fieldwork that I began to recognize the coherence of this community. For example, in 2009 I participated at the Regional Forum for Educação do Campo (FREC)—an event to which I will return momentarily—and met many of the educators, including Wagner and Denise, who were at the helm of the steering committee. In 2012, during my longer period of fieldwork, I ran into these individuals at various points in different contexts: participating in a movement plenary, teaching at the vocational institute and the university, participating in actions at the MST's pedagogical encampment. I began to realize that if you go to any series of educação do campo events in southeastern Pará, you will quickly run into the same individuals again and again—just as Wagner and Denise's lives intersected repeatedly.

The two interwoven examples of Wagner and Denise illuminate the political ecology of education in southeastern Pará. The origination of this community of praxis can be traced back to the demands of recently migrated small-scale farmers for agricultural education, which culminated in the creation of the center. The political opportunity created by the massacre led to the development of public policies and a variety of funded internships and scholarships that created training opportunities for emerging educators. Individuals, like Wagner and Denise, were formed through legitimate peripheral participation in these spaces, for example, through interning at the center, and coordinating a course at the family farming school. They are now integral members of a community of praxis, composed of individuals committed to social and environmental justice, and co-constructing knowledge through critical reflection on social reality. At a broader theoretical level, political-economic processes and the social history of the region came together to create the conditions for this community of praxis to form. In the next two sections I describe how this community of praxis has helped to scale up opportunities for critical food systems education throughout the region. I first turn to explore how Wagner, Jean Luc, Denise, and a broad network of educators and activists worked together to develop a new vocational agroecological secondary school.

Dialogic Space and the Creation of the Institute

Wagner, Jean Luc, and Denise have long been engaged in the Regional Forum of Educação do Campo (Forum Regional do Educação do Campo, or FREC), which I will refer to hereafter simply as the Regional Forum. The Regional Forum is a network of diverse actors, including rural peasants, indigenous communities, teachers, educational activists, and public institutions, who are committed to creating a system of educação do campo. The community that constitutes the Regional Forum is actively engaged in praxis through its critical reflections on the rural populations' educational and productive challenges and their efforts to develop locally relevant opportunities for educação do campo.

The Regional Forum is a clear crystallization of a community of praxis. For instance, one of the Regional Forum's principal activities is the (usually) biennial regional conference, which engages hundreds of stakeholders in thematic dialogues.[10] At the 2007 Regional Forum, whose theme was Curriculum, Public Policy, and Educação do Campo, participants agreed that there were very limited options for students from rural agrarian reform settlements to obtain professional technical training. Beyond a simple lack of technical training opportunities—one that could theoretically be filled by the state creation of yet another school—the group agreed that peasants and indigenous communities needed a special kind of school based in an alternative vision of knowledge and agricultural development. In the FREC participants' analysis, existing educational opportunities were largely irrelevant to the reality of peasant and indigenous communities because they were firmly based in the agroindustrial technological model that "seeks the extreme homogenization of local agroecosystems, searching for making artificial ones through chemical inputs, and industrial mechanization" (FREC 2011: 30). This quote comes directly from a political ecological analysis that the group authored about the effects of education, and its linkages to capital, on the landscape as part of that 2007 discussion, though it was not published until several years later.

Regional Forum members actively debated what pedagogies and forms of knowledge production would constitute the new school. One of their primary demands was for the school to help solidify a new regional science of agroecology. What they envisioned was an eastern Amazonian agroecology that would be specific to the region, although it would draw on general agroecological principles developed at the national and international levels. The desire for this "local science of agroecology" exemplifies how decolonizing education is intertwined with the construction of the social landscape.

These collective discussions about what kind of school was needed dovetailed with the rollout of new public policies. In 2002, when the newly elected Lula government promised to expand the professional and technological education system, the city of Marabá was proposed as the site for a new technical institute. As a result of the MST's position in the region's Educação do Campo movement, the MST's 26 de Março settlement was chosen as the site of the Federal Institute of Pará-Rural Campus of Marabá (hereafter I refer to it as the Federal Institute).[11] One of the first programs that the Regional Forum participants demanded for the new Federal Institute was a vocational high school degree program with a focus on agroecological extension.

Since Wagner had been intimately involved in region's early agroecological education courses and spaces as well as the discussions leading toward the creation of the Federal Institute, he decided to apply for a job there as a teacher. "I came through this trajectory, this trajectory of educação do campo and agricultural extension; I understood the reality of the settlements, so I decided to go and work at the institute and help in the process there."

In 2009, the first cohort of this agroecological extension program started, but they had no physical school in which to begin their training because the construction of the Federal Institute was plagued with delays. Without a school, classes were forced to meet in a variety of social movement spaces. They began in an intermovement organizing space known as Cabanagem in Marabá, which consists of two dormitories, an industrial kitchen, and a meeting pavilion. After several months at Cabanagem, the classes were moved to the MST's Florestan Fernandes National Training School–Amazônia branch, which is located just outside Marabá in São Felix do Xingu. Classes were held there for a month, but this also turned out not to be a satisfactory location for long-term study because it had no dormitories or classrooms, just two basic covered locations for hammocks and only the forest for teaching space. When it became clear this space was untenable, classes were canceled for several months. The Federal Institute's administration then reached a deal with the directors of a closed high school, known as Santa Terezinha, in Marabá. They spent a year there. By this time, construction at the Federal Institute's original location had reached the point where rough walls had been raised. However, progress on building the campus was still very slow, in large part because several of the contractors were embezzling money.

At this point Wagner and his colleagues decided to take their classes to the half-finished campus as a form of protest, and this was where they engaged praxis, or the combination of critical reflection and action, to create the pressure that would get the construction finished. As one student told me, "We came here to where they were building the campus, because if we're here, the process of construction could be accelerated, it can go faster, because we're here and we can see what's going on, we can direct our demands." The praxis of the Federal Institute's teachers and students ultimately paid off in the completed campus in 2015, seven years after it had begun and five years after the promised completion.

The Federal Institute (and its eventual construction) is significant to this region because it is committed to supporting the production of new forms of agroecological knowledge that are grounded in the histories and lived experiences of place. But bringing this new institute into existence was not simply a government initiative—although importantly, from a political ecology perspective, its origin was tied to national policies. Rather, it was a community committed to praxis that was responsible for bringing the Federal Institute into existence both conceptually and physically. Wagner, Jean Luc, Denise, and many others engaged in critical group reflections that developed the vision of the Federal Institute. Later, the first group of students engaged in praxis to pressure the defunct construction companies into finishing the Federal Institute's infrastructure. The Regional Forum for Educação do Campo conferences were one material form of this community of praxis; they were a process of becoming where individuals participated in actions, debates, and discussions with the shared end of transformative social, ecological economic, and political change. Whereas Wagner's story is intimately connected to the origination of the Federal Institute, Denise's is more closely tied to the development of educação do campo within the Federal University of South and Southeastern Pará, which I refer to hereafter as the Federal University.

Growing a Community of Praxis

Sitting in its courtyard in August 2015, I perceive the Federal University as characterized by an unmistakably radical aesthetic. The signs are everywhere: posters for a debate on Educação do Campo, the Expansion of Capitalism, and Mineral Extraction plaster one wall; a photography exhibit depicting the communist guerrillas "disappeared" by the Brazilian dictatorship during the 1970s is on display in the cafeteria.[12] These make the university appear as a sort of hybrid academic-political space. Its materiality is a function not only of the students but also importantly of the community of educators who have long been working within the institution to create social and agroecological change.

As a faculty member here since 2007, Denise had long been an important part of the fabric of the community of praxis that seeks to advance educação do campo and agroecology in the region. Denise described this complicated educational trajectory:

> Since I arrived here in Amazônia, in Pará, in the region of Marabá, from 1997 until now, I've been connected to the process of training teachers. I've accompanied the training of teachers. I've accompanied farmers working in the settlements, and in the course of Liceniatura in Educação do Campo, I've been doing extension work in the settlements. I've been part of the FREC. I've been part of a group that meets with the professors in the settlements every two months to try to work on the curriculum so that it contains the elements of educação do campo, to try to centralize discussions of agroecology, of food sovereignty, the questions of agricultural production in the settlements, of the culture of the settlements.

The central point of Denise's perspective here is that the struggle for land needs to be directly linked to this process of training teachers, but also at a broader level the strengthening of the struggle for land. By crafting curricula around food sovereignty, and addressing problems of agroecological production in the settlements, the community of praxis within the Federal University actively shapes the political ecology of education in the region. Denise was just one educator within the community of praxis who had long been waging this struggle within the Federal University. Gemeson Brito was another educator who worked closely with Denise, and I now turn to his narrative because it offers insight into how this community of praxis is connected by its epistemological and emancipatory convictions.

With his black coconut ring symbolizing his commitment to emancipatory social change and his MST movement shirt, Gemeson Brito contrasted from most high-level university administrators. Brito had directed nearly all of the region's PRONERA courses over the last two decades and was a pivotal member of the community of praxis that is advancing educação do campo and agroecology in the region. Sitting in his air-conditioned administrator's office, wearing both symbolically and literally the "shirt of the movement," Brito symbolized the presence of decolonial thought within the university.[13] He began by describing the relation between the learning community, epistemology, and decolonization. "Within the university there's not a singular form of thought; we have professors with different visions of the world, of society, of science." Here Brito emphasized the epistemological diversity among the faculty, which as a group recognized that there are not only other forms of knowledge but also other "visions of the world." Moving on, Brito argued that the integument binding this learning community together was its members' valorization of different visions of modernity and development.

> Today, we have a strong group within the university that is linked to educação do campo, and what unifies these people is two things: First, is a broad reflection on this region of Amazônia—of the Amazon as a whole, but of this region in particular, where you have different visions of development. And one of those is agrarian reform. The peasants in all of their diversity—the assentados, quilombolas (descendants of escaped slaves), indigenous—the various rural subjects who are capable of being a possible motor of a vision of development that is much more sustainable, from the perspective of nature, the distribution of economic resources, as well as that of the construction of a democratic society.

These professors have a broad analysis—one of Amazônia as a whole—as a transnational region defined by a plurality of visions of development, of myriad forms of possible modernity and material production. Scaling in on southeastern Pará, this vision retains its hybridity, composed of disparate groups with diverse relations to the colonial past: indigenous nations (the Kayapó and various other tribes have large reservations throughout southeastern Pará), quilombolas as well as various types of caboclos, such as breakers of the Babaçu palm, and the assentados (including those who live in both state and social movement settlements). The second element uniting this learning community was, according to Brito, the recognition that it must actively support this cultural, material, and epistemological diversity.

> This is a point of convergence for various professors at the university, and from this perspective we ask, how is it that the university is capable of acting with these groups? How can we strengthen this perspective of development with these subjects, at the same time as developing research that brings visibility to the conflicts, that brings visibility to the solutions that the very peasants themselves are developing. But it's not just about creating visibility, but at the same time bringing them into the university to create a dialogue, and the university is helping them assume a role as a protagonist in the process.

For these educators, it was not enough to be an ally. What united them was their motivation to be collaborators, or perhaps even co-conspirators, in a broad vision of transformative social and ecological resistance. Brito disentangled this relation with the movement:

> In terms of the definitions of roles, there's a certain clarity: even though we have a relation that is extremely close—for example we [professors] will go and live at IALA [La Vía Campesina's Agroecological Institute of Latin America] during the courses—there are things that the movement recognizes are *of* the movement, and we in the university recognize are the limits of our actions. But there are certain things that we in the university can help materialize, can help contribute to and do. The fact this group—me, Denise, Eduardo—are permitted by the university enables the social movement to enter the university, enables the movement to gain visibility, enables the possibility of joint actions.

Brito is not a member of the MST in a strict sense; while he, Denise, and other professors wear the "ring of the movement" (the black coconut ring) or its shirt and might live for a period in a settlement or encampment as part of a course, they are relatively privileged academic elites and will never literally sign the ledger and enroll directly as subjects in the MST's occupations. However, these individuals do see themselves as part of the broader Educação do Campo movement, and in this sense they are directly contributing to the MST's struggle. Brito understood this contribution in terms of curricular and extracurricular programming: "So from 2004, when the first MST PRONERA course took place at the UFPA, until now, these actions have continued. We've continued with these partnership actions in projects—well, beyond projects—in joint actions [too], such as seminars, in reflections, in debates, in productions, in processes that are really about the strengthening of the movement itself, beyond what the university, what the state, in fact, really formally authorizes." Professors like Denise and Brito at the Federal University and Wagner at the Federal Institute can be considered institutional activists—whom Pettinchio (2012: 499) defines as "insiders with access to resources and power—who proactively take up causes that overlap with those of grassroots challengers." These institutional activists were key players in social struggles, particularly those related to the politics of knowledge and progressive transformation of educational institutions. In Brito's narrative, we saw the core of what it means to be an institutional activist, advancing the aims and objectives of the movements through institutional pathways.

This was praxis at its core: Brito and the university's tight-knit community of activist educators were committed to action. As Brito corrected himself, these were not just collaborative projects with the social movements but rather joint actions, actions that perhaps seemed innocuous from an institutional perspective—a film screening one month, a public debate another—but were processes whose end was unquestionably beyond what the Federal University, and the state, would envision or ever authorize. They were at their core about advancing an alternative conception of development and modernity.

The relation between the university and the MST was not only constitutive for the grassroots and its political project; rather, it helped to constitute the community of praxis within the Federal University itself. One afternoon at La Vía Campesina's Agroecological Institute of Latin America–Amazônia, I ate lunch with Eduardo, who, along with Brito, was leading the certificate program on Agroecology, Educação do Campo, and the Agrarian Question in Amazônia that I mentioned in this chapter's introduction. We had just finished a morning session on the relationship between universities and social movements in the construction of Pan-Amazonian critical thought, and it seemed the perfect moment to ask Eduardo how he saw the relation between the movement and university. Eduardo told me,

This experience of IALA [the graduate certificate program] for us in the university is really important for two reasons. First, it enables us to consolidate these partnerships, which is a process that has been ongoing. Second, it enables us to the increase the number of professors that are part of this debate. For example, the course at IALA began with me, Gemeson, and Isabela, and then came Sandra, then came Saulo from geography, then came all these other people. This was a very positive point: that these experiences coalesce; they bring professors closer to this discussion. As you increase this number of professors, you make visible all of these questions within the university.

For Eduardo, these courses helped solidify partnerships with the grassroots, but they also worked to constitute a community of praxis. They brought others into the discussion. This produced an internal movement within the university itself. As Eduardo emphasized, collaborating with the MST enabled the broadening of a community of praxis. New individuals, who share the broad convictions concerning subaltern knowledge and collaboration, began entering the conversation. When this happens, the community grows ever more within the university and the scope of collaborative actions broadens. Wagner, Denise, Gemeson, Eduardo, and the others in this learning community recognized that their group was enduring. Eduardo concluded by telling me, "We've really built something here, a group centered around educação do campo. People come in and out; someone gets the opportunity to participate in a PhD program, and they go for a few years, but they come back and we're still at it, and it's like nothing ever changed." In this community educators are involved in intersecting relationships that persist over time and revolve around shared ideological and political projects of transformation.

Communities of praxis are sites of learning where knowledge is shared, ideas debated, and proposals discussed. But they are more than this; they are also sites of action. The transformation of educational institutions takes many forms and is a process occurring in disparate—albeit interconnected—times and places. Earlier in the chapter we explored FREC as one location where actions lead to the development of alternative education institutions in other spaces. In this chapter's last section I analyze how members of a community of praxis scale up change. I focus on the connections between the Federal University and the Agroecological Institute of Latin America (IALA-Amazônia), which is located in the MST's Palmares II settlement. I chart out how Gemeson, Eduardo, and other institutional activists engage in joint actions with the movement, working beyond what the state condones to build a multiscalar system of counter-hegemonic education.

Bringing Critical Food Systems Education to Scale

Dayze and Gemeson walked to the front of the auditorium at IALA and each took a microphone. Dayze was a dedicated MST activist, the longtime director of IALA, and a student about to graduate from the graduate certificate program in Educação do Campo, Agroecology, and the Agrarian Question in Amazônia, which I first discussed in this chapter's opening vignette. Gemeson Brito, the professor-administrator I introduced earlier from the Federal University, was one of the faculty members leading the program. The presence of these two individuals—one representing the university and the other the grassroots—facilitating this morning's session on "Movement-University Partnerships for Constructing Critical Pan-Amazonian Thought" (fig. 5.4) reflected the formative relations between the university and social movements in advancing new forms of critical food systems education.

Dayze handed the microphone to Andreia, a state MST leader, who offered an analysis: "The seminar, from yesterday, to today, to tomorrow, is a process for us to reflect about the necessity for the construction of a project, and the construction of a strategy." This seminar had a much broader purpose than its role in the graduate certificate program; it was intended to contribute directly to the development of a regional project of political education and agroecological transformation. Andreia noted, "One of the things that we've discussed through the weekend is that all that we've done at IALA up until this moment isn't sufficient to achieve what we've wished for, or for what we've been challenged to do . . . and for this we have the saying. . . ." Her voice slowed and she spoke the next words like a mantra: "IALA is a process of construction that is . . ." and the crowd collectively finished for her, "continual." IALA was a space of critical food systems education, but it was not a fixed entity. Rather, as a socially produced space, it was dynamic—a process whose production was ongoing. The university was playing a pivotal role in both the material and ideological construction of IALA.

Later that afternoon Eduardo and I visited the mandala at IALA. The mandala is an agricultural production area composed of concentric rings of crops grown in symbiotic assemblages; beans fix nitrogen for corn, which in turn provides a structure upon which squash grows. Walking through what felt like a labyrinth of paths that crisscrossed the mandala, Eduardo told me, "We are developing this place of IALA-Amazônica through relationships with

Figure 5.4. Movement-university partnerships for constructing critical Pan-Amazonian thought

the university, through the experiences of work parties [*multirões*]. As part of these work parties, for three days once a month, students from diverse disciplines will come from the university that want to better understand questions like, "What is the reality of the rural peasants?" "What are the large projects of capital that are being disputed in the region?" These students come and engage in debates; they come to understand the political project of IALA, but also to experiment, and to implement a new vision." Standing next to the center of the mandala, a circular water feature holding trout, Eduardo explained that the students would come and discuss, " 'What types of pests are common in the garden? What are the best types of vegetables that we can grow in this Amazonian biome? What type of organic fertilizer can we make?' But then they move from that discussion to action, and then it's like, 'So let's go, grab a shovel, grab a hoe, and let's implement it. Let's build bee boxes. Let's create the apiary. Let's create these structures,' and in the process debate how this can contribute to an understanding of the organization of agricultural production, of the improvement of rural income of rural peasants." What Eduardo described is the core of critical food systems education: education is being mobilized to contribute to food sovereignty. Students are gaining experiential knowledge about the political project of IALA, its emancipatory vision for creating agroecological system of production that will resist the expansion of capital. But these university students are not just consuming knowledge, they're coproducing knowledge while developing IALA itself, helping to build structures and systems to advance food sovereignty in their own communities.

During a break between sessions I grabbed a jelly jar of coffee and sat with Dayze, who helped me understand the role of the certificate program in the trajectory of IALA. She told me, "We began with the certificate because it was the only type of course that we could develop with the university, and because then it is easier to develop other types of training programs, whether at the level of certificate or even at the high school level. In addition, offering the certificate gives you a certain liberty to include in the course curriculum themes that help us to engage not only with the course itself, but to think about the challenge of the construction of IALA, what is it that IALA should be?" Starting with this certificate program was a strategic choice. By choosing to offer the certificate, the MST in partnership with its allies in the university had the freedom to shape the program in such a way that it contributed to the development of the institute itself. The key point to take from Dayze's sentiment is how scale gets produced in an educational context. By starting with the certificate program at IALA, the MST would be able to explore the creation of curricular opportunities at other educational levels. There was a scalar feedback loop between the creation of the course, the development of IALA, and its intervention in offering critical food systems education opportunities at various levels. This scaling up of agroecological education was not specific exclusively to IALA. In a separate context, Wagner, the educator from the Federal Institute, described the accretion of educational opportunities at the regional level:

> The first course was in literacy, and then it was like, "How can you have literacy training without teachers' education?" So then there was a program in teachers' education. "Okay, so you've got teachers' education, well how can you not have a technical course?" So the technical course was the first in Brazil, but then we said, "Okay, you've got a technical course, how can you not have a university level course?" So then we got a university-level program in agronomy and rural education. And then we asked ourselves, "How can you have a university-level program without a postgraduate program?" It was in this way that it kept developing in the region.

Taken together, Wagner and Dayze's perspective underscored how the relationality between educational scales is constitutive of gradual change. The creation of educational opportunities at various institutional scales—from high school to university to graduate certificate—enabled the "the vertical integration of courses," as Wagner described it. The metaphor of "vertical integration" was a tactical deployment of scale, as the local projects evidenced regional change. The stepwise manner in which social movements and their interlocutors advanced specific projects was one way they articulated a counterhegemonic vision of education. Similar to Wagner's description of "vertical integration," IALA was being constructed through an iterative scalar process that was built ever outward.

Throughout the seminar's weekend students, faculty, and international activists discussed how IALA could better reach not only the region's five hundred settlements but also the countless other rural communities in the Pan-Amazonian basin. These discussions were about creating new educational opportunities at various interconnected geographic scales—from the local to the regional, national, and international. From a political ecology perspective, the seminar was itself a product of scale in its multiple forms: financial resources from the national PRONERA program enabled a transnational convergence as scores of activists and academics came to debate the future of its evolving agroecological educational space. Activist academics drew upon their institutional power to mobilize political-economic resources and contribute to a subaltern process of scaling up critical food systems education. This portrait of IALA brings into focus how political economy and scale intersected to structure the political ecology of education in southeastern Pará.

Conclusions

In this chapter we have seen that scale is not only geographic but also intrinsic to the nature of education systems. A constellation of critical food systems education opportunities is emerging in southeastern Pará, running the gamut of educational scales—from elementary school through postgraduate programs. IALA, the Federal University, and the Federal Institute are creating connections between nested levels of the education system.

Several factors are responsible for the scaling up of critical food systems education in the southeastern Amazon. First, historical experiences, such as the center and family farming school, have served as central spaces for experimentation. New forms of agroecological education and research were developed within these institutions, which served as touchstones for the emerging

Educação do Campo movement. These spaces have also played an important role in training individuals committed to harnessing education's capacity to advance social, ecological, and political change. Second, the community of praxis that began in these early spaces has gone on to help develop new opportunities for critical food systems education at various interconnected scales. Through internships and other forms of legitimate peripheral participation, individuals have come to identify with and construct a broader movement for agroecological education. Third, this community of praxis was able to take advantage of political opportunities and emerging public policies to develop new agroecological education institutions, such as the Federal Institute. Developing these institutions is a long-term form of praxis, whereby individuals engage in various forms of dialogue and action to enact a shared objective of transformative social, ecological, economic, and political change. These educators are more than allies; they are accomplices who are acting in collaboration with the region's social movements to enact a broad vision of transformative social and ecological resistance. As institutional activists, these educators have been able to mobilize political-economic resources within the university and state to help build new agroecological education programs within social movement spaces. This contributes not only to the development of new spaces of convergence but also to the development of a broader community of praxis.

This chapter has highlighted how questions of scale are important to an understanding of hegemony. That which is hegemonic at the local level is a manifestation of higher scales. For example, in the 17 de Abril settlement, cauboi culture—consisting of particular forms of dress, foodways, and agrarian identities—draws its appeal from the fact that it is salient at the regional scale. Similarly, counter-hegemonic systems *must* be scaled up if they are to gain prominence themselves. A constellation of unconnected initiatives does not make a new system. Rather, relations between experiences and levels are pivotal. It is through the process of scaling up, through suturing an integument of relational experiences, that an alternative worldview becomes hegemonic.

CHAPTER 6

Fences around Knowledge

A student from an MST settlement placed a book in the center of a veritable cornucopia of fruits and vegetables that have been carefully arranged on the stage of a university auditorium. The book was titled *Breaking Fences and Constructing Knowledges* (Marinho 2016). I had heard secondary school teachers and university professors use a similar phase, "fence around knowledge," at various points during my research. Seeing the book take a central place in this afternoon's mística caused me to reflect about what meaning the idea of a "fence" related to "knowledge" might hold. In this chapter I draw upon two case studies to answer this question, demonstrating that reciprocal relationships exist between decolonizing land and knowledge. These case studies look at this relationship from opposing perspectives.

From one vantage, decolonizing education can contribute to a process of decolonizing land. In the first case study, I lay out the historical trajectory through which social movements and allied professors have begun the process of decolonizing the Federal University of South and Southeastern Pará (UNIFESSPA, previously and hereafter referred to as the Federal University). While this is a traditional state-funded public university that anyone can attend, as described in chapter 5, it has a palpable social movement presence. With state funding from the National Program for Education in Agrarian Reform (PRONERA), the MST and other social movements are able to partner with the university to offer undergraduate and graduate degree programs in federal universities. I focus on the university's graduate certificate program titled Educação do Campo, Agroecology, and the Agrarian Question in Amazônia, which exemplifies how social movements are partnering with activist professors to decolonize public education.

The second case study examines the relationship between decolonizing land and knowledge from the opposing perspective. Through an analysis of the Federal Institute of Pará–Rural Campus of Marabá (IFPA-CRMB; previously and hereafter referred to as the Federal Institute), I show that it is frequently necessary to first decolonize land—literally breaking up land concentration—in order to create new educational institutions, which are grounded in peasants' epistemologies and attentive to their livelihood concerns.

Both case studies highlight the complex relationship between the MST and the state in terms of education provision. Courses in either program might be taught by individuals with no affiliation to the MST, by activist professors who support the movement, or in some cases by state leaders within the movement itself. The state runs schools in MST encampments and settlements and offers degree programs intended for students from social movements in federal universities and vocational institutes. However, each of these initiatives requires diverse forms of grassroots struggle, ranging from direct occupation of federal offices to working with allies in positions of power to free up funding for the courses. Building these educational projects is a process of decolonizing education. I now turn to the first case study, where I explore the linkages between decolonizing knowledge and subsequently transforming land.

Decolonizing Education to Decolonize Land

The development of the Federal University has transformed the politics of knowledge on the frontier. This was the first federal university in the region, created in 1987 in Marabá as a satellite campus of the state's main federal university campus in the capital of Belém—a twelve-hour drive away. For Eduardo, an activist professor long affiliated with the Federal University, the creation of the campus was quite literally a "process of expanding the university's presence into the frontier." Eduardo elaborates, "The campus of Marabá was created to provide training in basic education to teachers, because this is a region that is very distant from Belém, isolated, forgotten, and so the schools don't have teachers." Far removed from the state's center of power, the rural schools in this area have historically lacked curricular and infrastructural resources, as well as trained teachers. Human geographer Neil Smith's classic concept of "uneven development" provides a helpful lens to understand Eduardo's description of the educational landscape of southeastern Pará. The state has differentially directed educational funding toward urban centers, as these are loci of power and capital. Southeastern Pará is a "forgotten" geography because capitalism transforms "the world after its own image" (Smith 2010: 198). Given this political-economic and geographical context, the creation of the Federal University exemplified the development of a new space of knowledge production on the frontier.

The Federal University's contemporary decolonial pedagogies can be traced back to the campus's origination. In the late 1980s and early 1990s, the Federal University did not have any permanent faculty. This created a highly malleable pedagogical environment shaped from the outset by its itinerant professors' engagement with social movements. French agronomist Jean Hebete, introduced in chapter 5, was one of these itinerant professors and a principal protagonist in beginning to valorize peasant agricultural knowledge systems within the Federal University. As discussed earlier, Hebete was a key actor in forming the Agroenvironmental Center of Tocantins (earlier referred to as the center). In 1999 the center and the Federal University partnered to create two programs for movement members: a Licenciatura program in agrarian sciences and, following that, an undergraduate degree program in agronomy. With the creation of these programs, the institutional connection between the Federal University and the MST began to grow. Whereas previously the Federal University simply had professors who were sympathetic to the region's social movements, with these new courses the MST began to have a voice in the constitution of the Federal University's degree programs.

During the 1990s the MST began what Eduardo, an activist professor at the Federal University, described as "territorializing itself in the region," in other words developing new encampments. One of the key ways in which the MST went about staking claim to the region was by integrating itself into the center of knowledge production—the new university. For the MST, developing this relationship with the university was a central priority. Eduardo remembered that the MST had its own ideas about what types of courses were needed and ways to conduct political education. The MST pushed the university to become engaged with geographic questions surrounding the frontier. As Eduardo reflected, "The MST challenged the university to think in critical ways about the relations between the production of space and capital. The provocation was for the university to think critically and tactically in terms of new types of courses that would help develop this critical territorial consciousness of the relation between the encampments and settlements, and the production of capitalism in the region, and its interconnections with broader spheres of globalization." As Eduardo described, the historical relationship between the MST and Federal University has been both grounded in and generative of the political ecology of education. The movement pushed the activist professors to develop new courses that focus on the material connection created by capitalism between this region and the broader world economy. New courses were, in other words, based in the region's political ecology. In addition, these relationships between the MST and the university professors also helped create a politicized form of education that was intended to shape students' critical territorial consciousness. Here, political ideology molds education about the agrarian landscape into a tool of resistance; it creates a political ecology of education.

After the early initiatives with the center, a host of other programs—all funded by PRONERA—began in partnership with the MST, including an agrarian residence program, a program in pedagogy, and one in literature. Throughout the 2000s the MST ideological and material presence within the university grew ever stronger as more courses were developed. The region's social movements have played a pivotal role in breaking down the fences around knowledge within the university.

I now turn to explore how activist professors strategically cultivate these relationships with social movements to decolonize the university on an everyday basis. Rosaldo Pinheiro helped direct the certificate program on Educação do Campo, Agroecology, and the Agrarian Question in Amazônia at the Federal University. Through this program he was creating a transformative relationship between the university and the region's social movements. As Rosaldo told me, "Educação do Campo is both a political and epistemological movement; through the partnerships between the social movements and university we end up developing new pedagogical principles." Rosaldo explained the process in more detail:

> The first step in developing these new pedagogical principles is to remove the hierarchy that comes from the perspective of Western knowledge. We need to not debase the knowledge produced through experience. Don't minimize the importance of the popular struggles, as forms of knowledge production, and pedagogical invention.
>
> We need to emphasize that knowledge is not created from a distance, but instead it is produced through dialogue, through the intentionality of various subjects, through informal knowledge, which has its own traditions, its own history. As a first principle, we can call this "interknowledge" [*interconhecimento*], which is the idea that a course isn't just a location for the development of academic knowledge, but a place for the convergence of experiences.

The process of decolonizing the university occurs through dialogue between the MST and allied professors. "What happens is that you begin to occupy the university with debates, with actions, with videos, with weeklong activities, which is part of their strategy, but which is also ours, right?" Rosaldo was explicit: social movements and faculty have a shared strategy of physically

Figure 6.1. Education and the expansion of capital in Amazônia: What is the role of pedagogy?

and ideologically occupying the university through the debates and activities they host (fig. 6.1). "In the way that you're bringing all this in, there's no way that the university can turn its back on it." Integrating and legitimating social movements' demands in the university's public consciousness is a process of taking a counter-hegemonic worldview and making it hegemonic. Much like the processual nature of decolonization, this is, and will always be, more an ongoing struggle than a completed projected. The following section highlights how allied professors mobilize political economy and engage in resistance and support this process..

Everyday Resistance and Political Economy

Gemeson Brito, the professor and upper-level university administrator introduced in the last chapter, exemplifies the crucial role allies play in decolonizing the university. I often met Brito at MST educational events. Brito has directed nearly all of the region's PRONERA courses, and when asked what his daily life is like as a coordinator of these PRONERA programs, he described the linkages between bureaucracy, financial instability, and the necessity of everyday resistance. Sighing, he took off his wire rim glasses to rub his eyes and told me, "In a variety of ways you simply have [long pause] . . . to struggle, because you have to get involved . . . when a course or degree program is approved by the government it guarantees funding, but in reality bureaucracy and financial instability often hold up the course. Liberating the funds requires active intervention. If you were just to send a memo requesting funds to be made available it can easily be forgotten." Brito continued, "So if you don't pick up the phone and call, and insist, and question—so many times I've had to personally go to INCRA, you understand? Because sometimes to get access to a [financial] installment you need to get approval at five levels." Every course or degree program has a budget, which includes stipends for students, faculty salaries, travel expenses for visiting speakers, and funds for meals and fuel, among other expenditures. While its presentation on a spreadsheet makes this budget seem neutral, I have no doubt that allies, such as Brito, helped direct the funds to implicitly support movement objectives. What Brito did was different than illegally redirecting the funds to finance land occupations, such as the case of the MST-affiliated extension service described earlier. Rather, the degree program supports the movement in indirect ways, such as by using funds to bring activists from other areas of Brazil to the Amazon to share experiences and strategies with the certificate program's students. Regardless of the use, the bureaucracy required to liberate the funds is often painfully slow. "So you send in the protocol, but the thing doesn't move forward in the nice way that it should, and so you call and they say, 'Oh, it's stopped at the first level,' and so you go there personally: 'What's the problem?'. . . 'Oh, it's missing this document, you need to correct this or that,' and so you need to exert this additional force, because if you don't these things take too long, you lose the window of time. There is an activist force, in the sense that you need to force the bureaucracy to function." Brito's determination is more than simply following up on his administrative responsibilities. His persistence is emblematic of quotidian forms of resistance (Scott 1987). Studies of such resistance, particularly among institutional activists negotiating bureaucracy (Katzenstein 1998; Arthur 2009; Banaszak 2010), highlight the importance of simple tactics such as picking up the phone. Perhaps it seems contradictory that Brito, an administrator, is involved in the decolonization of the Federal University; after all, he helps direct and maintain the institution's structure. I see this, however, as not a contradiction but rather a tactical choice on behalf of the MST. It takes an organized group of individuals to engage in the process of decolonization. Brito holds a position of power, and this gives him the legitimacy to help organize degree programs and mobilize the political-economic resources necessary to carry them out.

The specialization program in Educação do Campo, Agroecology, and the Agrarian Question in Amazônia, which Brito helps direct, is breaking down the barriers around knowledge. The program's cohort consists of twenty-seven students who hail from various social movements and civil society organizations. For example, in addition to the MST, there are students who have a relation with the Pastoral Land Commission (Commisão Pastoral da Terra, or CPT), others from the Movement of Those Affected by Dams (Movimento de Atingsidos por Barragens, or MAB), and others from the Federation of Agricultural Workers (Federação dos Trabhaldores na Agricultura, or FETAGRI). Aside from this political character and organizational diversity, there is also diversity in terms of disciplinary background. There are students whose training is in pedagogy, history, philosophy, social science, agronomy, and forest engineering. This diversity in students and disciplinary backgrounds is one signal that a broader process of decolonization is unfolding within the university. This is more than just an interdisciplinary program; it is challenging the coloniality of knowledge by decentering agronomic knowledge as a singular entity, replacing it with a pluralistic vision that is grounded in the experiences of subaltern youth.

The specialization program is organized around several pedagogical strategies that, as I described in the mística at the beginning of the chapter, break down the "fences around knowledge": generative themes, dislocation, and an alternating pedagogy. The concept of generative themes comes from Brazilian critical pedagogue Paulo Freire, who believed that it is necessary to identify the salient issues of people's daily lives. These are referred to as generative themes because they originate in people's lived experiences and are used to spark class discussions about political and economic inequalities (Freire 1973). One afternoon during the course Eduardo described to me the relation between generative themes and the course's organization around working groups,

> The first group focused on resource exploitation, such as mineral extraction and hydroelectricity generation. This group arose because these

projects are central elements of the students' reality. For example, we had a student from Maranhão that lives in a settlement where there are five hydroelectricity facilities. So he brought to the course this profound concern about hydroelectricity.

The second group arose out of concerns surrounding the struggle over land. These are ever-present processes—the occupation of land, the violent repression of the state and landowners. And the third group, it focused on agroecology. The ideas for the thematic groups arose from the shared and concrete problems in their respective communities.

The students' everyday experiences of political ecology—of environmental exploitation, of resource conflict, and of agroecology—were generative themes, shaping the organizational structure of the course and its discussions.

The second pedagogical strategy that helped break down the fences around knowledge was what human geographer Anna Godlewska (2013: 385) would call a dislocation pedagogy, involving "the removal of students from what has become familiar by disrupting their geography . . . and their assumptions about . . . the authority of academic knowledge." Throughout the two years of the program the cohort took a variety of field trips, ranging from two days to two weeks, visiting aluminum smelters, cattle ranches, and mines as well as farmers' markets, agricultural cooperatives, and encampments. During a trip the cohort visited one of the largest iron ore mines in the world in Serra dos Carajás. Diana, who was a student in the program and also a teacher from the 17 de Abril settlement's school introduced in chapter 2, recalled critically reflecting about the relations between places following this trip: " 'What space are we living in? What is happening here?' Because we live here, and lots of people say, 'Oh this [mining] is happening over theeeeere in Amazônia.' But hell, Amazônia is here, Amazônia is right here. They say, 'Oh that is happening way over theeeeere in the mines of Serra dos Carajás,' but you know what? Serra dos Carajás is right here." Diana's reflection typified a relational understanding of place. By asking "What space are we living in?" Diana called into question accounts of environmental change that see place as discrete and environmental devastation as distant. Rather, like human geographer Doreen Massey (1999: 22), Diana sees place as "open, porous, hybrid" and constituted through inter-relations. Diana visualizes how the strategies of extractive capitalism connect places in a "sphere of juxtaposition" (Massey 1999: 22). Evidencing the co-constitution of place, she emphasized how "that Amazônia [the one of extractive capital] is right here . . . Serra dos Carajás is right here." Although the scale of extraction is unquestionably different, Diana was correct: mining is a lucrative business in the 17 de Abril settlement. Farmers whose land borders the Rio Vermelho use small barges to pump sand from the river, which they then sell, a small-scale form of resource exploitation (fig. 6.2).[1]

Through dislocating pedagogy, students developed a relational understanding of place as grounded in spatially interconnected struggles. Places, Diana learned, are inherently relational and contested sites of marginalization and emancipation. They are "never simply local, sealed off from an outside beyond" (Moore 1998: 347) but are rather relationally connected to each other as well as hegemonic and subaltern worldviews. What's critically important about Diana's learning experience is that it was through comparative experiences in sites of environmental exploitation that she gained a critical territorial consciousness of how her own community reproduces hegemonic patterns of land use. Diana's experience of the connection between hegemonic and counter-hegemonic spheres of production sheds light on how place can be reimagined from a political ecology of education perspective.

The third way the certificate program breaks down the fence around knowledge production is its alternating pedagogy (*pedagogia de alternância*), where students spend alternating periods of time in both their home and school communities.[2] Alternating pedagogies are grounded in the recognition that

Figure 6.2. Serra dos Carajás is right here

learning is not a singular activity in either a spatial or a temporal sense, occurring only within the confines of the school and its school day. For the MST
learning is perhaps better understood as a hybrid process, which ideally should
serve as a bridge between the home and school environments, thus deconstructing the supremacy of academic knowledge and validating the importance
of knowledge gained through experience.[3] The certificate program's alternating
pedagogy enables the students to design critical field-based research projects
during their school time, which they then carry out in their home communities.

Lucinede, who was profiled in chapter 3, is both a student in the program and
a teacher in the 17 de Abril settlement's school. When I asked her about how she
came to choose her research project, she slapped her knee and leaned forward,
exclaiming, "The tendency in our settlement is ranching! In a little while, we
won't be producing anything; we're simply going to be raising cattle for milk."
Lucinede's frustration with the transition to cattle ranching motivated her research project: "I began to observe this two years ago, and I talked about it with
my friend, and it annoyed me. When I began the course, I wrote several assignments about this, talking about this irritation I had, and our professors proposed
some assignments for our time in the communities, and the assignment was for
us to work to identify the form of production in the settlement and through
researching it, work to understand both hegemony and counter-hegemony."
When Lucinede's professors encouraged her cohort to focus on conflicting com-
modities, she first chose milk production. Her professors then encouraged her
to research an alternative product, asking her, "What is it that you have in your
settlement?" In response, Lucinede went out in in the roça (rural area), conducting site visits with various farmers. What she found shocked her:

> I discovered so many things, so many lovely things, so many interesting
> things. I discovered that there is a farmer who has milk cattle, but he also
> has a mandala agricultural planting; he works with agroforestry, he has
> cacao trees. There's another farmer who works doing beekeeping, but he
> also produces cupuaçu fruit. There's another farmer who is working with
> agroforestry and is working to reforest his land with native Amazonian
> forest species. And so I discovered within the settlement a universe that I
> had never seen, which was so broad, so vast and so marvelous, filled with
> diverse experiences of production.

Drawing upon Stahelin's (2017) Gramscian analysis, I see Lucinede holding a
territorial consciousness characterized by common sense. Like many others,
she has internalized the dominant narrative in the settlement that "it's only

extensive cattle ranching." Yet through critical field-based research, Lucinede starts to challenge this assumption. Her narrative highlights how researching the relations between hegemonic and counter-hegemonic forms of production leads to the development of a critical territorial consciousness. Having discovered this unknown universe, Lucinede felt driven to action: "When I discovered this I thought, 'I need to do something to show these people the potential that exists within the settlement, the potential for the diversification of production,' and I realized that someone has to do something, and I thought that I can do this." As an educator, Lucinede knows she has the power to help her students bring a more diversified agricultural system into existence. In the next vignette I explore how Lucinede and her colleague Diana used education to transform their students' territorial consciousness.

In August 2012 I witnessed how teachers drew upon their critical training to help students challenge the common sense of hegemonic agricultural practices. The Youth Journey is a week in August when normal classes are canceled and in their place MST activist youth and teachers lead lectures and workshops in the municipal public schools located in MST settlements and encampments throughout the region. During a workshop on agroecology during the Youth Journey in 2012, Diana and Lucinede presented findings from their research projects. Diana told the students, "Sometimes you'll hear people talk about certain things as if they were something that only took place really far away; but sometimes, those things are actually occurring quite close to you, it's just you're not able to realize it." Diana's description was strikingly similar to Lucinede's previous comment about discovering a "marvelous" and "unseen universe" of agroecology in her own community. The students began to learn about these invisible landscapes, as Diana continued, "Through our research we were able to learn many things, to discover many things here in the settlement. We observed a variety of agroecological initiatives going on, which are barely known by the population of the settlement." Photographs projected at the front of the room showed students this unseen geography through a critical lens. Lucinede picked up from Diana:

> I'm going to tell you all two stories from our research. One is from an inhabitant in our settlement, and another is from another MST settlement, which we visited as part of our course.
>
> When we were visiting that other settlement, Mede took us on a tour of his lot. And he told us that the first thing he did was try to use the lot to raise cattle, but the lot was very small and it didn't work to raise cattle, which is often the case here.

None of her students had been to this other settlement, but Lucinede painted a relational vision of place by using a description of *that* place to educate students, critically, about *this* place. She indicated that MST settlers in both settlements face similar constraints with the land and its small lot sizes, which are inadequate for cattle ranching. Lucinede also used her experience to instruct the students about how both settlements' inhabitants had similar agroecological opportunities available to them. Lucinede went on to describe, in exquisite detail, the ecological richness of Mede's land and how he was able to sustain his family through the agroecological products he and his wife sold from it, ranging from fruit pulps to natural cosmetics to orchids. Challenging the students, she asked rhetorically, "Now, where is all this taken from?" "From their lot," a student interjected. "From their lot is correct," Lucinede responded, "from Nature, exactly correct, so it's a different form of producing. They are able to survive without destroying the rest of Nature that still exists there." Lucinede created a relational geography, highlighting the similarities between the Mede's land and that of the 17 de Abril, in order to help the students realize that forms of agroecological production that work in other contexts can succeed in the 17 de Abril. One of the core ideas of the political ecology of education perspective is that pedagogy can shape conceptions of nature and ultimately land management practices. By employing a relational geography, Lucinede deepened the role of place within this framework, showing that transformations in conceptions of specific landscapes can be affected by recognizing the connections between landscapes (fig. 6.3).

Lucinede's presentation then shifted from illustrating a relational geography to explaining her critical place-based learning about hegemonic and counter-hegemonic production in the 17 de Abril settlement. "Another place where we did research was here in our settlement. And sometimes you see someone's land plot that has a lot of forest, really high forest, and you say, 'Man, he's lazy,' right?" She stopped and emphasized her next statement, meting her words out slowly to describe a hapless imagined individual: "We . . . see . . . them . . . as . . . lazy, now don't we?" Without missing a beat, the auditorium responded in unison, "We do." "Right," Lucinede continued, "we see them as lazy because they've been on the land for fifteen years, and you can see from the beginning to the end, it's just forest, just forest." Lucinede drew upon the students' own experiences, setting them up for a problem posing moment by asking what seeing "just" forest on someone's lot indicated about that person. "But I don't think this is laziness," Lucinede offered. "You know what it is? It's a choice to engage in a new form of production. Do you think economically he just survives on cattle and pasture?" "No," the students all replied again.

Lucinede probed further, "Do you think that he just knocks down the forest to burn so that he can then plant crops?" "No!" shouted the students, getting into the exercise. "There are other forms of production," Lucinede emphasized, filling in the other half of the contradiction she had created: having one's land covered completely in forest is not a sign of laziness, as many believe; rather, it can be an intentional means to diversify one's income, not degrade the land, and generate food for self-consumption. Lucinede continued, "What is lacking amongst us is knowledge of how to do this. That's the reason we did this research. Through this research we learned that this individual has açaí, mahogany, cedar, cupuaçu, cacao, goiaba, he has a huge list of tree species, including Castanha do Pará. He has planted more than five thousand trees on his land." Lucinede's research was, as she described it, a process of discovering the counter-hegemonic forms of production. It was a process of developing critical territorial consciousness. Lucinede concluded her presentation, "These examples can be a way of encouraging our parents to work in a type of production that is not simply ranching. This new form of agroecological production is in equilibrium with nature, because one thing depends on the other. This type of work is gratifying because it creates in the person a perspective of a

Figure 6.3. Shaping conceptions of nature

future that is more healthy, and that is much better than having someone take a land plot and mechanize the entire thing and plant pasture across it. And so these two experiences bring for us a new hope for life." Lucinede's pedagogy exemplified territoriality because it communicated "information in order to affect, influence, and control the ideas and actions of other and their access to resources" (Sack 1986: 26). Territoriality is a core aspect of the political ecology of education because it is a mechanism whereby the production and circulation of knowledge transform conceptions of nature and access to and control over natural resources.

In this section, I have highlighted one way of understanding the relationship between decolonization, education, and the fences around knowledge. Decolonizing education can take place by recognizing that important learning happens outside of the university. Degree programs have been created from historic partnerships between the MST and allied professors at the Federal University. These programs begin decolonizing education by breaking down the barriers around knowledge; learning happens as students conduct comparative research on hegemonic and counter-hegemonic spaces of production. The students take lessons learned from this critical place-based research and impart them in their communities, seeking to transform territory. Decolonizing education has the potential to result in the ongoing decolonization of land. The next section approaches the relationship from the opposite perspective; I show that decolonizing land can lead to the decolonization of education.

Decolonizing Land to Decolonize Education

The MST's 26 de Março settlement, which houses the 354-hectare Federal Institute campus, is the product of a process of decolonizing land. In 2004 the National Institute of Colonization and Agrarian Reform (INCRA) created the 26 de Março settlement from the Fazenda Cabaceiras, which had been owned by the Almeida family—one of the most powerful, and feared, families in the region. The Almeidas' principal activity in Fazenda Cabaceiras was the extraction of Brazil nuts, which they sold to international markets. Like many fazendas in the Amazon, the Almeida family did not legally own the land of Fazenda Cabaceiras but maintained a hold on it primarily through intimidation and violence. They contracted migrant workers from other states under the promise of good housing, fair pay, and safe working conditions and then used hired gunmen to prevent the migrant *castanheiros* from escaping. Between 1982 and 1989 these gunmen murdered forty migrant workers. In

1989 the Almeida family sold Fazenda Cabaceiras to the Mutran family—another of the region's powerful oligarchies. With the sale of the property, the form of labor changed from Brazil nut harvesting to the cutting of the Brazil trees and the conversion of the forest to pasture land. The repressive violence continued under the new owners, as the fazenda's gunmen once again murdered migrant workers who protested the working conditions, burying them in unmarked graves in the forest. After decades of illegal activity under both families, in 2004 INCRA finally managed to put a stop to it. The state expropriated the land and created the MST's 26 de Março settlement. The community allocated a section of the land to be used to create the Federal Institute. This was truly a manifestation of the knowledge frontier: the Federal Institute arose materially from a conflicted landscape and is now a subaltern epistemological space—recognized and funded by the state—that seeks to challenge enshrined systems of agrarian violence and environmental devastation like those that were carried out on this very land for more than twenty years.

The Federal Institute is well aware of this central historic relationship to the epistemological and material contradictions of the frontier, and it uses these roots to define itself as an institution. An analysis of the school's political and pedagogical project document (*Projeto Político Pedagógico*, or PPP) captures this perspective.[4] The PPP is an institutional plan for creating a transformative educational institution. The document begins with a regional context section that reads like a treatise in political ecology. It situates the Federal Institute's origination as beginning with national development projects that opened up the Amazon through road-building projects (Foweraker 1981; Branford and Glock 1985). These projects, the PPP explains, further entrenched agrarian inequities by promoting consolidation of land, which led to large-scale land violence, including assassination and torture (Simmons 2005). In the face of this history of oppression, the PPP asserts that family farmers remain important social, political, environmental, and agricultural actors. The PPP describes how these small-scale farmers have resisted the hegemonic narrative of technological progress and development, instead emphasizing the importance of diversified production (Campos and Nepstad 2006). It situates the Federal Institute at the intersection of two visions of rural space: one of capital and the other of family farming as a counter-hegemonic force.

Against this analysis of the linkages between political economy and agrarian landscape change, the PPP's regional context section then describes how the Federal Institute is an extension of the two-decade history of educational activism in this region, involving various social movements, indigenous communities, and professors from the Federal University. This activism also gave rise in the 1990s to the agricultural education center I referred to in chapter 5 as the center, with an accompanying school for the children of small-scale farmers. In the early 2000s the MST and Federal University professors entered into dialogue with the Secretary of Professional and Technological Education about the need for a new vocational high school where students could learn about agroecology, and in 2008 these discussions culminated in the creation of Law 11.892, which brought into existence the state-level Federal Institute of Education, Science, and Technology of Pará (IFPA) system, and with it the Federal Institute.

This two-decade process of creating the Federal Institute is about more than developing an educational institution that attends to social movements' needs; it also concerns the decolonization of land. As the PPP documents, social movements have helped create more than five hundred settlements in the region, providing access to land and the opportunity for diversified production to more than eighty thousand families. The PPP explicitly describes the Federal Institute as a key contributor to this process of resistance by working with students to develop a place-based model of agroecology that is relevant to Amazônia and is the product of hybridized knowledge. Its stated objective is to train students to "organize their territories according to the reproduction of their existence," contributing to family subsistence, community life, and the larger sustainability of southeastern Pará (IFPA-CRMB 2011: 21). It aims to reproduce a novel vision of society by stimulating horizontal working relationships—encouraging cooperative initiatives, workers' associations, and solidarity economies (IFPA-CRMB 2011: 21). This is a model that attempts to recast knowledge as not purely academic but rather as part and parcel of students' life experiences. Throughout the PPP's contextual sections, the school is presented as a product of and response to the frontier, originating from a history of educational activism that sought to redress environmental degradation and rural residents' lack of opportunity for training in sustainable agriculture.

On a Saturday visit to the Federal Institute in November 2012, I gained firsthand knowledge of how the process of decolonization advances subaltern forms of agroecological knowledge and ultimately results in the transformation of the landscape. When I arrived at the Federal Institute, Helix, a student in the agricultural extension high school program, offered to show me the cohort's experimental agroecology projects. We entered a garden area and found a tarp-covered piece of ground. A PVC pipe was stuck into the center of the tarp. This, Helix proudly told me, is a biogas generator. "We just finished it, so no gas yet, but it would come out here," he indicated, pointing at a valve. "We bring the food waste from the school and mix it with manure, drop it under the tarp and let biodegradation do its work. When methane rises, the tarp will billow, and the only byproducts will be rich compost and a liquid that is high in nutrients." Impressed by the students' ingenuity, I turned around and found Marcos, Helix's agroecology teacher, bending down in some bushes a short distance away. Seeing Helix and myself, he called us over. In his agroecology class today they would be talking about nitrogen fixation, and Marcos wanted to show his class an example of rhizomes. "I want to show them what rhizomes look like. It can't just be in theory, it needs to be in practice as well. The students need to be able to see and feel the rhizomes." He reached down and pulled up a bean plant, gently fingering its roots. "This will do." We continued walking and came to an area where beans were planted in among the grass. Marcos remarked, "We're doing research on these beans, looking at them as a method of combating the pasture grass. Rather than burning, farmers can plant beans, which not only give food, but also provide nitrogen to the soil. Early results look promising." As we walked, I reflected on how I had just witnessed the reciprocal linkages between the decolonization of land and knowledge. What once was a landscape characterized by agrarian conflict and environmental degradation had now been reshaped through decolonization into a landscape of generative agroecological experimentation and learning. The transformation of this landscape had been simultaneously material and epistemological. The transformation was striking and, frankly, inspiring.

We headed from the field toward the auditorium, where the director of the Federal Institute was beginning a presentation to a group of parents. Infrastructure remains a challenge, the director noted, with the road to the school unfinished and a dorm only half constructed. There had been many small but substantial victories over the last year, however: they had successfully constructed a series of experimental areas for agroecological research and extension, such as those that Helix was just showing me. Flashing rapidly through a series of slides, the director drew our attention to the apiary, seed laboratory, and other spaces where students were raising pigs, cows, goats, sheep, and fish as part of an integrated agroecological system. There were also areas, the director told us, for creating value-added products such as yogurt and facilities for processing manioc and fruit pulps.

These spaces evinced the Federal Institute's commitment to helping train students in economically and ecologically diverse systems of production. They also demonstrated that education is playing a direct role in repeasantization.

Van der Ploeg (2012) describes six mechanisms of repeasantization, and the Federal Institute is engaged with each one.[5] Students worked on experimental agroecological plots in cooperative groups, learning to create highly diverse agroecosystems that reduce the use of external inputs. These were spaces for careful research and experimentation in which students developed new technologies—such as the biogas generator—suited to their realities and needs. They were recognizing that through utilizing the apiary to produce artisanal beeswax candles in addition to honey they could diversify their livelihoods (fig. 6.4). In describing this as a "project of construction" (*projeto de construção*), the director used the word *project* to signify an overarching objective, as in "the project of social transformation." The "project of construction" here was developing an educational institution that would advance food sovereignty by transforming rural livelihoods, economies, and ecologies.

Advancing this project required negotiating political economy and resistance. The director's next slides provided insight into the complicated financial maneuvering necessary to offer these diverse courses and fund these agroecological experimentation plots. The Federal Institute financially invested in the students' success, providing small scholarships to each secondary school student to defray travel costs associated with its alternating pedagogy. It also

Figure 6.4. Learning to diversify

provided funding for them to participate as a cohort in regional and national conferences on agroecology. All this money had to come from somewhere, and at present most of it came from the state. The director provided context for these figures by describing the ongoing struggles, victories, and setbacks that occurred in the process of securing the state's promised education funding. The audience erupted into applause as the director concluded his presentation with a picture of him hugging Brazilian president Dilma Rousseff. "That was just three days ago in Brasília!" he smiled.

As the director finished, I reflected on his presentation, which highlighted the collective trials, struggles, and partial victories in keeping the campus fiscally solvent. The overarching message for parents seemed clear: the Federal Institute's administration was directly linked to the seat of power and would traverse geopolitical scales in order to pressure the government to fulfill its financial and political obligation to funding necessary to keep the Federal Institute going and advance educação do campo (figs. 6.5 and 6.6). Through struggle, it would obtain the resources needed to continue the dual "projects" of advancing locally relevant education and creating agroecological education opportunities—going all the way to the president if necessary.

The public face of the Federal Institute highlighted the reciprocal struggle

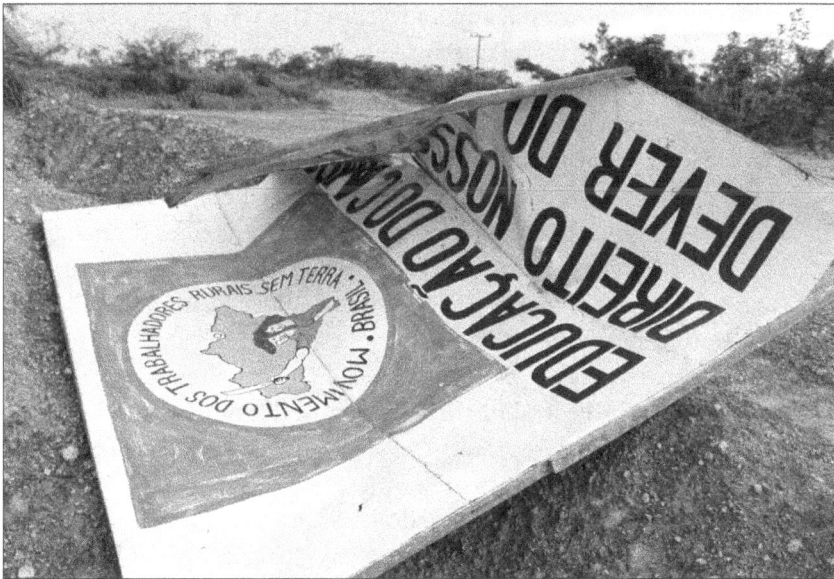

Figure 6.5. Educação do campo: Our right, the state's obligation

Figure 6.6. Signs of an ongoing struggle

involved in transforming land and knowledge. This was a bidirectional process—land transforming knowledge and knowledge transforming land—and it was ongoing in conflicts that persist into the present over material and immaterial territory. For Brazilian geographer Bernardo Mançano Fernandes (2009), material territory is the physical landscape (hills, rivers, forests) as well as infrastructure (buildings, bridges, roads). Immaterial territory, by contrast, is the landscape of ideas. It is the system of knowledge that structures the manipulation of material territory. Like much of the frontier, this material territory has been marked by cycles of violence and environmental exploitation. When the MST successfully pressured INCRA to expropriate the land and create the 26 de Março settlement, the process of decolonization—of transforming material territory—began. The Federal Institute continued this process, further transforming material and immaterial territory through a novel system of education grounded in agroecology.

This was not just a set of theoretical lessons. Rather, alternative systems of knowledge were materially structuring the landscape of the Federal Institute itself, as in the example of the agroecological experimentation plots at the Federal Institute where people were developing new methods of working with land (such as planting beans instead of using fire to clear land). These experiments hold the potential to be translated and transferred by the students in their own regions. In contrast to the earlier example of the Federal University, which highlighted how decolonizing education led to the decolonization of land, the case of the Federal Institute highlights the opposite: decolonizing land can lead to the process of decolonizing education. However, a core question for political ecologists of education remains unanswered: what factors either enable or preclude students in these programs from putting their critical food systems education into practice, transforming their agricultural systems, and in turn the landscape? In this chapter's last section, I address this question, which is central to understanding the political ecology of education in the 17 de Abril.

The Potential and Pitfalls of Political Economy, Ecology, and Education

During an agricultural cooperativism class at the Federal Institute in October 2012, I learned about how political economy can provide opportunities for students to put their agroecological learning into practice. Francisco, the teacher, explained how their final project would serve as their personal application for a new credit project known as PRONAF-Jovem, a government credit program intended to fund sustainable agriculture for small-scale farmers.[6] Francisco told the class,

> You all will be doing a final project titled "Improving My Land." The objective of this class project is to put together a document that can serve as your proposal for the PRONAF-Jovem credit initiative. To put forth your vision for your land, we want you to describe in detail the historical production of the landscape. I want you to do this in three ways.
>
> The first is a history of your lot. Your objective is to understand the historical production of this agroecosystem. Think about what have been the social, economic, political changes in the system. When did electricity arrive? When did the road reach your house? What changes did this precipitate?
>
> Second, what are the technological practices that your family uses? You need to understand what practices a family uses, because it won't work to propose activities where a family doesn't have knowledge of a particular type of agriculture.
>
> Third, what are the rationales for the changes? How have they maintained their life within that space? For example, your land was already cattle pasture, and PRONAF came along and you got cattle because that

made sense. With this understanding of the history of your landscape, and your family's role in its transformation, you'll be able to better describe your vision for that landscape.

Class projects such as this taught students to approach extension from a spatially and temporally nuanced perspective. Students' critical reflections were part of the learning process that results in reformulating their spatial imaginaries, or particular ideas of how landscapes should be spatially ordered, what forms of production are intuitive, and what constitutes nature (Larner 1998; Golubchikov 2010). Spatial imaginaries are learned, and this learning can be structured by financial subsidies. Course projects provided students a concrete opportunity to think outside the confines of their taken-for-granted spatial imaginaries, envisioning what a more diversified landscape might look like. When political-economic incentives, such as the PRONAF-Jovem project, intersect with these innovative courses, students gained the capital to transform their production systems. For them to achieve this potential, however, required that they themselves negotiate hegemonic systems of land management.

I learned about how families navigate hegemonic land management practices when I made a visit to the family farm of Josemá, a Federal Institute student, in 2012. In the 17 de Abril settlement, I joined Josemá and his father Misael on a walk around their lot to discuss its history, his family's role in its transformation, and his vision for the future. When Misael originally got the land, it had been part of the old fazenda and was mostly pasture. Although some of the original forest remains today, Misael complained that they have had trouble preserving it. He pointed to the remaining forest with a sweeping motion that encompasses the entire area: *picado* (burnt through). Misael reached to the ground and made a spider-like motion with his hand. "A neighbor will set a fire at sunset, and it will pass under the ground, coming up again and burning everything. We tried to maintain a forest reserve, as we had a lot of native cupuaçu and cacao, but every year it becomes more and more picado." The landscape's historical usage for cattle, and the reckless burning practices of neighbors, limited Misael's efforts to maintain an area of preservation that he wishes could be an agroforestry system.

It was not supposed to be this way. Similar to Arnoldo, profiled in chapter 3, Misael had always envisioned engaging in agroforestry on his land. In the beginning Misael had taken part in the PRONAF-A credit program for agroforestry. It was a group credit project, in which he had to enter with a set of neighbors. However, this meant that they had to pay as a group, and so when one member didn't pay, they all remained in debt. The agroforestry project failed in part due to the cultural politics of negotiating the repayment of credit.

In 2009 Misael signed up for the PRONAF-A program again—this time for cattle. The money was enough to build a watering hole for the cattle, construct a corral, and build a fence. "Was there technical assistance?" I asked. "Perhaps, but only to create the project. Here, it is really rare to see a technician," Misael responded as we walked the property. Similar to most residents, Misael participated in the cattle project because it seemed like a sure thing, especially after the failure of the agroforestry project. Plus there was money to support it. Extension provided Misael access to political economy in the form of a financial incentive that connected his spatial imaginary with the landscape's historical usage for cattle ranching. As I explained in chapter 2, cattle are imbued with symbolism in this region: as a system of financial security—a living "bank"—as well as a symbol of social status. People also saw them as something that just makes sense, given the fact that many of their plots were already cleared of forest and growing pasture by the time they got hold of them. Moving away from ranching and toward agroecology will inevitably be a contest of values and cultural politics.

As we walked Josemá told me that his family had given up on subsistence agriculture because it was too hard to prepare the land without machinery. We talked about the dependence on machinery and its apparent contradictions within the context of agroecology. "We are all *maquinarios mesmos* [literally, 'machine people, ourselves,' meaning technologically oriented people]," he responded with a smile. "It's very difficult to work agroecologically." Here he was reflecting the broader conception I described in the introduction: to reject cattle ranching and attempt to remove pasture and remediate the soil for other purposes takes more work than just leaving it as is and attempting to eke out a living in small-scale agriculture. Josemá gave me an example, pointing to the shrubs growing up through the pasture. "My father wants to use herbicide to clean out this pasture, but I think it would be better if we just worked the land by hand." Josemá told me that he was interested in greening his family's production on the lot; as part of his "Improving My Land" course project, he envisioned trading in some of the meat cows they currently had for milk cows and beginning milk production. Cattle, Josemá indicated, can be integrated into a diversified agroecological system, providing fertilizer for the land with their manure and urine and obtaining food and shade from the land if it is set up as a partial agroforestry area. Josemá would have liked to use the PRONAF-Jovem funds to help create such an agroforestry area within the small forest that persisted on their land, picado though it was. However, there was another familial conflict here: Misael wanted to convert it into a swidden area to plant manioc. Drawing upon his experiences in the agroecological extension program, Josemá thought that planting cupuaçu, coconut, and açaí would have made much more sense because they would have diversified his family's income and been more environmentally sustainable than cattle ranching.

The tension between Josemá and Misael concerning manual labor versus herbicides and swidden cultivation versus agroforestry underscored the larger cultural politics surrounding the agroecological transition in this region. In particular, Josemá and Misael's conflict over the value of different forms of production mirrored the contest that was going on in the settlement, as extension agents and MST students pushed for diversified production while the community relied almost exclusively on ranching. Underlying these cultural politics were the interwoven historical and political-economic forces—ranging from Green Revolution policies to agricultural subsidies—that have shaped the landscape, enshrining ranching as the hegemonic form of agricultural production. From a political ecology of education perspective, agricultural extension focused on the promotion of cattle ranching has served as a constraint to diversifying production. Yet education—even that provided by agricultural extension—held the potential to help usher in an agroecological transition, if it was pitched correctly. Josemá's cohort was being trained in a new model of agroecological extension designed to do just that. As this chapter's earlier case study of the Federal University graduate program highlighted, education had the potential to transform territorial consciousness, agricultural practices, and the landscape itself. Decolonizing education helped advance the decolonization of land.

Conclusions

This chapter has addressed how the breaking down of fences—both literally and symbolically—is central to the MST's related goals of decolonizing land and education. Given the MST's primary characteristic of direct action land reform, the phrase indexes the literal breaking down of fences to get access to land (Branford and Rocha 2002). Yet as I've shown in this chapter, the metaphor also underscores the common perspective that knowledge is produced in authoritative places, such as universities, rather than on rural farms (Mignolo 2009). Access to quality schools and universities, like access to land, has historically been concentrated among elites (Plank 1996). Given this context, I believe the symbolism of the mística at the Federal University auditorium that opened the chapter is much clearer. A graduate cohort, composed entirely of students from agrarian social movements, used this mística to create a moment of reflection before opening a plenary session where they would be presenting their own field-based research surrounding educação do campo. A student's placement of a book titled *Breaking Fences and Constructing Knowledge* symbolized that barriers of knowledge have been—at least in certain circumstances—broken down.

Scholars are increasingly recognizing that the historical and current contexts of colonization have structured access to both education and land (Tuck et al. 2014). These two case studies contribute to this emerging discussion by demonstrating that the struggle over land must also involve breaking down the barriers to education. My work among students and educators in southern Pará led me to realize that the decolonization of land and education exist in a mutually constitutive, bidirectional relationship. As the two case studies demonstrated, breaking up the concentration of land can provide the impetus to decolonize education, but also decolonial education can generate new decolonizing land practices that people may adopt after exposure to such education. Decolonizing education is an epistemological and political process, involving a direct challenge to the primacy of academic knowledge by drawing on rural students' embodied nonacademic community experiences and engaging with social movements' lived experiences of material struggle. By decolonizing education, students can gain the critical territorial consciousness necessary to transform the landscape itself. Turning this relationship on its head, decolonizing land can also lead to decolonizing education.

As both case studies highlighted, questions of national-level political economy are central to realizing the transformative potential of education. PRONERA, for instance, is a national-level public policy that provides crucial funding for critical food systems education programs, such as the course Educação do Campo, Agroecology, and the Agrarian Question in Amazônia offered by the Federal University. Similarly, PRONAF-Jovem is a relatively new national financial incentive that students can access to help put their critical agroecological learning into practice.

This chapter is closely tied to the themes of political economy and place that have arisen at other points in the book. As described in chapter 2, agricultural credit incentives helped solidify the hegemony of cattle ranching, making it akin to what Gramsci terms "common sense." By contrast, as outlined in this chapter, financial subsidies, as exemplified by PRONAF-Jovem, have a counter-hegemonic potential, as they are capable of facilitating the transition to agro-ecology. Taken together, these two chapters have highlighted that an analysis of the ways in which political economy structures dominant and subaltern land use practices is central to understanding the political ecology of education. Similarly, this chapter has deepened the analysis of place, which has been a central thread in this book. For example, as highlighted in chapter 3, a critical conception of place was one of the central differences between the competing educational visions of Educação do Campo and rural education. As described in this chapter, a dislocation pedagogy—referred to in Brazil as an "alternating pedagogy" (Ribeiro 2008)—helped students recognize that places are inherently relational and that hegemonic systems of extraction connect ostensibly disparate places such as the 17 de Abril and large-scale mines.

Similarly, this chapter has shed new light on the contradictions of place, which have emerged in many of the earlier chapters. There is irony in the fact that places like the 17 de Abril were founded with a vision of alternative agriculture yet ended up being constituted from the start by a hegemonic system of production (i.e., cattle ranching). Isabel, for example, opened chapter 1 by lamenting that "it wasn't supposed to be this way"; the movement's vision was not for a landscape defined by cattle ranching. In this chapter we saw how this contradiction of place can be profoundly instructive. Lucinede's recognition that "in a little while, we won't be producing anything; we're simply going to be raising cattle for milk" led to a profound pedagogical opportunity. Through her critical field-based research, Lucinede made startling discoveries about an invisible world of alternative production happening right under her nose. She drew upon these experiences to help transform local students' understandings of their own landscape and ideas about the range of viable land management strategies that a person could use in this community. Within this example place and education exist in a circular relationship: the contradictions of place, which spawned a critical pedagogical opportunity, end up intervening through education in a new constitution of place.

This dialectic between the politics of place and education is much broader than just Lucinede's research. It speaks to the reciprocal transformations that constitute the frontier itself. As a region southeastern Pará is peripheral to centers of established knowledge production, but it remains central to the exploitation of workers and natural resources that funds a large portion of Brazil's economy. Without established universities along the rapidly expanding frontier, the state sought to establish an ideological presence. The opening up of new material territories on the frontier therefore sparked the need to develop new educational institutions. In a way the Federal University and Federal Institute are both products of frontier expansion. They highlight how transformations in material and immaterial territory are intrinsically related. Focusing on immaterial territory, it becomes clear that the type of education—an alternative system of knowledge production grounded in agroecology—is itself a product of the material struggles on the frontier.

CHAPTER 7

Learning through Movement

We left the 17 de Abril settlement in a packed school bus. The atmosphere started out fairly subdued as people sat on laps and stood shoulder to shoulder. But soon someone broke out a tambourine and began to sing. The environment immediately transformed, and nearly everyone began to sing. As was common in the MST, the young activists transformed the lyrics of a popular contemporary song to echo the movement's dominant themes. "I just want to live with no worries, and with healthy rice and beans too, and this way I'll live well."[1] Repeating the chorus about healthy food three times, the tone of their voices changed to a softer melody, suggesting *saudade*—the common Brazilian expression for longing and nostalgia. We rocked with the music, as the bus jostled back and forth on well-worn shocks, negotiating a narrow bridge hewn from rough timbers. Passing through the city of Eldorado dos Carajás, we saw a ring of towering burned *castanha* (Brazil nut) trunks in the distance. These trees are the S-curve monument. They memorialize the massacre of nineteen MST activists killed by paramilitaries on April 17, 1996, at this sharp bend of highway PA-150 known as the S-curve.

The sight of the castanhas at the S-curve is always striking. Maybe it's their gnarled, almost sculptural shape, or maybe it's that one normally encounters them as lone trees left in a cattle pasture (figs. 7.1 and 7.2). In the early 2000s several arts educators partnered with youth from the 17 de Abril settlement to construct this memorial, which consists of the burned trunks of nineteen Brazil nut trees that are entombed in a circle. Nineteen tree trunks to commemorate the nineteen activists murdered on April 17, 1996. The monument usually invokes in me a sense of devastation because these lone trees standing in pasture are a sign of deforestation..

As we sit in a line of traffic—our bus held up by MST activists who have blockaded the road ahead—Edinilson tells me that this was part of the intention: "The idea behind the monument was to represent the massacre in the most appropriate form—it represents the massacre of the peasants, the massacre

Figure 7.1. Verdant and scorched Brazil nut trees

Figure 7.2. Brazil nut trees entombed at S-curve with pedagogical encampment in background

of the miners many years before, the massacre of biodiversity, of the forests, of the land, of the Brazil nut trees. A decade after the massacre we began to think about creating a pedagogical youth encampment, about reconstructing this space, which was a theater of death." Once the site of a grisly massacre, the S-curve has been transformed into a pedagogical space of resistance. In the early 2000s, several arts educators partnered with youth from the 17 de Abril settlement to construct this memorial, which consists of the burned trunks of nineteen Brazil nut trees that are entombed in a circle. Nineteen tree trunks to commemorate the nineteen activists murdered on April 17, 1996. Every year since 2006, hundreds of youth activists have participated in this annual "pedagogical encampment," a learning space where political consciousness and agroecological knowledge are enmeshed together. This year, approximately four hundred high school students and I would be participating in the MST's week-long Oziel Alves Perreira pedagogical encampment.[2] We would live in rudimentary shelters made of black plastic tarps, sleeping side by side in hammocks strung from a bamboo frame. From morning to night we would engage in diverse critical learning opportunities, from seminars on the agrarian question to organizing road blockades and writing poetry about agroecology.

With a shuddering lurch, our bus moved forward—I could see in the distance tires and tree trunks being rolled off the road by youth wearing red shirts and waving red flags. The barricade was lifted, and there was movement. We drove forward, finally entering the pedagogical encampment.

This chapter focuses on how place, learning, and political participation intersect in the pedagogical encampment and 17 de Abril settlement to bring new conceptions of the world into existence. It comprises three sections. The first and last are short sections that illustrate how the politics of place constrain political participation. The middle section is an extended vignette that centers around the pedagogical encampment. Although it might appear a success story for nonformal educational practices like those at the pedagogical encampment, the third section details the substantial obstacles to realizing the transformative potential of nonformal education. Rather than an unabashedly celebratory account, this chapter takes seriously the prospects and pitfalls of place. I now turn to explore how political participation intersects with both informal and nonformal education.

Place, Experience, and Formation

Opportunities for learning through political participation are so extensive that scholars of adult education describe them as a "learning iceberg" because the learning is frequently invisible but extensive (Crowther and Shaw 1997).[3] Brazilian social movements use the term *formação* to describe the embodied experience of learning that takes place through political participation.[4] I tend to think of formação as "formation" and envision it as a process of molding, or quite literally *forming*, individuals. In this section I focus on how individuals, which Gramsci terms "organic intellectuals," are formed through pivotal life events. I advance our understanding of these organic intellectuals by underscoring the role of place as part of an ensemble of relations in shaping political consciousness. I provide a case study of Raul, a thirty-four-year-old MST leader, to show how informal learning that occurs in particular places structures our political consciousness.[5]

Here, I distinguish informal learning from nonformal education. Informal learning takes place in quotidian moments, which are "outside of formally structured, institutionally sponsored, classroom-based activities" (Marsick and Watkins 1990: 6–7). Nonformal education, by contrast, also takes place within a broadly defined pedagogical space, but one that is not necessarily state sponsored. The pedagogical encampment is characterized by nonformal education: it has an explicit pedagogical purpose, involves active study, but does not yield credentials, involve assessment, or take place within a traditional educational setting. One of the broader arguments of this book is that political formation exists on a spatial continuum, involving interconnected experiences of learning ranging from formal education to informal learning. I now return to Raul to explore how his experiences of informal learning shape his political formation and in turn structure subsequent opportunities for both nonformal and formal education.

Raul and I sat outside his small tent at the pedagogical encampment. Behind us were the towering castanhas that form the memorial to the massacre. I told Raul that I was interested in learning about the history of the pedagogical encampment and its role in educating youth. Reflecting for a long moment while he hand rolled a cigarette, Raul told me that first it was necessary to talk about the effect that the massacre at Eldorado dos Carajás had played in his life.

Raul, who was sixteen years old when he survived the massacre, said that the experience formed him (*me formei*), unequivocally, as a political subject: "It was a very difficult time. I saw a lot of children and their parents dying, falling to the ground. Women and children trying to save themselves. Children running without knowing where their parents were. And there was a little church, and children were running towards it for safety. Other children climbed a tree to try to escape the bullets, and their parents were dying there on the ground beneath them. And that for me was the biggest shock of my life. And, in truth, it was what transformed me into what I am today." Raul made a decision at that point to formally enter the movement. Although he had been at the massacre because he was accompanying his parents and living in an encampment at that time, he had not really felt committed to the movement prior to that moment.[6] Following the massacre, however, Raul emerged very quickly as a leader within the MST. Although he was just a teenager, he became immediately involved in coordinating the encampment and facilitating discussions. He was eventually nominated to serve as a state coordinator of the MST. He remained in the state coordination for three years, but then moved on to pursue opportunities for training, both within the movement and in formal school as well. "These spaces of formation prepare leaders of the MST. The formation is so that you can understand how society functions, how do relations of power function," he explains.

Between 1999 and 2002, Raul participated in a teacher-training course at the Federal University of South and Southeastern Pará (UNIFESSPA), which was funded by PRONERA and affiliated with the MST. The course was a powerful experience of formação for Raul, in which he was exposed to new forms of political ideology, music, and poetry. The teacher-training course—in which Raul participated in everyday moments of political formation alongside the educator training—helped form his political identity. Raul came out of the course and began to advance the movement at a structural level, taking on "some of the grandest tasks of the movement: carrying out occupations, helping to organize settlements, broader mobilizations. My responsibility wasn't just to look after my community as a particular space, but to remain watchful over the other communities and occupations in the region." Fanning his fingers out, Raul continued, "My responsibilities grew like a folding fan, and I became involved in coordinating various state level collectives. I stayed at the state level working for ten years. And last year, I was elected to the national level of the MST for the state of Pará." Finishing his cigarette, Raul remarked, "What we need is to recognize that all of these companheiros [students at the encampment] are also subjects of this same process of formação. And the settlement, the encampment, and the massacre have been this in my life, but principally the massacre; these have been the 'school of life' [escola da vida] where I learned many things, and I'm reproducing this in the various spaces in which I exist."

Raul would be very recognizable to Antonio Gramsci as an organic intellectual, coming from the masses, a public orator and permanent persuader, committed to raising popular consciousness and organizing. Raul's narrative provides crucial insight into how informal learning and place co-constitute the "organic." Intellectuals are organic when they are formed by the web of social relations in which they exist. As part of a challenge to conventional conceptions of the intellectual, Gramsci (1994: 8, emphasis added) argues, "the most widespread error of method seems to me that of having looked for this criterion of distinction in the intrinsic nature of intellectual activities, rather than in the *ensemble of the systems of relations* in which these activities (and therefore the intellectual groups who personify them) have their place within the general complex of social relations." What defines the intellectual is not particular ideas but this ensemble of relations. I argue here that these relations can include not only individuals but also places. The S-curve will forever be a place characterized by direct action and violent repression. Places, and our experiences in them, become nodes in a broader ensemble of relations; they are moments of formation that shape individuals, who, once mobilized, go on to participate in other formative spaces. Informal learning conditions other moments and spaces of formation that are both nonformal and formal.

Raul is the archetypical individual *formed* through the movement. The experience of living through the massacre itself was powerfully formative, as Raul stressed at both the beginning and end of his narrative. It was a "school of life," a moment that forever changed him, providing in his words a "shock" that elevated his consciousness and shaped his life trajectory. The massacre solidified Raul's identity of Sem Terra, of being at once marginalized as well as committed to social change. Moving forward from this experience, he made a decision to enter the movement, and pursue opportunities for formação both within the movement and the formal education system that would help him develop into a leader. The spatial continuum of learning experiences, ranging from informal learning gained through movement organizing to nonformal experiences in movement workshops and formal education through coursework, is an ensemble of systems of relations; these are relational spaces of education and militancy. Seen as an ensemble, this diverse ecology of spaces of knowledge production organically produces militants, such as Raul, who are dedicated to using education as a tool for social mobilization and transformation.

Not everyone, thankfully, endures the kind of trauma that propelled Raul into this new phase of life. But even for those who have not been through such trauma, place shapes political consciousness. For Raul, the massacre was not the only space of learning. In addition, the encampment and the settlement have been, for him, a school of life.[7] Likewise, for the tens of thousands of individuals living in MST encampments and settlements throughout Brazil, these are important spaces where there is a freedom to develop new forms of social organization. Throughout my research MST activists spoke nostalgically of their time in encampments; although these were incredibly difficult circumstances, they inevitably shaped their understandings of how to work in a cooperative, develop consensus, and engage in creative resistance. Similar to Crowther and Shaw's description of social movements as "learning icebergs," I argue that these disparate occupied spaces are important places through which MST members are shaped.

We can take from Raul's case study the lesson that our experiences in places can transform us. It's not just surviving a massacre or squatting on land that forms individuals; rather, for those in the Global North, interning with a food justice organization, cultivating an urban garden, and working in solidarity with grassroots groups can also be politically formative. As Raul described, these experiences can build upon each other organically, leading to ever-greater political participation. In the ensemble of relations that produce organic intellectuals, place is an important relational node—this place can be an encampment in Brazil or a campus organic garden in the United States. Here I've highlighted the voice of one individual—Raul—to underscore how informal learning happens within place, shaping one's engagement with both nonformal and formal education, and ultimately one's political consciousness. In the next section I present various voices of educators, students, movement leaders, and myself to provide a broader picture of what nonformal critical food systems education looks like at the pedagogical encampment and how it decolonizes place.

Agroecology, Education, and the Agrarian Question

I left our black plastic roofed *barraca* (tent) and headed across the highway, entering the encampment's large white seminar tent. Hanging around the edges were an assortment of solidarity flags: the Palestinian, Cuban, and gay pride flags, flags from rural unions such as the Confederation of Agricultural Workers, flags from other national movements like the Movement of Those Affected by Dams, and flags from international movements like La Vía Campesina (fig. 7.3). Student art hung between the flags—paintings of peasants with hoes, of fields, and of movement flags. Large banners with images of Frida Kahlo, Antonio Gramsci, and Paulo Freire hung from the sides of the tent, providing several feet of much-needed shade. Although it was only eight in the morning, the temperature was already beginning to rise under the relentless sun (fig. 7.4). The burned Brazil nut castanha trees provided a backdrop for this scene, their shadows crisscrossing the roof of the tent and serving as part of the background for this space.

Figure 7.3. Signs of movement

Figure 7.4. Dialogic learning

The music inside the tent was contagious, and several hundred youth were singing, dancing, and jumping in unison, seemingly unfazed by the heat (fig. 7.5). At the front of the tent two teenagers with a tambourine and a drum set a rhythmic beat. A young woman wearing a red T-shirt depicting Che Guevara's hand-screen-printed profile held the microphone. Pacing back and forth, she leaned into the microphone, body arching toward the ground, and sang the "call" section from a parody of an affectionate early twentieth-century ballad called "Mommy, I want" ("Mamãe, Eu Quero").

> Bad food no one can stand,
> This is Syngenta putting venom in every corner.
> This is Monsanto!
> This is Monsanto killing thousands of people.
> Agribusiness! The lie of Brazil!

Hundreds of teenagers rose up and responded in unison:

> Stand up, youth!
> The youth have to fight, and build the people's power.

The teenagers repeated this chorus two times, and then the young woman took the microphone from its stand and began to yell:

> MONSANTO!
> CARGILL!
> Murderers, SYNGENTA!
> You all are in the crosshair,
> In the peasants' crosshair!

The parody of the song, like many others sung at the encampment, frames Syngenta and Monsanto—two exemplars of international agribusiness—as evil and grants agency to youth who are at the center of the struggle. The pedagogical coordinating committee, which organizes the encampment, scheduled moments for these songs throughout each day, keeping youth physically and mentally engaged in a collective process of political formation..

As the song ends, a group of youth worked their way through the crowd. They were wearing black T-shirts that they recently screen-printed to say "Education is not a crime!" The group handed out homemade tote bags, constructed out of the same brightly colored floral fabric that adorned the plenary table. In the bag was a folder containing the schedule of events as well as a

Figure 7.5. The spirit of youth

notebook and pencil. I looked at the schedule for today and noticed that we were about to start the lecture on "Agroecology, Youth, and Development."

Clarice, a young teacher from the Federal Institute of Education, Science, and Technology of Pará–Rural Campus of Marabá (IFPA-CRMB, or the Federal Institute), was going to lead this morning's lecture. Unlike many of the teachers at the Federal Institute, Clarice was actually raised within the movement. Along with her parents, she occupied land and grew up in one of the region's agrarian reform settlements, only to get a higher education through a movement-sponsored course at the federal university in Marabá. Wearing a T-shirt depicting Mexican painter and political activist Frida Kahlo, Clarice made her way slowly through the crowd to the plenary table where she took the microphone. As the daughter of peasant farmers and an educator formed within the movement, Clarice used her oral history as a point of departure.

Today, I want to talk with you all about youth and agroecology, and the challenge of work and education in the countryside. And I want to start out with my own story.

I am a farmer's daughter. And since I was a little girl, my mother and father kept pushing the idea that I needed to study, to study very, very,

very hard so that I wouldn't end up working on the farm. Because farming is an exhausting type of work, and it doesn't guarantee anybody's future.

So, my parents, even though they were farmers, even though they had knowledge of the art of how to deal with the land, unfortunately ended up assimilating, and reproducing in a very intense way, this devaluation of farming, a devaluation of their own work that they have accomplished.

Principally this was directed at us women; because I came from a family with ten siblings—five boys and five girls—and the girls were being educated to leave the farm, because it wasn't a profession that could guarantee our future. And, as a woman, I obeyed.

Education and agrarian change are interconnected in fraught ways, as Clarice highlighted. For many peasants education becomes a depeasantizing force, as children like Clarice are pushed to study "very, very hard" so that they "don't end up working on the farm." This version of education is a driver of hegemonic agrarian change. While many families I knew saw education as a pathway to an ostensibly better future, I learned that their sons and daughters frequently ended up unemployed, living in precarious conditions and making ends meet through work such as selling snack foods on the street in nearby urban centers. Education's unforeseen proximate results are the depopulation of the rural countryside and the disintegration of traditional modes of social reproduction.

Although her parents saw education as way to ensure their children had a better life—a means to move their children out of the countryside—this provoked an identity crisis for Clarice: "Education broke my relationship with my mother, my father, and with the way of life that I've learned from them, the way of life that I've got from my family. When people asked me at the school where I was from, and where do I live, I was ashamed of speaking about my origins. Has this ever happened with any of you? I don't think so, right?" I read Clarice's interjection as sarcastic, knowing that the stigma associated with rural culture, and especially with living in agrarian reform settlements, is widespread. As highlighted in chapter 3, urban teachers often denigrate rural culture in both implicit and explicit ways. For Clarice, this stigma further drove a spatial and cultural wedge within the family, expanding the distance between the rural and urban realities. Clarice's lecture suggests that conventional education not merely is a vehicle for bringing rural youth to urban areas but also advances processes of depeasantization by breaking the bonds between generations and negatively stigmatizing rural livelihoods and spaces. She goes on to emphasize the linkages between the devaluation of rural culture and depeasantization:

"We know that many youth end up not making their way back to the rural areas, because they feed off the idea that this is how things are supposed to be. The farmworker is devalued; we all know that many don't even consider it work—to be a farmer is not considered a profession because it is not valued socially." Clarice distilled the commonsense view of agriculture—it is brutish labor, not a skill, and certainly not a vocation. Mainstream education, Clarice argued, functions as social reproduction.[8] It reproduces commonsense ideas that include the stigmatization of farming and services the needs of capital by legitimating particular professions while denigrating others. Wiping the sweat from her brow, Clarice took a drink of water and created a prolonged pause in what I began to realize was a structured logical argument.

Up until this point, Clarice had narrated an analysis of the ways in which mainstream education contributes to depeasantization; now, she pivoted to argue for an alternative conception of education, one that advances repeasantization. Labor, learning, and the transformation of nature are intertwined, Clarice instructed us. We learn as we work, and through labor we reciprocally transform both nature and ourselves. "The common idea that 'farmers don't have to study to be a farmer, because in the end it is just manual work' only reinforces what we were just talking about, which is the reduction of the comprehension of what work actually is. Because labor in a broader sense, it's humans, about men intervening and transforming nature. The moment that man acts towards nature, he transforms nature, but he doesn't just transform it, he's also being transformed."[9] What Clarice told the audience next about labor is critically important: "This relation produces knowledge. That is the reason why education and work are inseparable, because it's in the practice of transforming nature that knowledge is acquired. It's an essentially educational process." Clarice's argument was building upon itself, moving from a critique of the dominant education system and its role in depeasantization to an analysis of labor's capacity to produce knowledge and transform nature.

Political ecologists have long debated how knowledge of nature—and even the concept of nature itself—is produced.[10] I employ Gramsci's ideas surrounding the relationship between labor and knowledge production to inform this debate and in so doing advance political ecologists' understanding of the role of education in mediating the political transformation of the environment and society. For Gramsci practical activity is "fundamental to the generation of new ideas out of which the world may once again be transformed. Just as thought and action are internally related moments within the socionatural whole, so human and nonhuman are mutually constitutive and co-evolving" (Loftus 2012: 184). Clarice's narrative underscored this point: both nature and the self are produced through labor—and this process itself is pedagogical. We develop new conceptions of the world through labor—through the dialectical process of transforming nature and the self. Education—in this light—takes on a radically different significance for political ecologists: education is key to shaping the "person"—but the person is relational, inherently connected to the natural world through specific socionatural relations in particular times and places. Gramsci's work is powerful in highlighting the linkages between labor and education, the transformation of nature, and the shaping of the individual; yet like much of Gramsci's insights, these are disparate threads. From a political ecology of education perspective, however, they are part of a larger tapestry—where education is central to a broader political project of transforming space, society, and the relations of production.

Clarice's argument now begins to come full circle. She's moved from an analysis of the relation between education and depeasantization to its dialectical opposite: the relationship between education and repeasantization. Agroecological education, which teaches students to diversify production, reduce external inputs, and create feedback loops between different production systems, is a way to make peasants more peasantlike by becoming more autonomous. Education contributes to peasants' struggle for reexistence by providing critical analytical skills and practical agricultural techniques for developing a differentiated form of existence based upon alternative forms of production.

Clarice began to develop this argument by laying out what repeasantization means at a local level and its relations to the future of the peasantry. "If we look at history, we notice how incredible the farmers' capacity is to remain, to reexist [re-existir]." The concept of reexistence (re-existência) is at the core of agrarian social movement struggles across the globe.[11] Reexistence occurs when peasants use agroecological techniques that strengthen both their peasant identity, which is fluid and historical, and the permanence of their tenancy on the land. For Clarice, the struggle for reexistence was central to grappling with the future of the peasantry. "Because when we look back in history, all the forces are contributing for this category [the peasantry] to be vanished. Some have started to forecast its extinction even before they disappear."[12] Clarice began to push her students to critically reflect on this commonsense perspective that family farming is unviable. "This idea of changing according to what capitalism dictates is impacting the youth so they will have changes in their personalities. And to change oneself in line with the forms of the capitalism, you have to neglect your origins. . . . When they talk about the extinction of the peasantry, it's a form of them saying, 'Let's end this group because they are not important . . . or because they need to feed off the idea that they are in fact inferior.' " Clarice was trying to encourage the students to realize that they have likely internalized a false consciousness of their own inferiority, a self-stigmatizing prophecy of common sense. Clarice would undoubtedly bristle at the idea some scholars have published: that peasants have "disappeared" (Bernstein 2014). She would probably agree, however, with Desmarais (2007), who suggests that the question of their existence can be easily resolved if one listens to peasants' own perspectives. Despite all of the historic forces seeking to destroy the peasantry, Clarice emphasizes, "farmers keep existing and resisting. This is a very important aspect of peasant family farming. These farmers exist despite all the contrary conditions that they are facing."

Education shapes the agrarian question and the lives of rural smallholders in southeastern Pará. Conventional education reinforces what has become common sense in rural areas: an understanding of reality that matches the dictates of development and agroindustry—being a family farmer is not a profession, it's not even a viable livelihood because the peasantry is dead. This disappearance thesis, Clarice argued, is all too common. It's become a false consciousness that circulates as common sense. Clarice knows it's all too common because it's her life story. As a young woman, education served as a driver, what Araghi (1995) terms an "invisible foot," that pushed her off the land. Clarice took a long sip of water from a glass on the table and began the culminating stage of her argument: education doesn't need to contribute to the self-fulfilling demise of the peasantry.

Education can play a different role in the agrarian question. Rather than acting as a depeasantizing force, education, if envisioned from the grassroots, can contribute to repeasantization. This is the argument that Clarice wanted to end with. "So, and here I'll conclude my talk: if education has historically been used for transformation and taking men out of the farms, destroying and devaluing our culture, it's also through education that we will use techniques to do the opposite and resist." Education can function as a form of alternative social reproduction, supporting repeasantization and reexistence. Education can help students assert a vision of modernity that can be described as the "peasant way," one that "rejects the temporality of capitalist modernity that regards peasants as pre-modern, and the spatiality that removes and divides humans from nature" (McMichael 2006: 478).

For education to achieve these alternative ends, it needs to be decolonized. Conventional rural education produces the illusion that rural areas are "places of non-thought" (Mignolo 2009). Within this logic, rural areas are the periphery where knowledge is consumed but not produced. Clarice told us, "This is one of the biggest challenges of the rural area: to provide education, and access to education for the children of farmers, but from a different perspective." Educação do Campo is such a perspective; it is a form of situated knowledge constructed in a particular geographic context. Within the system of Educação do Campo, knowledge is grounded in, developed by, and relevant to those who constitute rural areas. It is both spatially and materially opposed to conventional rural education, which has long sought to prepare students for manual labor in emerging capitalist industries. Educação do campo is an example of decolonization. It is a pedagogical process of "waking up from the long process of westernization" (Mignolo 2009: 161). Subaltern groups learn to think about new forms of formation, new models of knowledge production, and new ways of transforming the environment (McCune et al. 2014).

From Clarice's perspective, agroecology is key to decolonizing education. The state, development agencies, and philanthropic organizations have long promulgated a vision of agronomic education that delegitimizes peasant knowledge systems and agricultural practices as "backward." This is what many teachers and activists told me was the Green Revolution model of education, which promulgates high-input, large-scale, heavily mechanized production (Cleaver 1972). The MST's vision of agroecological education is counterposed to this Green Revolution model because it is grounded in an epistemology that is alternative to that of agricultural modernization. Clarice told us, "The question of agroecology ends up being key in this formation process. Because it causes us to think about a type of formation which is different, a type of formation in which we think about other types of relations with the rural areas, and with natural resources; relations that won't be so degrading, so inhuman and devastating as the model presented by the business owners in the Green Revolution." In her last point, Clarice shifted from an analysis of her own educational history to the broader production of subjects through agricultural modernization. She was making a subtle—yet profound—argument: broader political and economic histories of knowledge production associated with the Green Revolution structure hegemonic education systems as well as their antitheses. For Clarice the Green Revolution was not responsible for advancing just a system of agriculture but a particular view of how knowledge is produced, circulated, and applied (Cleaver 1972; Goldman et al. 2011). The model of agroecological education that Clarice asked us to envision is a critical response to the vision of knowledge production associated with the Green Revolution. Educação do Campo, like other decolonial strategies, starts "from the principle that the regeneration of life shall prevail over primacy of the production and reproduction of goods at the cost of life" (Mignolo 2009: 161). Building upon

Clarice's insights, we can see that critical food systems education is an ideological and material response to the modernization of agriculture and agricultural knowledge; it is a form of education that emerges out of a process of resistance to broad-scale political-economic processes of agrarian change.

Clarice concluded by describing the first step in developing a new education system: critically analyzing common sense: "I know each of you has various ways of thinking about what peasant labor means, about what the life of a peasant is about. Your heads are full of these ideas—and these are not ideas that are tranquil and peaceful. Rather, they are contradictory as well."[13] Clarice believed that her students' task is an empirical analysis of how history and political economy constitute these contradictory forms of common sense: "To deal with these ideas, we have to firstly identify them, to know exactly which are the contradictory ideas that each of us holds. And we need to understand them as being contradictions in the sense of being consequences from the capitalist model. We need to identify: 'What is the prejudice that I have, concerning the relation between youth and peasant work?,' 'What prejudices am I feeding in relation to understanding peasant work?' I consider this to be a fundamental question." To combat what Clarice terms "contradictory ideas," there needs to be a process that Raymond Williams refers to as "unlearning," whereby we question the "inherent dominant" truths.[14] Through unlearning, individuals actively reshape their "conception of the world . . . with the labors of [their] own brain" so as to "take an active part in the creation of the history of the world" (Gramsci 1994: 323).

When we scale out, it becomes clear Clarice was arguing that education and the class transition in agriculture are tightly interconnected. Conventional rural education plays a role in depeasantization by denigrating rural livelihoods and valorizing urban professions. This perspective has become an unquestioned reality, or common sense. In deprecating farmers, the education system both denies the needs of agrarian communities *for* education and fails to recognize that knowledge is often produced in other nonschool contexts, such as through working the land. By paying attention to agricultural labor as a means of knowledge production, we recognize that education is a relational process involving the transformation of both the individual and the landscape. Peasants are struggling to advance new forms of knowledge production and new relations with nature. This is a struggle for reexistence, which at its core is about identity and the ability of peasants to retain their tenancy on the land. New forms of education based in agroecology help to advance a new conception of the world by valorizing the peasantry and rural livelihoods. The first step for this new vision of education is unlearning common sense.

As Clarice concluded her talk she handed the microphone to Santiago, who was helping to coordinate this morning's session. "If anyone has a question, or maybe wants to share an experience," Santiago noted, "we probably have time for just one or two folks to share before its time for the discussion groups." Spaces of dialogue like these, which are structured into the MST's nonformal education practices, provide opportunities for collective unlearning. Throughout my research I observed students using these spaces to explore contradictions in their own lives. They often voiced frustration with their parents' taken-for-granted assumptions that normalize chemically intensive forms of agriculture. It became clear that the cultural politics of the family often operate as constraints toward advancing agroecology.

In one of these discussion sessions I gained crucial insight into how the family manifests common sense, the potential for agroecological education to create dialogue, and the ongoing need for decolonizing education. Pedro was the first speaker in this discussion session. He wore a white and green polo shirt with the name and logo of the Federal Institute on the front. He took the microphone and explained to the audience, "The question of agroecology is very difficult. Agroecology has incredible potential, but today it is largely only on paper. In practice, there are very few concrete experiences that exist." Pedro was repeating the commonsense perspective that I heard virtually every time I asked about agroecology: it's an embryonic worldview that has yet to be actualized. Pedro's purpose in taking the microphone was to peel back the layers and offer his analysis of the barriers to advancing this emerging worldview: "Why is it that agroecology is largely only on paper? As a student in the institute's agroecological agricultural extension program, I can tell you there are many barriers to agroecology, and *one of the principal barriers is our family*. We study agroecology, but when we reach our farm and try to work agroecologically, our families don't let us. Why? It's because they only know of the dominant methods. And as a result, for us it's very difficult to change the practices in our own houses." Pedro's cultural analysis provides us a window into subaltern thought, which is defined by overlapping and contentious traditions. Pedro, like virtually all other young activists I worked with, grew up by learning "the dominant methods"—an approach to agriculture characterized by swidden cultivation and pesticide usage. These dominant methods are historical artifacts—products of lifetimes of working as agricultural laborers on fazendas. As Pedro described it, the dominant methods were synonymous with common sense. What Pedro has learned at the Federal Institute is a hybridized conception of the world—one where peasant traditions and agronomic science are brought into dialogue. Yet Pedro related that the crucial challenge in advancing agroecology was negotiating the cultural politics of the family and creating dialogue across the kitchen table.

"Events like these are really important for the youth," Pedro continued, "but what we need to do is bring our parents into the discussion, so they can understand what is this process, what is this process of transformation directed towards, because without this process of transformation we won't make it anywhere." I saw Pedro, in describing the need to develop dialogue across the kitchen table, function like Raul as an organic intellectual, encouraging the audience to do the everyday work of challenging common sense. Talking with one's parents about their usage of pesticides, or practices of deforestation, is not easy. Pedro described these methods as common sense, and it will require both critical reflection and an alternative vision of the future to move beyond them and develop new ways of being in the world. It will require these students to actualize their function as organic intellectuals.

The struggle to advance new forms of common sense requires more than negotiating familial politics; it is also necessary to continue decolonizing education. As Pedro went on to emphasize, "This is a process that begins within the school. We go to a school that has a focus in agroecology, but still uses certain traditional methods. For example, our teacher who is responsible for the lab where we raise chickens told us that we need to have a ratio of seventy females to one male. But we know, who among us small farmers has the financial means to have large-scale production like this, so what we need is to have a different process, where we begin small and gradually increase using agroecological methods." What is perhaps surprising in Pedro's narrative is that even at the IFPA-CRMB, an agroecological school located in an MST settlement, many of the professors come from other areas of the country and have been trained in the dominant methods. Listening to Pedro, I interpreted his call to transform what agricultural techniques students learn and the pedagogies through which they learn them as a demand for further decolonization of the Federal Institute. Decolonizing—whether of land or of education—is not a single event, such as building a radical agroecological school or breaking up a fazenda to create a settlement—rather, it is an ongoing process that requires continuous political mobilization.

The intention of the pedagogical encampment was not to be a singular space for learning, where youth travel once a year for just a week. Rather, the coordinating collective that organizes the encampment envisioned it as a relational space, a node within a network of knowledge production. The organizers hoped that the youth would take the lessons learned at the encampment and return to their settlements, where they would give presentations at school, have discussions with their parents, and share insights with their neighbors. I conclude this section by exploring what these lessons look like.

On the last morning of the encampment we assembled for a collective self-evaluation of the encampment. Raunir, from a nearby settlement, was critical of the food—there wasn't much variety. He noted, "We should have more diversity next year." Rosa, one of the MST state leaders, responded, "That's correct, we should. And this is all of our responsibility. It's each of our responsibility to organize. Each of the settlements and encampments is responsible for donating food, and the objective is that this food is produced in that community. But look at what we've had here: store bought rice, store bought beans, store bought squash. It is the responsibility of the settlements and the encampments to diversify. It's our collective responsibility to challenge the systems of production." Rosa hammered home the disjunctive reality: for the last week we had been discussing agroecology and food sovereignty, yet the settlements, which had largely transitioned to export-oriented dairy production, were no longer producing the necessary basic foodstuffs even to provide for the one-week event. Rosa stressed that it was the responsibility of the youth to serve as agents of transformation, bringing about a new hegemonic system based around diversified production.

Renildo, from the 17 de Abril, built on Rosa's critical rejoinder about food sovereignty. He reflected on how he had learned about new approaches in the encampment that weren't taught in conventional rural schools. "For example, when we got here many people didn't know what was agroecology. What did agroecology mean? They didn't know. But here we learned. We need to take this back to our areas to continue these debates and disseminate knowledge." Helenira, one of the MST state leaders who was facilitating the discussion, chimed in,

> This is the point; to bring the knowledge, the learning gained here, to your areas. Youth were here to learn, but also to bring knowledge back to your communities. This is an organizational form within the movement—you all will discover themes, and then you will create groups within your own encampments and settlements, working with these themes. So the discussions begin here, but they then reverberate in the encampments and settlements, with your families, with your friends, within other spaces that you as youth participate. So, in a sense it's a way that something can be awoken here, but which you all will continue working on in your own collectives. Continuing to work on, to debate, to construct experiences

around. During this week, many debates occurred that were transforma-
tional. The transformation is permanent.

Raul, the MST state level leader who survived the massacre at age sixteen,
concluded the discussion with a question: "What I want everyone to leave and
think about is, 'How do we begin debates?' . . . [long pause] The encampment
isn't an end; it's a process, a process of participation. Our job is multiplying.
Our job is to organize here, and form youth collectives in each area." As Raul
suggested, the encampment was a space of political formation—one in which
the youth were molded into permanent persuaders, organic intellectuals who
would be capable of multiplying the struggle within their encampments and
settlements, continuing the process of building a new common sense based
in agroecology.

We then broke into small groups composed of the youth from our respective settlements and encampments. We were reuniting with our comrades to
foster a discussion about bringing the lessons from the encampment home.
Our group of seven students from the 17 de Abril gathered some plastic chairs
in a circle. Renildo, one of the charismatic leaders in the settlement, started
off, summarizing where we left off and how we needed to move forward: "We
need to figure out ways to carry out the things that we have been studying
here at the pedagogical encampment. We need to choose a path, a methodology for working with these topics, so that they don't become abandoned, so
that the encampment doesn't end and everyone just goes home, but instead
that what we keep constructing is the process of construction. Who has ideas?"
After a long pause, Raunir suggested, "We need to revive our youth group, the
Evolução Juventude Camponesa [EJC]." Renildo was taking notes and repeated
Raunir's suggestion as a bulleted point for discussion. Victor then offered his
perspective: "We need to figure out a way to engage with the school, utilizing
the school, and its auditorium, to show photos, to share the experiences that
we had there, and to discuss the subjects as well, to choose one or two subjects
and work with them." Samuel agreed, noting that maybe "there should be a
set day, where every week we could to go to the school and make a presentation to the students on an MST topic, we could do a mística." Victor scaled out
and tried to get at the bigger picture: "Right, so what we really need to do is
to start a dialogue, to bring more people in. So how are we going to do that?"
Samuel thought for a moment and then responded, "We need to think about
what youth want, what will excite them. Here, for example, we had music and
films. That was great." Jumping in, Renildo pointed out, "While that's true,

remember, the films this week—they were politically oriented. This can't be just a time for playing around. We can't just get together, play some soccer, and watch some random movie. This needs to be a time where people are experiencing formation. That's the point." Victor nodded his head vigorously in agreement: "Remember, these groups are incredibly important for helping transform people. People change. Take Francisco as an example. I can hardly remember an example of a meeting where he spoke up. But he participated in these groups, changed, he grew. He's now a state coordinator, known throughout all of the MST encampments and settlements."

The pedagogical encampment drew into focus both the contradictions facing youth as well as the possibilities for transformation. Recognizing the prevalence of store-bought food underscores the need and capacity for youth to be agents of diversification. These students, many of whom came to the encampment unfamiliar with agroecology, learned over the course of the week how to critically analyze the agroindustrial system and the ways in which alternative forms of production can reinforce the permanence of the peasantry on the land. According to the encampment's organizers, for these youth this learning was a permanent personal transformation. But how can this new knowledge be disseminated throughout the settlements and encampments? To function as organic intellectuals, the students need to challenge common sense in their own homes. After all, this is the broader purpose of the encampment—advancing a revolutionary consciousness that is grounded in a novel conception of the world. A central lesson that youth took from the pedagogical encampment is that education can be a central tactic in transforming common sense. The potential for the 17 de Abril's school to be a vehicle for broader social change was one of the central themes that arose in our group reflexive process. But learning requires participation. As Victor indicated in that group reflection, political participation—among individuals and the community at large—is highly dynamic. I conclude this chapter by exploring how these youths' vision of bringing the lessons of the encampment home is constrained by the vicissitudes of daily political participation. Critical food systems education, which seeks to use education to advance food sovereignty, and political participation exist as a set of mutually reinforcing positive and negative feedback loops (fig. 7.6).

Participating politically in the MST, which involves not only occupying land or the offices of INCRA but also attending the movement's myriad events, provides access to critical agroecological learning that has the potential to transform common sense and influence the permanence of the peasantry on the land. This is the process of learning in the movement. But the flip side is

Political Participation

Permanence
of Peasantry

No Change

Change

Common
Sense

−

−

+

+

Critical Food Systems Education

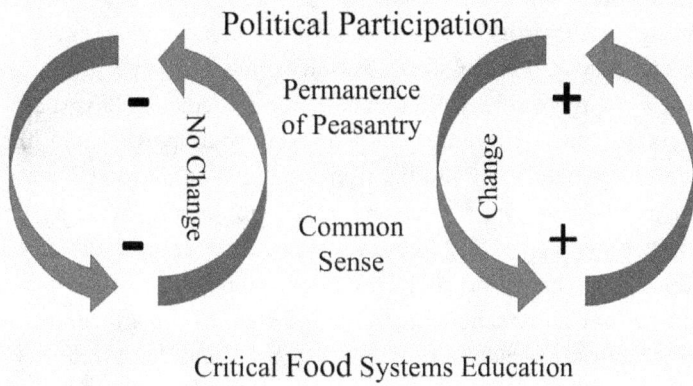

Figure 7.6. Dialectic of political participation and critical food systems education

the negative feedback loop—without political participation one never enters these critical learning spaces and education fails to make an intervention in the future of the peasantry. I conclude this chapter by outlining a conversation with Francisco—the young adult Victor just described as having transformed from apolitical into an MST leader—to explore how the spatial continuum of education—ranging from informal learning through nonformal to formal education—intersects with the politics of place and political participation.

The Struggle's Over and Now There's Just Victory

One late afternoon a week later Francisco and I sat outside his home, waiting in the shade for the magical moment when the desperate heat of the day would begin to dissipate. To me there was a discordant feeling in the air. The pedagogical encampment felt like a fever; a sense of movement, of explosive energy, pervaded each and every day. The encampment seemed to be the beginning, or perhaps the annual reawakening, of primal energy at the core of the movement. The encampment had ended with rich discussions about how to take its lessons back to the settlement and into the school, reinvigorate the youth collective, and build a broader political awakening. Perhaps it was just today's suffocating afternoon heat, and that the street was deserted save for a limping dog, but there seemed to be a sense in which that movement had stopped, in which *tudo está parado.*

Leaning back against the house in a plastic chair, I asked Francisco about the ebb and flow of political participation within the settlement. He began by noting a divergent reality. "Remember, our settlement is less than twenty kilometers from the S-curve, but fewer than ten youth participated. The 17 de Abril has a large number of youth, but most ended up not participating." The problem, he explained, wasn't that the school prohibits them from participating in the encampment. "No," Francisco told me, "the school always frees the youth up to participate, but they end up not going and prefer to stay in the settlement. They go to school at night, and then in the afternoon, and the rest of the day, they're just relaxing, just relaxing. They don't want to go. They were born here, the parents survived the massacre, but they end up just not sympathizing much with the MST. If you give them the option they won't participate in the MST's actions." "Why is that?" I asked, pressing Francisco to explain from his perspective, as a young adult, how youth relate—or not—to the movement. "It's a question of an individual's own consciousness and ideology; people think they don't need to participate in the MST's actions anymore. The youth don't participate very much because they believe that they already have everything: in the afternoon they play soccer, at night they go out to parties, they spend the day watching TV, maybe driving around on their motorcycles." For Francisco, the recently concluded pedagogical encampment encapsulated the broader dynamics of political participation in the community. Very few students participated in the encampment because, like their parents, their basic material needs were met. They didn't see a need to be active in the movement. As Francisco concluded his description of the various excuses youth offer for not participating in the encampment, the refrain from the Brazilian pop song "The Struggle's Over and Now There's Just Victory"—came into my head. It seems like the song's title encapsulates the status of the MST in this settlement—one in which collective grievances have been satisfied and there is no longer a need to be politically active.

The sun dipped below the horizon, and youth began to congregate with their motorcycles in the central square, grabbing the cell signal where it's strongest. The community radio crackled to life; Osvaldo, the announcer, reminded the community that the EJC group was scheduled to meet now at the settlement's headquarters, just off the central square. The EJC was the youth group we had discussed resurrecting at the conclusion of the encampment. We had agreed this group would be the principal vehicle for working with the school to disseminate the lessons learned at the encampment, and I was excited to see this group of organic intellectuals converge to plot out the next steps in organizing the community. Francisco and I leaned our chairs forward, slipped on the ubiquitous rubber thong Havaiana sandals that everyone wears—his were a commemorative MST edition with the movement's flag on the foot bed—and headed down the dusty street. When we arrived at the meeting room there was no one there, and Francisco asked Osvaldo to make the announcement about the meeting again on the radio. We waited a half hour for youth to arrive, playing idly with our phones. When it became clear that no one was going to show up for the meeting, we started to head home. A young boy pushing a re-purposed wheelbarrow that held a cooler of homemade popsicles approached us, asking if we'd like to buy one. Francisco and I each select an açaí-flavored one and stopped to enjoy the coolness it provided. The evening light bathed a group of youth playing soccer in a golden glow. The suffocating heat had dissipated. Perhaps so too had the movement, I thought, as I nibbled on the almost painfully cold popsicle. Francisco seemed completely nonplussed that no one showed up for the meeting, which I interpreted to mean this was an expected outcome. It seemed that this moment exemplified the end of the struggle and the challenge of remaining politically active amid the feeling of victory.

Savoring the last of my popsicle, I tried to make sense of what seemed to me a series of fundamental contradictions. The encampment felt to me like a space and time of pivotal political formation. But did it mean anything in the lives of the settlement's youth? What about those ten who had made it to the encampment? Where were they now? If they were so engaged at the idea of bringing the lessons home, why couldn't they organize themselves to come to the meeting of the EJC? Recognizing contradictions in one's own activism, and in the process of organizing, is a very important activity within the MST. The contradictions do not point to the failure of the encampment nor to that of the youth's commitment but highlight that actualizing the transformative potential of agroecological education requires an ongoing process of transforming common sense. For Gramsci, this process requires an analysis of the relationship between culture, knowledge, and revolutionary change.[15] Culture, from a Gramscian perspective, consists of "critical self-knowledge focused on understanding one's relations to others, including one's 'rights and obligations' in relation to them, and one's place in history" (Crehan 2016: 76). Gramsci saw this knowledge as so important because he believed that every revolution first requires individuals to engage in the difficult process of self-critique, diffusing new ideas about how to be in the world among their compatriots who might be complacent, fixated on attaining their immediate needs, without recognition of how their own situation is tied up with that of others out of solidarity (Gramsci 1977: 10–13). Gramsci is instructive for helping think in new ways about the political ecology of education because his theories refocus one's analysis away from formal education and toward the pedagogical work of everyday critical self-reflection and informal dialogue between activists as they grapple with enshrined hegemonic ideas. Education becomes part and parcel, from a political ecology perspective, of the "war of position," a long-term process of transforming common sense and grassroots mobilization.

Conclusions

This chapter has highlighted how place and transformative spaces of formal, nonformal, and informal learning are interconnected in complex ways. Informal learning, which occurs in quotidian spatiotemporal contexts, can form us, shaping our life trajectory and political consciousness. Youth become organic intellectuals through participating in this assemblage of relations with other nonformal and formal spaces of education. Youth decolonize spaces of repression into places imbued with hope and resistance. Places, as the S-curve highlights, are political and powerfully pedagogical. As we have seen, decolonizing education, decolonizing place, and decolonizing the self are interwoven processes. Both Clarice and Pedro exemplified this tripartite vision: critical food systems education can transform the relation between youth and the land, but first common sense needs to be transformed. The MST offers opportunities for transformative nonformal learning. This nonformal education challenges assumptions about agrarian development. But if individuals see no need for personal or broader social transformation, they won't take advantage of these nonformal educational opportunities. Only through political participation and challenging the already existing terrain of ideologies, through transforming common sense, do new conceptions of the world emerge.

This chapter has provided novel insights into how education shapes what Gramsci terms the "terrain of ideologies." These ideologies are forms of domination that are historically produced and must be transformed through political struggle. As a "terrain," ideologies are akin to a superstructure upon which individuals become aware of how they have been historically marginalized but also of their power and capacity to coalesce as a distinct social group. Becoming aware requires both identifying and redefining common sense. In this chapter Pedro noted that the "dominant methods" or forms of agriculture, such as using pesticides, that have historically become commonplace are some of the major barriers to farming agroecologically. Education, Pedro argued, is necessary to move beyond this commonsense vision of agriculture and toward agroecology. However, education must be continually decolonized. This process was described in chapter 5 where Brito and Eduardo, university professors, partnered with the MST to develop courses that valorize subaltern forms of knowledge and alternative visions of Amazonian development. In chapter 6 it became clear that struggles over the production of knowledge on the frontier require engaging in the reciprocal processes of decolonizing both land and education. Taken together, these three chapters have demonstrated that the terrain of ideologies is a contest over both immaterial and material resources. Drawing upon the political ecology of education framework, pedagogical spaces in southeastern Pará—ranging from the Agroecological Institute of Latin America–Amazônica's radical agroecological training center to the Federal University—are sites of resistance on the terrain of ideologies. They are a frontier on which a struggle is being waged to advance counter-hegemonic knowledge practices and agroecological production.

CHAPTER 8

Revisiting Territory

This book opened with Isabel's critical question: "Why are we no longer producing food?" In the intervening pages I've synthesized the voices of educators, youth, and community leaders with archival aerial photographs and longitudinal satellite images to provide a series of answers to this question. In this final chapter I begin by offering a thematic synthesis of the factors constraining agroecological production. I then offer a theoretical recap, highlighting the broad contours of the political ecology of education perspective and reviewing how it made sense of the diverse voices presented in this book. While the end of chapter 7, when no one showed up to the MST youth meeting, portended a bleak future in the 17 de Abril, I offer one last vignette that provides a glimpse into alternative futures. I conclude the book by reflecting on what lessons social movements and policy makers might take from a careful reading of its chapters.

Scaling out, the constraints to agroecological production in the 17 de Abril can be thematically grouped into politics, economy, space, and culture. Given that the MST is an agrarian social movement, it might have been a surprise at the outset of the book to learn that low levels of political participation are an obstacle to advancing agroecology in general and agroecological education in particular. As Edison acknowledged in chapter 3, however, "It's really quite complicated, this relation between the school and the movement." Edison's warning drew attention to the fact that educators' political participation in the MST is not consistent. Some educators are explicitly anti-MST, and with their everyday resistance other educators' efforts to advance critical food systems education get stalled out too. However, it's not only the teachers that are an obstacle to the movement's education initiatives. Some parents constrain the potential for youth political formation too, complaining to the school's administrators if the teachers discuss the movement's history in class. The MST's critical food systems education initiatives within the school are virtually destined to fail unless everyone is on the same page. This is most clearly manifested at the pedagogical encampment where very few students from the 17 de Abril participate. These problems with political participation reverberate beyond the school and throughout the broader community; as Raunir described in the same chapter, "Everyone's got their television . . . they have enough food. What need do they have for the movement?" With the ebb of the MST, the settlement's inhabitants increasingly lack contact with the movement's mobilizations, literature, and calls for agroecological production. They become shut off from the formative nature of the movement itself.

Agroecological production is also constrained by the interrelated political economies of agricultural modernization, agricultural credit, and agricultural extension. Together these factors have helped solidify the hegemony of cattle ranching in the region. When this vision was supported by credit initiatives (Special Credit Program for Agrarian Reform [PROCERA] and PRONAF-A), the proliferation of projects directed toward cattle production fomented a shift in the 17 de Abril from subsistence agriculture to where it is currently just "gado, gado, gado" (cattle, cattle, cattle), as Lucinede complained. Adriana, the extension agent in the 17 de Abril from chapter 3, agreed: "Since the settlement's creation, the projects have been set up for ranching." Credit projects and agricultural extension have engendered distrust among the inhabitants of the 17 de Abril toward agricultural extension (chapter 2). As indicated by the example of Dona Maria and Seu Antonio (chapter 2), whose investment in fish production floundered, improperly planned credit projects and nonexistent extension can trap people into insurmountable debt. Adriana lamented, "It's gotten to the point where farmers are cynical about agricultural extension. They don't believe in the companies working in agricultural extension, seeing them as just promising and not doing anything." Through no fault of their own, farmers' disillusionment with extension can act as a constraint to advancing agroecology within the settlement. As Adriana, who is interested in developing unorthodox reforestation projects, indicated, "You could be telling the truth. You could be there with a project in hand already approved by INCRA, but the farmers just don't believe it." Adriana's perspective brought to light an important critique of the MST's broader agroecological education project. Whereas from a grassroots perspective agroecological education can be understood as helping usher in a new counter-hegemony, from the vantage point of most of the settlement's residents it is a form of imposition.

The spatial history of land use—long-standing patterns of deforestation and cattle ranching—is yet another factor that constrains the advancement of agroecology in the region. It does so literally, by creating degraded soil, but also symbolically, by shaping the spatial imaginaries of those who come to try to make a living out of this depleted landscape. Spatial imaginaries, or collective understandings of how space should be used, determine what forms of agricultural production are commonsensical and what forms are perceived to be aberrant. As Arnoldo, the settlement's president, reflected (chapter 2), when the settlement's inhabitants received land in 1997 it was already largely degraded. My results from a longitudinal spatial analysis of archival aerial photographs and LANDSAT imagery support Arnoldo's perspective: by 1997 (when the 17 de Abril settlement was created) approximately 70 percent of the landscape had been deforested. This was a process that had already begun by the 1960s with large-scale mechanized forms of land clearing. The farmers' efforts at agriculture were largely unsuccessful, according to Arnoldo, "because the land had already been prepared for cattle ranching." The constraints of landscape history were reinforced by the combination of credit incentives and agricultural extension activities. As Arnoldo explained in chapter 2, "One project came, and then another, that only supported cattle. And so the type of land use didn't really change." The constraints of the political economy of credit and extension and their effect on landscape change were augmented by cultural beliefs about land management. Cattle ranching has become enshrined as a territorial consciousness characterized by common sense; as Genival boiled down (chapter 2), "It just made more sense to leave the land as pasture." The hypervisibility of ranching excludes other forms of land use. Agroforestry and small-scale agroecological gardens are invisible in the context of pasture's long and strong shadow. However, through critical forms of food systems education, students are learning to see alternative futures existing within the present. Through her critical place-based research, Lucinede discovered an unseen universe of agroecological production within her own community (chapter 6). This realization pushed her to action. She and Diana held workshops in the school to help students visualize this unseen geography and recognize that it is not some far-off possibility but one that currently exists.

The flip side of the equation is equally important. It's not just that space structures social life, but, as I pointed out in chapters 3 and 6, social life structures space as well. Cultural traditions are deeply embedded in the minds and bodies of those who inhabit the 17 de Abril and are a significant factor that constrains both the potentiality of critical food systems education and, in turn, the advance of agroecology. Samuel (chapter 2), for example, described how all his parents knew was what they learned growing up: that one needs to "cut the forest, burn, plant, harvest . . . cut the forest, burn, plant, harvest."

These embedded systems of cultural knowledge provide obstacles to advancing agroecology. As Pedro, an IFPA-CRMB student, described during the

MST pedagogical encampment (chapter 6), "one of the principal barriers" to agroecological production is "the family." Alan experienced the family barrier in a different form (chapter 7). For Alan, his father's interest in using herbicides was a hurdle to overcome in putting his agroecological learning into practice. Cultural traditions structure space in other contexts too. Financial insecurity means that cattle ranching is seen as a safer form of land management than subsistence agriculture. As Luis indicated (chapter 2), "Cattle are a constant, they're a bank. If I need money, I can sell a calf in an hour and have money in my pocket."

Isabel's question about the loss of food sovereignty within the MST's 17 de Abril settlement is undoubtedly a thorny one. Answering it requires that two optics must be kept in parallax: the spatial production of the social and the social production of the spatial. Neither approach by itself is sufficient to explicate processes of agrarian transformation in the 17 de Abril. While the history of the landscape is a driving force shaping present land management options, so too are the embodied cultural traditions and spatial imaginaries. Space and society are intricately intertwined forces. Political-economic processes, operating at multiple interconnected scales, shape both of these lenses. From national-scale visions of agricultural modernization and Cold War geopolitical maneuverings that opened the Amazon to a series of credit initiatives intended to consolidate cattle ranching as a hegemonic form of land use and the everyday financial calculus of extension agents, it's unquestionable that capital structures the reciprocal production of space and society, shaping agrarian identities and livelihoods.

Before meeting people like Diana I had not specifically planned to study food systems education, landscape change, political participation, or political economy. Rather, it was through long conversations with her, participating in road blockades, and exploring what unifies the movement's diverse educational opportunities that I recognized food systems education as an emerging tool to reshape agrarian relations and the permanence of the peasantry on the land. What Diana and other activists helped me to see is that food systems education, when reimagined from the grassroots, looks very different from what many readers will be familiar with. Sure there are raised-bed gardens at schools, similar to what one finds in the United States. Undoubtedly there is an emphasis on the local, as exists in Europe and increasingly throughout Asia. What Diana, Zé, Lucinede, Haroldo, and the various educators profiled in this book are struggling for in the streets and promulgating in the classrooms is something qualitatively different.

Throughout the book I've described this approach as critical food systems education. What distinguishes this vision of education is its goal of food sovereignty, which is characterized by autonomous systems of production based around workers' rights, cooperative values, and ecological techniques. This approach is *critical* because it moves beyond traditional forms of knowledge production that are based in monologue and deconstructs the effect of traditional forms of agricultural knowledge and technology in shaping both peasant production systems and the landscape itself. In Brazil critical food systems education is a direct response to top-down forms of agricultural knowledge production that are a product of neocolonialism. Rather than reproducing forms of knowledge from Brazil's South or disseminating technology as a means to generate capital (as described in chapter 2), educators throughout southeastern Pará are decolonizing knowledge. Decolonizing education in this context means recognizing the linkages between systems of knowledge production, processes of capital accumulation, and their effects on advancing processes of depeasantization. Decolonizing education also means recognizing that knowledge production can be reimagined from the grassroots and be made directly relevant to rural realities.

Decolonization is at the core of Educação do Campo (education of the rural area) as a pedagogy, as a set of teaching practices, and as a vision for education reform. Educação do Campo begins from the recognition that rural areas and subjects have long been subjected to the imposition of forms of knowledge produced in urban areas, which simultaneously denigrate rural livelihoods and differentially valorize urban ones. As I discussed in chapter 3, traditional approaches to rural education are predicated on a particular vision of space, one where there is no cultural or geographic specificity. Educação do Campo seeks to disrupt this urban capitolocentric logic. It draws upon diverse pedagogies that transform the spatiality and temporality of the school system. Rather than simply learning within the confines of the school's walls, students spend alternating periods of time in their home and school communities, conducting their own research projects on pressing issues surrounding agrarian change and resistance. The lessons from this research, as chapter 7 showed, can be transformative. Lucinede and Diana discovered a universe of production of which they had never heard; drawing upon these findings, they sought to challenge students to think critically about their landscape and role in its transformation.

Throughout this book I've made a case for rethinking education from a political ecology perspective. This is because time and again I was confronted with the centrality of education to conceptions of agriculture and nature— not just the counter-hegemonic education promoted by the MST but also the mainstream education to which virtually every child in Brazil is exposed through public school. Decolonizing education, as each of these examples shows, is not simply about decolonizing knowledge. Rather, it is about transforming the linkages between knowledge, agricultural practices, and the landscape itself. This basic insight—that knowledge, political economy, land management, and the landscape are intertwined—is the foundation for a political ecology of education. This approach draws upon four core insights from political ecology but directs them to education.

First, I've explored the importance of political economy at multiple scales in mediating access to, usage of, and control over the landscape. As highlighted in chapter 2, the landscape of southeastern Pará has long been structured by political-economic incentives; credit incentives that encouraged ranchers from the South were in many cases responsible for the opening of the Amazon. The history of the landscape was a major factor influencing settlers' spatial imaginaries and perceived land management options. Genilson and Arnoldo, for example, described how the prevalence of established pasture in the settlement helped normalize cattle ranching as common sense and also precluded the pioneers from engaging with agroforestry. These experiences underscore how political economy and histories of land use change intersect to structure mental geographies and provide formidable obstacles to sustainable agriculture. These spatial imaginaries were further informed by agricultural extension and codified by additional credit incentives that favored cattle. Genival, for example, described how the system of agricultural credit reinforces cattle production, as extension agents make more income from ranching projects than those devoted to agroforestry or subsistence agriculture. When taken together, these examples demonstrate that political economy, and its focus on the interrelations between political institutions, the political environment, and the economic system, is a central factor that has shaped knowledge and the landscape. This attention to political economy makes sense for those interested in the politics of knowledge, as scholarship within the political economy of education has long been attentive to the power of funding circuits in mediating neoliberal education (Carnoy 1985; Torres and Schugurensky 2002). Merging the concerns of the political economy of education with more traditional political ecology provided a lens for analyzing how particular funding packages and the policies that promote them either differentially enable or preclude particular pedagogical practices. This shifted theoretical lens also laid bare the effects of these practices on conceptions and practices of land management.

Second, this book has sought to disrupt accepted environmental narratives. All too often peasants are placed at the sharp end of the machete, perceived as driving environmental degradation—especially in the Amazon. There is certainly some truth to these accounts. As highlighted by the cases of Charlés and Genival (chapter 2), who, like many others, deforested their newly won land in order to plant subsistence crops, those who join the MST are by no means ecologically noble individuals. However, a more nuanced analysis is needed of these individuals' land management practices. First, the cycle of land conversion, whereby forests are knocked down in order to plant a quick season of subsistence crops and then pasture, has been promulgated by large-scale farmers, supported by political-economic incentives (agricultural credit) and processes (commodity supply chains) operating at various scales. But in addition to political economy, one needs to see this cycle of land conversion in the context of individuals' life histories. Coming from incredibly marginalized positions, many of the 17 de Abril's founders reproduced what they knew, re-creating an embodied geography that they had learned from their parents and while working as "farmers' cats." Last, I've sought to problematize these narratives by expanding the time scale through which we make sense of environmental change. The pioneers of the 17 de Abril did not receive some primeval tract of land. Rather, the presence of indigenous artifacts and the stands of Brazil nut trees show that the landscape of the 17 de Abril had long been modified by anthropogenic forces. Drawing upon longitudinal spatial data enabled me to expand the time scale of land use and landscape change. Archival aerial photography and longitudinal satellite imagery highlight that the process of land conversion began in the 1960s and that by the time the MST got the land it had largely already been converted to pasture. These spatial histories are incredibly important because they highlight the constraints facing the critical food systems education initiatives that the MST activists work so hard to promote. As a form of decolonization, the MST's critical food systems education pedagogies provide a set of tools whereby students can critically read the landscape, empowering them to question histories of landscape change and their role within those narratives (Gruenewald 2003).

Third, the narratives within this book have helped synthesize, and contribute to, long-standing debates within geography and education surrounding place. Place is multivocal; whereas for some it is inherently local, for others it is neither strictly local nor strictly global but rather "the grounded site of local-global articulation" (Biersack and Greenberg 2006: 16). As a national movement for education reform, Educação do Campo challenges educators, students, and parents to critically question the differences between rural and locally relevant education from a place-based perspective. Educação do Campo is a place-based pedagogy, but unlike many conceptions of place that are

apolitical, this one is critical at its core. Through critical place-based pedagogies, students like Alan (chapter 7) were able to peel back the layers of place and
hone in on histories of colonization and structural marginalization. It is also
through these pedagogies that students like Lucinede (also chapter 7) began
to engage and mobilize their students to participate in a process of reinhabitation—making degraded places livable using new forms of land management
(Gruenewald 2003). More than multivocal, place—and our conceptions of it—
is entangled with questions of hegemony. Critical food systems education in
this context becomes a process of decolonizing this history, recognizing how
political economy, structural violence, and the politics of knowledge come to
constitute what is natural and then recognizing the potential for education to
reclaim that history. Highlighting how political economy can be differentially
mobilized to redress histories of colonization, Francisco, for example, directed
students to use their class project to both uncover this history of exploitation
and imagine a new pathway toward more sustainable production (chapter 7).

Fourth, I've emphasized how the interdependence between political institutions has structured agrarian knowledge and landscapes. Political institutions are understood broadly in this context as entities of the state, which
include both public universities and research centers. Political ecologists recognize that political institutions are interrelated and the connections between
these networks structure transformations of the environment (Hempel 1996).
In this book I've explored the relations between educational institutions at
various institutional levels, such as municipal secondary schools, federal vocational schools, and public universities (chapters 1, 3, 6, 7). Each of these
institutions is an object of the state, whether in an MST settlement or an urban
center. Yet each is also connected with nonformal nonstate spaces of critical
food systems education, such as La Vía Campesina's Agroecological Institute
of Latin America–Amazônia (IALA) (chapter 7), and nonformal but recurring
spaces, such as the pedagogical encampment (chapter 6). When insights from
political ecology are brought into conversation with educational studies, we
gain a better understanding of how these interconnections themselves come
to transform educational spaces. As Dayze and Brito indicated (chapter 5), the
Federal University's certificate program was designed to help develop IALA
ideologically as well as materially in terms of its mandala garden, apiary, and
aviary projects. Similarly, as Eduardo and Rosaldo indicated at the Federal
University (chapter 6), it was the process of bringing the movement into the
university through debates, documentaries, and course programs for social
movement members that was transforming the university from the inside out.

This movement, the circuits between the spaces, is transforming these institutions. For political ecologists attuned to education, the focus on political institutions naturally intersects with the idea of coproduction (Jasanoff 2004), which analyzes how institutions of science and technology mediate understandings of nature and how the politics of knowledge order society and the environment. Coproduction focuses on the relation between scientific methods and instruments that reconfigure nature, and other social devices, such as laws, financial incentives, and interest groups that reorder society. Schools are important instruments for the coproduction of environmental knowledge because they are where conceptions of what constitutes scientific methodologies and knowledge are continually inscribed, thus affecting how students create boundaries between the social and natural. The Federal Institute's internal political pedagogical project document (chapter 6) emphasizes how the school is designed to train its students in a regionally specific science of agroecology, which in itself helps to promote new forms of social organization.

This eastern Amazonian agroecology would be specific to the region, although it would draw on general agroecological principles that have been developed at national and international levels. It would be created at the intersection of academic and popular knowledge amassed from small family farmers and indigenous organizations. The desire for this "local science of agroecology" is exemplary of how knowing nature is intricately caught up with the construction of the social landscape. At the Federal Institute the reorganization of time and space associated with the alternating pedagogy is closely linked to affirming the hybrid nature of the school and the coproduction of knowledge. As students engage in agroecological experimentation and devise new forms of cooperative production, "the workings of science and technology cease to be a thing apart from other forms of social activity, but are integrated instead as indispensable elements in the process of societal evolution" (Jasanoff 2004: 17). Through the process of coproduction both science and society are constructed.

This book is a preliminary foray into the intersections of political ecology and education. With an eye to dynamic transformation of lives, livelihoods, and landscapes in the 17 de Abril, I've focused on thematically highlighting the importance of political economy (Greenberg and Park 1994), the relations between political circumstances and environmental degradation (Stott and Sullivan 2000), place as relational and an arena of both marginalization and emancipation (Gruenewald 2003; Biersack and Greenberg 2006), and the interconnections among political institutions (Hempel 1996). I define the political ecology of education as a perspective attuned to how the distribution of power and resources among connected political and cultural entities in related places mediates pedagogical processes—from tacit to formal learning—and related knowledge systems, mediates access and control to natural resources, interactions with the cultural landscape, and conceptions of nature-society relationship. Recognizing that this definition is not all encompassing, I invite others to similarly develop political ecologies of education attuned to multiple axes of difference, including, but not limited to, ethnicity, race, ability, multispecies, and sexuality.

Policy Implications

Although this book focuses on a very specific time and place, the results of this research have direct implications for agrarian reform policy in Brazil. The National Program for Education in Agrarian Reform (PRONERA) is a major policy affecting the landscape of rural education in southeastern Pará, Brazil. My analyses demonstrate that this program has been instrumental in funding educational initiatives that have the potential to help rural communities develop more environmentally and economically sustainable forms of production. These PRONERA-funded programs, which are based in an alternating pedagogy, also enable students to remain both in residence and gainfully employed within their communities, thus stemming the rural-urban migration and depopulation of rural areas. However, the demand for these opportunities far exceeds the spaces available. This research supports expanding the PRONERA program's funding and scope so that it continues to be a source of funding for developing equitable and innovative forms of education for marginalized communities. My exploration of the historical role of credit in fomenting livelihoods and environmental shifts is also pertinent to ongoing discussion of agricultural development in Brazil. PRONAF-Jovem is a government credit program that has enormous potential to enable youth to influence their families' transition to sustainability. However, this research finds its potential is quite limited, as it is open only to students who have completed a vocational agricultural program. I recommend changing the conditions of the PRONAF-Jovem project so that other agrarian youth can individually and collectively advance credit projects; one way to do this would be to designate innovative mentors in the agrarian sciences who could advise these youth in developing their projects.

Grassroots Implications

My research results are significant not only for the MST but also for the other grassroots movements both in Brazil and globally. One of my central findings is the importance of institutional partnerships between the MST and activist-oriented professors in creating educational opportunities for agrarian settlement youth. I believe that this finding has broad applicability beyond both the MST and education reform. Grassroots movements should understand that the state, in its many guises, is a powerful arena for fomenting social change. Movements can reach their objectives of wider social transformation by forming partnerships with individuals who have an affinity for social and environmental justice. In my research the arena of education was an important locale for developing these partnerships. Individuals in strategic positions can help mediate movements' access to state resources and grant legitimacy to grassroots projects.

My findings on political participation also directly support grassroots movements' efforts to reach their objectives. Movements must maintain the active political participation of their members in order to be effective at creating change. However, political participation often wanes following a movement's initial success in addressing a social grievance. My results illuminate recursive relationships between political participation and educational opportunities. Movements that provide educational opportunities to their most active members enable the training of activist leaders who will be the future of the movement. When these educational opportunities are designed as continuing education opportunities for educators, movements strengthen these leaders' abilities to effect change on a much wider scale by training their own students. Movement educational spaces are key incubators for larger scale processes of educational, social, and environmental change. I find that these educational spaces are often interconnected. Dialogues that begin in one space will be taken up in another, and this accretionary process will ultimately result in significant change. Movement educational spaces are also important because they create an arena in which to develop institutional partnerships. Grassroots movements can foster long-term partnerships by inviting activist professors and administrators to participate in movement activities in these movement spaces. Additionally, these spaces can be important temporal bridges, providing movement courses a space to function when the state fails to meet its educational obligations. Although creating and maintaining these spaces undoubtedly requires extensive movement resources and commitment, doing so is extremely valuable in the long term and should be continued.

My research suggests that the agricultural extension system is at odds with the objectives of agrarian reform movements. In southeastern Pará the MST has been quite successful in advancing a new conception of agricultural extension education in state educational institutions; however, the larger political and institutional system in which these students will ultimately work is driven by a short-term project-oriented system that is at odds with the realities of agrarian reform communities. I encourage social movements to take a two-prong approach to transforming agricultural extension. The first element is to continue transforming the educational institutions that train extension agents, moving these institutions from an agricultural modernization paradigm to one grounded in community development, food sovereignty, and agroecological methods. The second element is to begin a difficult debate about how to create a fundamentally different vision of extension that is community-based and does not rely upon production-maximizing projects. This latter aspect might take the form of extension collectives that fund themselves through value-added agricultural production (e.g., yogurt, cheese, fruit pulp) or through a community tax. By developing nuclei of trained community extension agents, or what Freire would simply term educators, agrarian reform settlements will be able to work toward developing knowledge sovereignty.

Concluding Moments, Emerging Futures

The story of the 17 de Abril is anything but a happy one. Born from one of Brazil's most violent massacres of landless workers, the settlement has, by many accounts, been a series of failures. This includes many people who live in the 17 de Abril itself. As Isabel framed it in chapter 1, "Our settlement was supposed to be a model. We had a great opportunity here for the history to be different." From the dilapidation of the various government projects to the continued outmigration of the original inhabitants, the immigration of nonpoliticized newcomers, and the subsequent transition away from subsistence agriculture, there is a significant disjuncture between the reality of the settlement and the original vision of either its early inhabitants or the MST at a national level.

The school still flies the flag of the movement. This is highly symbolic, suggesting that the movement still has a presence within the school. As illustrated in chapters 3 and 7, Lucinede, Zé, Diana, and Isabel, among others, are actively trying to recuperate the presence of the movement, its pedagogy and ideology within the school. However, at the same time one finds few teachers interested in *teaching the movement*, and those that do largely limit their content to the month of April and covering the massacre. Even if the teachers were interested in teaching the story of the struggle, it's not clear that students or their parents would actively participate in either the movement's educational events or the struggle for land itself. The movement's flag flies today outside the school, but for how long? Perhaps soon it will be forgotten—much like the movement's sign at the entrance to the settlement (fig. 8.1). Walking through the settlement, down streets nearly abandoned, one wonders what it will look like in twenty more years (fig. 8.2). Will all of its youth have left, its elders died, and its lands been reconsolidated into mini-fazendas as many suspect might be the case? Perhaps. While that may be the overarching trajectory, there are numerous points of pause in which another future might be evolving. I conclude this book by offering a glimpse at some potential futures, futures that are embryonic in the present.

Youth are leaving the settlement, but not all are moving to nearby urban centers. Several of the more active MST youth leaders have left the settlement and joined the movement's encampments. Two of my closest informants, Fabío (who worked at one point as my research assistant) and Diana (the educator from the 17 de Abril who participated in the Federal University's graduate program), have joined an MST encampment known as Hugo Chávez—named after the socialist Venezuelan president—which is outside the city of Marabá.

The access road to the Hugo Chávez encampment lay almost directly across the highway from the entrance of the IFPA-CRMB, which was located in the MST's 26 de Março settlement. The encampment was situated fifteen kilometers down a heavily rutted dirt road. A giant wooden sign with Hugo Chávez's

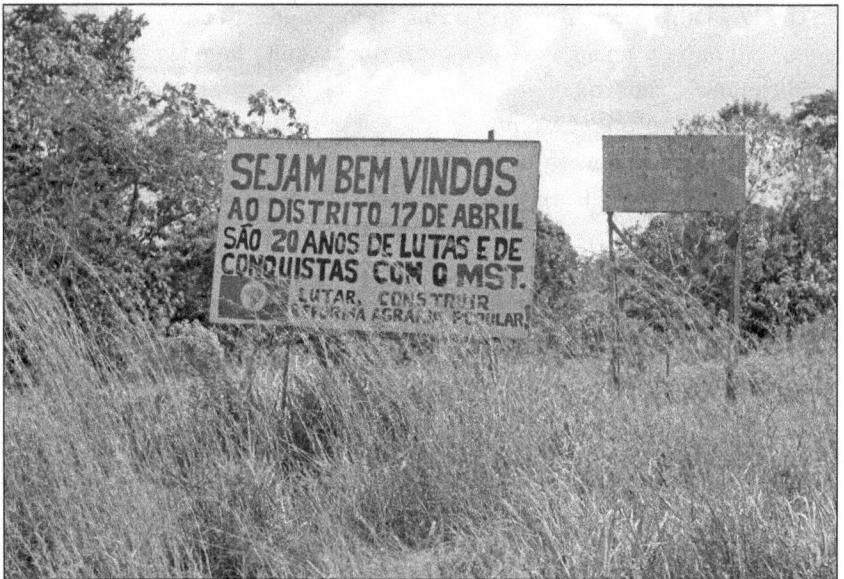

Figure 8.1. Twenty years of struggle and conquest

image painted in black-and-white marked the encampment's entrance. When I visited, the encampment consisted of around 350 families. Fabío told me that it was earlier up at around 800, but many had left over the last year since the community's founding. "They come, but are really just interested in getting a piece of land, selling it, and moving on," Fabío informed me. "They're not interested in spending four, five, six, maybe ten years in the sun, rain, living under the black plastic tarp."

The encampment's school graced the middle of Hugo Chávez's central square. Behind the school there was a mandala planting. Diana was the director of the school, and Haroldo was a teacher there. As heavy afternoon clouds coalesced and raindrops begin to fall, we rushed toward Diana and Haroldo's shelter, which was located across the street from the school.

Through slats in the ceiling rain fell in a steady stream, spattering onto the kitchen table. It was the first time I had seen Diana and Haroldo in nearly two years. In 2013, during my previous period of fieldwork, Diana was living in the 17 de Abril and teaching at the school; Haroldo was finishing up his vocational secondary school program centered on agroecological extension at the Federal Institute. I was surprised upon returning to the 17 de Abril in 2015 that Diana had left her coveted teaching position at the Escola Oziel Alves and

Figure 8.2. A forgotten future

joined the encampment. Sinking into a cavernous hole in the broken frame of her run-down, albeit dry, couch, I asked her why she chose to move here (fig. 8.3). Diana told me that although her mother had been officially settled by the National Institute of Colonization and Agrarian Reform (INCRA) after the massacre and legally had a house and land, Diana never had any land of her own. Her decision to leave the 17 de Abril and move to Hugo Chávez was actually motivated by a desire not for land itself but for change. Diana was intensely frustrated by stagnant local politics and hoped that she might find a more rewarding existence in a new community. "I lived in the 17, but I felt the need to live in a place where I could make a difference; I thought that in the 17 it wasn't going to be possible to make a difference. There were too many problems with the militancy." Diana, like Francisco in chapter 7, was frustrated by the complacency; levels of political participation within the settlement plateaued as people gradually got basic needs addressed and as newcomers changed the demographics. Diana might be frustrated by the state of political participation in the settlement, but she still has hope—a persistent belief in the possibility of radical social transformation in her new encampment, if not in 17 de Abril. Diana's persistent hope was a product of her formação. She felt an obligation to actualize the potential of this education, and it seemed that the more fertile ground of an encampment would provide that opportunity.

Rather than a stagnant space, the encampment was a fresh territory, where the energy and commitment to social change remain palpable. "The encampment is full of possibilities," Diana said (fig. 8.4). In the encampment, Diana recognized that the "17 de Abril had transitioned, it had already gone through a process of transition. It's that old story: if you want to have a settlement that's good, you need to do this in the initial phase, which is the encampment." Diana had decided that her capacity to effect long-lasting social transformation, to actualize the potential of her political formation, to pay back her investment to the movement, needed to take place in the encampment. "In the encampment you plant some seeds, the seed of production, the seed of belonging to the movement, this seed of respecting others, all of these things that you work on in an encampment." What Diana was describing is a process of formation—helping to mold the political subjectivities of those who have joined the encampment.

This educational work is directly imbricated with the ultimate sustainability of the movement. "If you're able to work really well with the social base in the encampment, then the essence remains. And the essence is just this: the sense of belonging to the struggle, the solidarity with the social movement, this part of one's identity remains." Having witnessed the transition in the

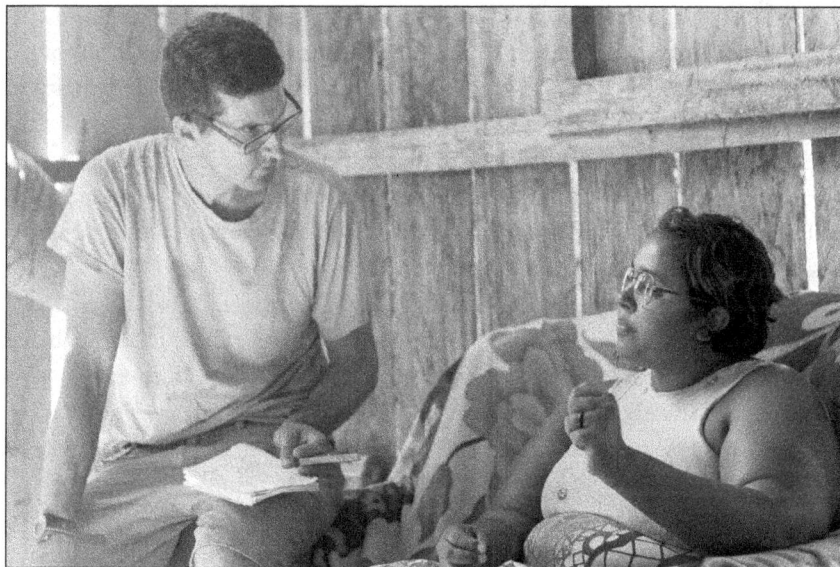

Figure 8.3. A desire for change

Figure 8.4. A landscape full of possibilities

17 de Abril, Diana recognized that this work is crucial to the future of the movement. "If you're not able to have these debates at the higher levels of the encampment, you lose this. And this is what occurred in the 17 de Abril. It lost the essence. It lost many other things as well, but above all what we lost in the settlement is the essence, which we had."

Diana understood that her potential to plant this seed of political sustainability is grounded in her history of political formation. "I can take my fourteen years of experience of struggle within the social movement, and work with the encamped community on this. Everything that I studied, everything that I learned, everything that I know, I can use to help make a difference for them." Diana was thus primed for a new opportunity. "When this occupation arose here, I felt the desire, I said, 'I'm going to go there, because I know there, I know that I'll feel more complete. I needed to feel that I was really making an impact in the lives of others.' " Diana realized her vision of being an integral part of forming the new encampment. "On the first day of the occupation I came, and I've been here until today." Being a leader within the encampment has been incredibly fulfilling for Diana.

> I feel really satisfied, with myself; I feel very happy, the entire day, knowing that my life is very complete here. In terms of my activism, I returned to my militancy, which is something that I've been wanting to do for a very long time. I returned to this question of being in dialogue with the people that are so close to my community. I have helped many people, and it feels very positive. For example, in terms of the school; from the beginning we've been working with the question of what it means to be an escola do campo, and this has left me very happy.

Throughout this book, I've made a case for critical food systems education having the potential to stem depeasantization and, through political formation, lead to a process of repeasantization. Perhaps that's no longer possible in the 17 de Abril. Perhaps, as Diana suggested, that essence is lost. But that does not mean that the movement's vision, or its efforts to transform the education system, is a failure. Perhaps they're working exactly as intended. The struggle is not over. Diana has been formed and is drawing upon her political formation to plant the seed for sustainability—for the long-term political, agroecological, and organizational sustainability of the movement itself. Diana's perspective forces a radical rethinking of how the success or failure of the movement, and its vision of critical food systems education, is evaluated.

It is not only in Diana that the movement's aim was achieved: through his own process of political formation, Fabío has emerged as a leader. Soon after returning from a three-month movement course in political leadership at the MST's Florestan Fernandes National School, the Hugo Chávez encampment was formed, and Fabío was called by the movement to go help direct the encampment. As Fabío and I waited at the entrance to the encampment for my ride to return to the 17 de Abril, I asked him about how he negotiated the decision to the leave the 17 de Abril and come to the encampment. Fabío explained the calculus that youth face, an analysis that we've seen various youth offer in different ways throughout the book:

> There are no jobs in the settlement, there's no means of subsistence for the youth. The culture of agriculture production is being lost in the settlement. So the youth see two options: one is to leave the settlement and go work for a large company. It might be a boring day-to-day job, but you're going to earn a decent monthly income; you can buy food, clothes, a motorcycle. Or the other option is that they spend three or four years struggling for land?
>
> What are they going to see as better: one option where they're spending three or four years living on the land, surviving on a cesta básica, facing violent conflict with landowners, living under the sun and rain all the while struggling for land. Or the other—which is a much easier life to opt for, because they want money, they want to dress nicely, and so they're going to opt for this.

Fabío's assessment was nearly identical to the perspective Clesío offered in chapter 4. The options facing youth are as plain as day, and for many they don't really constitute a choice. As Fabío recognized, young adults have to provide for their families and there are no jobs in the settlement. But it's a perception of lack of choice that is structured by one's reading of reality, one's consciousness. I asked Fabío how he reconciled these choices.

> I reached the point where I stopped, sat down, and analyzed the situation: I can be an alienated worker, leaving to the side everything that I've been able to earn through the struggle since I was three years old, leaving all this to the side. But my mother struggled for this; everything that I know, I earned through this movement, everything that I've won, which isn't very much, but in terms of knowledge—which in my perspective is the only thing that one can take with them—throughout one's entire life, knowledge is only thing that can't be stolen from you, and

knowledge is what I've been able to achieve through this movement. For one to understand what are the contradictions in life, to understand what alienated labor is, to understand exploitation, and then to go and work for a massive company, it's really contradictory, but at the same time it's necessary for many.

Fabío shared with me a window into his assessment of reality. Fabío illustrated that his choice was predicated on a critical reading of the world, more than simply a representation of his options. Would he become merely another cog characterized by alienated labor, working for Vale—one of the most disreputable multinationals in Brazil? In Fabío's analysis that would be contradictory—at least for him. Fabío's assessment is structured by his formation he's received through the movement.

For Fabío there really was only one choice. "I remained thinking about it, and decided, I'm going to keep going, I'm going to join the encampment, because I can't break with the movement. I was forged within the movement, and I need to continue within the movement. I'm a subject of the movement, and so I decided to join the encampment." Fabío described the rationale behind his choice—to leave the relative comfort of the settlement and to not opt for a stable job in the city but rather to join the encampment—as a product of his formation within the movement—forged, literally molded by the movement, Fabío saw himself as a *subject* of the movement.

As a subject of the movement, Fabío was now able to actualize his potential as a leader, and being a leader is in many ways about teaching.

I arrived at Hugo Chávez about a month after it was first formed; but it was all still very preliminary, there was no school, no health post, the roads hadn't been made, people were still arriving every day; maybe thirty people a day. Do you understand? I arrived during the heat of the moment: People just kept coming, and coming, and coming.

I looked at the situation, and realized I had never been a part of the base, doing the work of bringing people in, and giving them a perspective on life that is different. I had never lived in an encampment, I didn't really understand what an encampment was, it was all very new. And I found it very mystical, very magical. People arriving, and me having to explain, "Look, the struggle for the land means this," "It means that," "It means that you'll struggle not just for land, but health, education, transport," that there are benefits, like technical assistance.

Fabío needed to do this base work, educating people about the movement, because much like the pioneers who formed the 17 de Abril, they were largely unaware of what was the MST. These were marginalized people on the periphery, many coming from the city of Marabá, who just wanted access to land.

> When people arrive, they need to register that they are living in the encampment, to officially join the movement, but they have no idea about that. They have no idea about how to do it. It's not just about writing down their name in a ledger, telling them where they can build a shelter, but rather saying, "We're a movement that has a social and political character; we're a movement of struggle—we're a movement of the struggle for land, for agrarian reform, and socialism." And to arrive at the second [agrarian reform], you need to be engaged in the first [struggle for land], and there's no way to the third [socialism] without the other two. And so we won't achieve this without the struggle for land.

Coming full circle, Fabío provided the very same type of formação that was necessary for Lucinede and all of the other pioneers when the 17 de Abril was first founded. Much like Diana, he too was very intentionally using his training to help plant the seed for the long-term political sustainability of the movement. This involved molding the pioneers of Hugo Chávez in the culture of the movement.

> We say, "Look: here you'll be encamped, you'll receive a cesta básica [box of basic staples from the state], you'll need to construct a shelter, and be responsible for it. You're going to participate in místicas." You need to tell them about the culture of the movement, which is very strong. Tell them that: "You're going to study, your children will study, there will be the opportunities for courses. You're going to struggle for what's yours. And we, we'll accompany you with education. With our model of education, you're going to learn to plant in a new way, which is form of agriculture that is sustainable, and known as agroecology, you're going to pass through a process of acculturation." All of this we'll be talking about with them, teaching them, so that they'll understand what they are entering into, so that they have a sense of belonging.

Much like for Diana, this has been incredibly rewarding for Fabío. "I've found all of this very magical—me, a youth of twenty-one years of age, helping

people that are fifty or sixty years old understand what this is, how it all functions. And that's when I had this sense of certainty, that I've accepted—I've
opted to continue the struggle, to continue walking with the organization."
Fabío is now a leader within the movement; he's at once an organizer and an
educator; the two are not separate. He's helping bring those new to the movement directly into the movement. He's helping them understand what the
movement is; he's beginning the process of acculturation, helping to create a
sense of belonging for them. And this experience, which was entirely new, is
magical, helping him realize he'd made the right choice.

Epilogue

Helix, a student in the Federal Institute's vocational agroecology program, uses one finger to carefully apply red paint to my face, tracing letters onto a base of white clown makeup. Holding a handheld mirror, I can read the letters. On my left cheek: *Fora!* [Get out!]. On my right: Temer. It is October 2017, and one month ago Brazilian President Dilma Rousseff was ousted in what many political commentators describe as a coup. Michel Temer, a right-wing conservative, had taken power and begun a process of rapidly rolling back public funding for agrarian reform and educação do campo. Here in the Palmares II settlement the MST is holding its Jornada de Sem Terrinha—a week of political education workshops for youth from agrarian reform encampments and settlements. It has been four years since I completed my main period of fieldwork in the 17 de Abril and two years since I last returned to present preliminary results to MST leadership and settlement residents in a community forum and at public events at the Federal Institute and Federal University. Helix is adorning my face, as I am about to participate in a mística surrounding Temer's attack on Educação do Campo. Properly costumed, our núcleo de base, or base group, begins. Adinete enters, shrouded in black fabric, mimicking the ethereal movements of a haunted spirit. She reads out excerpts from Temer's recently proposed constitutional amendment—the PEC do Teto dos Gestos, or PEC 241, which would freeze social spending on education and other public sectors for twenty years. As she concludes, whispering begins from each corner of the room, escalating in volume. "PEC-241?!?" the group repeats in a lamenting tone as they shake their heads, pretending to cry, and console one another. They halt their chant as three students enter, circling around the middle of the room. The first student carries a makeshift tombstone fashioned from cardboard reading: "PRONERA." Another student enters holding a similar prop; as she slowly turns around we can read the words: "Educação do Campo." A third student slowly walks in, holding her sign above her head, at which point the students read it out loud in unison: "Food

Sovereignty?!?" At this point a young child joins the circle and asks the audience, "What will become of our future?" Helix stands beside her and slowly pumps his left fist in the air: "Fora Temer! Fora Temer!! Fora Temer!!" This morning's mística felt significant as more than another moment of political formation within the MST. Rather, the mística underscored that MST youth see the intersection of public policies, political economy, and power as structuring the fate of educação do campo and possibilities for food sovereignty. I read the mística, which connects local struggles over education to national politics, as highlighting that the political ecology of education framework can shed light on not simply the struggles over agroecological education in 17 de Abril but also the threats facing educação do campo in the contemporary political conjuncture and possibilities for resistance.

As I have shown in this book, a careful analysis of political economy and the opportunities and constraints it provides to agroecological learning is a core feature of understanding Brazil's political ecology of education. The rise of the Temer government and succession by that of Jair Bolsonaro signals the return to a neoliberal system after the post-neoliberal governments of Luiz Inácio Lula da Silva (Lula) and Dilma Rousseff. One of the major narratives that Brazil's conservative forces mobilized in the lead-up to the coup was that the state's spending on social services was exorbitant and responsible for Brazil's growing economic crisis. Following Dilma's ouster, Temer's response was to pull hard from the neoliberal playbook and initiate austerity measures. What this represents is the transition away from seeing education as a human right and instead viewing it as a service that must be bought and sold. The implication is that for the Temer and now Bolsonaro government, services, such as education, are better delivered by the private sector, which absolves the state of the financial responsibility as a service provider. This rollback of the state is a key feature of neoliberalism. These austerity measures will have a particularly dramatic effect on emerging forms of popular education in rural areas. Drastic spending cuts to PRONERA pose a grave threat to educação do campo. PRONERA's funding has been slashed from approximately 30 million Brazilian reais in 2014 to less than 100,000 reais in 2019. Why is the Brazilian state actively undermining educação do campo, an education system, which as I have shown in this book has the capacity to advance sustainable livelihoods and landscapes? For Gilmar Felipe, a representative of the MST's Education Sector–Paraíba, "Educação do campo is a transformative instrument, and that is why its threatened. Recently, educação do campo has helped demarcate an important space within the last few years, in which the peasantry can organize itself, to think of new possibilities for society, a new methodology for a pedagogy that makes possible the liberation of human beings, it is for that reason that the right is threatening it" (MST 2018). Drawing upon the political ecology of education perspective, specifically its focus on the intersection of political economy, agroecology, and alternative social reproduction, provides further insight into why Brazil's conservative governments are targeting rural education. As Felipe noted, educação do campo has helped to create a network of spaces in which society can reimagine itself. Cutting the funding that supports these spaces is part of an effort to close down dialogue. By defunding programs like PRONERA, the government is seeking to politically and economically neutralize the transformative potential of educação do campo and its project of reenvisioning rural livelihoods and ecologies.

Second, in this book I underscored the pivotal role of Federal University professors and administrators who are political allies of the MST in the struggle to expand educação do campo and opportunities for agroecological education. These individuals recognize that education is a political project, and as allies they are able to harness their positionality to propose new graduate programs and access funding for scholarships for those students from agrarian reform communities. Since the ouster of Dilma, throughout Brazil these individuals have begun to face political persecution. Temer has helped fuel a movement known as Escola Sem Partido (School Without Parties), which seeks to publicly identify and penalize teachers and professors who are seen as engaging in political and ideological indoctrination. In this neoconservative context, schools are locales not of education but rather of instruction; education is the purview of the family and church; a teacher's job is instruction, consisting of the unidirectional transmission of knowledge. Drawing upon the lessons from this book provides insights into why university professors and teachers are being targeted. Many of these individuals are committed to a vision of political transformation and recognize education as a tool for shaping political consciousness. By penalizing these educators the state is trying to create a landscape of fear within the Federal University context in which educators will no longer work to support the collaborative projects of grassroots movements. If the government continues in this direction, the implications of blacklisting educators and creating a repressive Federal University environment would be huge for grassroots movements. Universities have been pivotal spaces in which the Educação do Campo movement has arisen and developed. Shutting down the possibility of critical political debate would stymie the cross-pollination of ideas between movements, the articulation of novel policy proposals, such as those that led to the creation of the Federal Institute of Education, Science, and Technology of Pará–Rural Campus of Marabá, and the collective mobilization that is necessary to bring these proposals to fruition. Here, the political ecology of education perspective provides insight into the spatiality of this recrimination. The MST and other Brazilian social movements are adept at creating dialogic spaces, which involve critical forms of communication between social movements and society and are intended to mobilize education to advance emancipatory social change (Rule 2004). Dialogic spaces include Federal University fora, like panel discussions with movement leaders, but also those like the Regional Forum for Educação do Campo (FREC), which are where new forms of common sense are articulated. Allied professors and teachers have the institutional power and legitimacy to create and nurture these spaces as part of a broader process of decolonization. By targeting these institutional allies, the state is seeking to control the nature of space, ostensibly stripping it of any political character. However, as Freire points out, all education is political. The government's actions in this context are explicitly political and part of an effort at suppression of alternative epistemologies and agroecological imaginaries.

Last, and perhaps most gravely concerning, is the environmental transformation that is taking place in the current political conjuncture. During the 2018 presidential campaign deforestation rates rose approximately 50 percent, signaling to many that Bolsonaro's supporters were awaiting a rollback in environmental protections. In the year since the election it has become clear that many have taken advantage of this political shift. In August 2019 the National Institute for Space Research reported it "had detected 39,194 fires this year in the world's largest rain forest, a 77% increase from the same period in 2018" (Andreoni and Hauser 2019). Bolsonaro has fanned these fires through his public messaging and political appointments. In his September 2019 address to the United Nations General Assembly, Bolsonaro argued that it is a "fallacy" to conceive of the Amazon as global patrimony and a "misconception" that its forests are the lungs of the world; taking a line from US president Donald Trump, Bolsonaro then criticized the liberal media for sensationalistic reporting, arguing that it was responsible for escalating deforestation. Bolsonaro's political appointments demonstrate his commitment to violent anti-environmentalism. Ricardo Salles—who ran for federal Congress with a political ad that displayed bullets from a rifle as his solution to environmental activists— was chosen to head Brazil's environmental ministry. Unsurprisingly, shifts in Brazil's agricultural-political landscape are intertwined with these environmental transformations. Bolsonaro appointed Tereza Cristina as agriculture minister; Cristina is known for her vehement support of pesticide deregulation and fast-tracking the socioenvironmental licensing of large infrastructure projects such as dams, industrial waterways, and mines. This spiraling political and environmental crisis will undoubtedly have long-standing implications for the future of small-scale family farming in the Amazon. One of the major insights of this book is that the history of the landscape plays a central role in structuring smallholders' land management decisions. Contemporary environmental devastation is transforming not only the ecological present but also the potentiality that still exists for a more agroecological future. To make sense of what is at stake and the potential for an alternative future, I end with perhaps one of the most important lessons from a political ecology of education perspective: the transformations of material and immaterial territory are intertwined. The escalating environmental devastation in the Amazon is not simply physical but also ideological—we are witnessing the expansion and consolidation of a reactionary and far right common sense. Pushing back against this common sense, which preaches the necessity of environmental exploitation and industrial agriculture, is undoubtedly a long-term struggle, but it is one that the MST and other social movements understand how to wage. It is in the classrooms, in the fields, and across the dinner table that minds will be changed and new forms of agroecology will take hold. If the voices of the educators and students from the 17 de Abril can still be heard, their reminder is that education is bringing an emerging conception of the world into existence, and our job is to nurture it.

Notes

Chapter 1

1. Since the 1934 Constitution articulated the need for land to have a social function, this mandate has been a part of every succeeding constitution (Ondetti 2016).
2. This debate is far from settled. Connor (2008, 2013), for example, argues that the studies of Badgley et al. (2007) and more recently Seufert et al. (2012), which showed that organic production in certain contexts nearly approximates the productive capacity of conventional agriculture, are dangerously misleading because their assessments of the potential of organic agriculture to feed the world do not take into account the energy and resources required to produce organic manures, among other purported miscalculations.
3. Scholars debate whether or not, and how, agrarian reform is contributing to agricultural productivity. Sparovek and Maule (2009), for example, suggest that Brazil's agrarian reform program has resulted in increased agricultural production for smallholder beneficiaries. López and Valdés's (2000) quantitative analysis, by contrast, did not find a linkage between access to land and short-term increases in agricultural production; however, they do argue that the security of land tenure stabilizes household income and increases food access. Similarly, Campelo (2014) argues that assessing the productivity of agrarian reform requires recognizing that the process supports the diverse agroecological initiatives of small family farmers, which contribute in various ways to social and ecological justice. Taken together, these scholars signal that assessing the social function of land requires a critical analysis of how productivity is operationalized.
4. Political ecology is a broad and evolving research program that examines how power relations and political economy impact human-environmental interactions. Overviews of political ecology include Forsyth (2003), Zimmerer and Bassett (2003), Robbins (2004), and Biersack and Greenberg (2006). Goldman et al.'s (2012) volume is particularly relevant to the present work for its focus on the politics of knowledge in political ecology.
5. Recent exceptions include Meek (2015a, 2015b) and Lloro-Bidart (2015, 2016). See also the 2017 special issue in the *Journal of Environmental Education* (48, no. 4), which focuses on the political ecology of education.
6. This question is the focus of chapter 4 and is also addressed in chapter 7.
7. Recent interventions and reviews of this debate can be found in Bernstein (1996, 2004), Akram-Lodhi and Kay (2012), and McMichael (1997, 2007).
8. The decolonial turn in social theory began to consolidate throughout the second half of the twentieth century, following the second wave of decolonization in Africa, the Caribbean, and Asia, the rise of the civil rights movement in the United States, and indigenous movements throughout the world.

9. Antonio Gramsci was an Italian Marxist political theorist and politician who lived from 1891 to 1927. While imprisoned by Benito Mussolini, Italy's fascist leader, Gramsci wrote more than three thousand pages in a series of notebooks that have come to be known as the Prison Notebooks. For an accessible introduction to Gramsci's life and work, see Schwarzmantel (2014). It may seem inappropriate to draw on Gramsci to help understand decolonization, particularly within a peasant movement. Gramsci, after all, saw peasant culture as archaic and fragmentary. He was very critical of the political potential of subaltern movements, seeing Italy's southern peasants as accepting hegemonic values and trying to emulate the characteristics of ruling classes (Gramsci 1994: 327). Yet he also believed that these peasants could inject nonhegemonic values into the dominant worldview. In sum, Gramsci saw Italy's peasants as a class that maintained itself in subordination through internal weaknesses and its acceptance of the social, political, and moral leadership of the ruling classes. Yet it could also become a revolutionary class through alliances with workers and the development of a class consciousness (Arnold 1984: 158–59). In making a case for Gramsci's relevance in a decolonial context, it is important to note that his concepts have been applied in diverse international contexts. Feierman (1990), for example, translates Gramsci's concept of the organic intellectual to rural Tanzania, exploring the formation of peasant intellectuals. Perhaps most important in the present context, Karriem (2009) draws on a Gramscian approach to understand the interplay between space, ecology, and politics in the Brazilian MST.

10. Gramsci's writings on nature are diffuse in the Prison Notebooks. In recent years, however, geographers have developed various analyses of Gramsci's understanding of nature (Jessop 2005). As Loftus (2012) encourages us, rather than searching for a singular conception of nature in Gramsci's scattered notes, it is perhaps more productive to see the concept as part of his broader philosophy of praxis. Conceptions of the world are spatial because they concern how consciousness structures forms of material production and in turn the landscape itself. Ideas about how space is organized are part and parcel of hegemony and closely tied to particular forms of knowledge.

11. The task of developing alternative conceptions of the world is a political process of active learning, characterized for Gramsci by the "labors of one's own brain."

12. As Mayo (2008: 419) argues, education is a central element of Gramsci's vision of social transformation because for Gramsci "every relationship of hegemony is an educational one."

13. The Gini coefficient is a metric for inequality in a frequency distribution. A Gini coefficient of zero represents perfect equality—everyone having the same amount of land. A Gini coefficient of 1 (or 100%) highlights complete inequality among values— only one person owning all the land.

14. For more comprehensive analyses of the MST's origination and development, see book-length treatments by Branford and Rocha (2002), Wright and Wolford (2003), Ondetti (2008), and Wolford (2010).

15. See Borges (2010) for a Brazilian perspective on the agroecological transition within the MST.

16. The movement began in July 1997, when educators and leaders from these movements converged in the capital of Brasília for the First National Conference of Agrarian Reform Educators (ENERA). For greater details on the history of the national Educação do Campo movement, see Munarim (2008) and Breitenbach (2011). Tarlau (2015) offers an excellent analysis of the institutionalization of Educação do Campo at the federal level and the threats of co-optation to the movement.

17. For more detailed histories of the MST in Pará, see (in Portuguese) Bastos (2002), Silva (2003), and Rocha (2010).

18. In chapter 2 I provide a deeper examination of these histories.
19. Many place the total at twenty-one, but the bodies of two individuals were not accounted for at the morgue and have never been recovered. For an analysis of the event in the context of larger regional land violence, see Simmons (2005).
20. Throughout my fieldwork, this university was known as the Federal University of Pará (UFPA). The name of the university was changed in 2013 to the Federal University of South and Southeastern Pará (UNIFESSPA). Throughout the book, I use the current name and acronym to avoid confusion.
21. I refer to this space as IALA rather than IALA-Amazônica because it is the only one of the IALAs that I discuss in the book.
22. I was unable to pinpoint when these photos were taken but was able to narrow the time period to between 1965 and 1969 due to the organizations involved in the aerial survey and when the photos were entered into the archive.
23. I obtained the images from the USGS Global Visualization Viewer (http://glovis.usgs .gov), search criteria: WRS-2 Path 22, Row 64, percent cloud < 10%. I used the ATCOR extension within Erdas Imagine to conduct atmospheric correction on the imagery.

Chapter 2

1. This was not the first mass migration of northeasterners to the Amazon. During the Second World War, the United States subsidized mass labor migration to the Amazon from the Northeast to increase rubber production (Garfield 2014).
2. *Roça* is the Brazilian version of couscous, simple dish made from steamed corn meal.
3. These currency values are approximately $1.75 million and $4 million, given the 1998 exchange rate.
4. The other remainders of the project are less visible but no less present: the Association, the key social institution linked to the MST, is permanently discredited in the eyes of many both within and outside of the settlement.
5. For several reasons, it would be problematic to assume that the pioneers *would* engage in sustainable agriculture by nature of their role in the MST. First, in the mid-1990s the MST was just beginning to turn toward agroecology at the national level; it wasn't until the MST's sixth national congress in 2000 that it adopted agroecology as its agricultural approach. Second, as I will highlight in chapter 3, "membership" in the MST is a slippery concept; more often than not, individuals simply "signed the ledger," entering the movement out of a desire for land rather than any knowledge of, or commitment to, the movement's political or agricultural vision. Third, the movement is composed of individuals who have independent perspectives and desires; there is no homogenous group mandate.
6. As Balée (1998) indicates, stands of Brazil nut trees are an exemplar of long-term indigenous management; this is unsurprising given the contemporary proximity of indigenous territories (largely Kayapó) and the presence of indigenous artifacts, such as arrowheads, that have been found in the present-day settlement.
7. Equal to approximately $1,000.
8. In 1999, the PROCERA was renamed the National Program for the Strengthening of Family Farming (Programa Nacional de Fortalecimento da Agricultura Familia, or PRONAF).
9. Equal to approximately $3,250.
10. COOMARSP is an abbreviation for Cooperativa Mista Dos Assentamentos de Reforma Agraria da Regiao Sul e Sudeste do Estado do Para.
11. Cupuaçu (*Theobroma grandiflorum*) is a tropical rainforest tree related to cacao.

Chapter 3

1. While I did not attend this conference, I conducted semistructured interviews concerning the major themes with five of its attendees.
2. What Luz is describing is a change in political administration boundaries that recently took place; the settlement itself was recently declared a sub-prefeito, basically a geographic area that is smaller than a municipality but has its own political representation.

Chapter 4

1. One translation of the Portuguese *militantes* would be "activists."
2. I generally use the term *peasant* over *farmer*, as *camponês* was much more common than *agricultor* among the individuals with whom I worked.
3. The pedagogical encampment is the subject of chapter 6.
4. Some within the movement's vanguard would likely critique this—indicating that state- and national-level service positions are two years in duration, precisely to ensure that activists can continue to engage in settlement-level organizing. However, in my experience, these activists' engagements with state-/national-level organizing are simply some of many movement-level obligations.
5. The course focused on agricultural extension from an agroecological perspective.

Chapter 5

1. The quote is usually attributed to Chilean president Salvador Allende and reads, "Being young and not being revolutionary is a biological contradiction."
2. The song, titled "America Livre," was written by Jacir Strapazzan and featured on the MST's CD *Arte em Movimento* (www.landless-voices.org/vieira/archive-05.php?rd=FREE AMER034&ng=p&sc=2&th=49&se=0).
3. Due to the number of institutions and acronyms, I've elected to introduce them by type so as to not confuse the reader. The nonformal agricultural training center is the Agroenvironmental Center of Tocantins (Centro Agroambiental Tocantins, or CAT). The public university is the Federal University of Para (UFPA). The vocational secondary school is the IFPA-CRMB (Federal Institute of Pará-Rural Campus of Marabá). La Vía Campesina's agroecological training center is the Agroecological Institute of Latin America–Amazonian branch (IALA-Amazônia). Last, the regional conference is known as the Regional Forum for Educação do Campo (Forum Regional do Educação do Campo, or FREC).
4. The CPT maintains a database of land conflicts in Brazil that has been a pivotal resource for social movements and scholars (see, for example, Simmons et al. 2007).
5. This nonformal educational institution was known as the Agroenvironmental Center of Tocantins (Centro Agroambiental Tocantins, or CAT).
6. CAT comprised three elements: a training center (the Escola Familia Agricola, or EFA), the Agrarian Foundation of Tocantins Araguaia (Fundação Agrária do Tocantins Araguaia, or FATA), an entity that helped rural trade unions to network, and an agricultural research body known as the Socio-Economic Laboratory of the Tocantins (LASAT). FATA sought to organize the peasantry by networking emerging rural unions together, helping them develop new forms of production, marketing, and credit. LASAT,

the third leg of CAT, conducted research on peasant farming systems, attempting to identify and promote agroecological practices.

7. This school was known as the Escola Familia Agricola (EFA) and was associated with CAT. EFA was significantly inspired by educational experiments taking place both in Europe and in Brazil's south surrounding alternative forms of agricultural education. It drew upon pedagogical methods, such as an alternating pedagogy where students rotate between school and their home communities, that were first developed in France in the 1930s and then brought to Brazil as part of the Casas Familias Rurais movement in Brazil (see Gnoatto 2006).

8. Extractivist settlements have a different legal designation than agrarian reform settlements. These communities are intended by the state to pursue sustainable forms of resource extraction, such as Brazil nut harvesting and palm nut processing.

9. This program—Youth and Adult Education (Educação dos Jovens and Adultos, or EJA)—was the mainstay of PRONERA at this time.

10. Forum conferences occurred in southeastern Pará in 2001, 2005, 2007, 2009, and 2011.

11. On October 25, 2007, Law 11.534 formally created the Federal Agrotechnical School of Marabá. However, this new school existed only in name and was never formally built. A year later, on December 29, 2008, Law 11.892 was passed creating a new federal technical institute system in the state—the Federal Institute of Education, Science, and Technology of Pará (IFPA). The IFPA system now included the Federal Agrotechnical School of Marabá together with the Federal Agrotechnical School of Castanhal and Federal Center of Education and Technology of Pará. What was the Federal Agrotechnical School of Marabá changed its name to the Federal Institute of Education, Science, and Technology of Pará- Rural Campus of Marabá (IFPA-CRMB).

12. The graffiti references Brazil's unelected and right-wing president Michel Temer, whom Brazilian social movements see as orchestrating a coup to replace democratically elected and left-leaning president Dilma Rousseff.

13. As discussed in chapter 3, individuals are described as being politically aligned with the MST if they are proud enough to wear "the shirt of the movement," particularly in public places that might engender scorn, such as on public transportation or in a government office. They then represent the "face of the movement."

Chapter 6

1. The sand is subsequently sold to construction contractors, who use it to make concrete.

2. The alternating pedagogy predates the Educação do Campo movement. It was developed in France in the 1930s by educators associated with peasant communities and brought to Brazil as part of the Casas Familias Rurais movement in Brazil (see Gnoatto 2006).

3. The MST and other agrarian social movements frequently organize courses around an alternating pedagogy because rural youth provide indispensable agricultural assistance to their families during harvesting, sowing, and other parts of the local agricultural calendar and the social movements recognize that these experiences have pedagogical value (Ribeiro 2008).

4. An analysis of the phrase *projeto político pedagógico* provides insights into this document's potential for social and environmental transformation. It is defined as a project because it visualizes a new horizon for education and seeks to explicitly move the school, students, and faculty in that direction. This project is political because it is grounded in a particular population's sociopolitical reality and their demands. As Veiga, a Brazilian education scholar of PPPs, writes, "It is political in the sense of commitment to the training of citizens for a type of society" (2005: 15). The PPP is political because it seeks to reproduce an alternative vision of society. It is pedagogical because it defines

the educational actions and characteristics of the school necessary to achieve its particular proposals.

5. The six mechanisms that Van der Ploeg (2012: 49) highlights are (1) diversification, (2) changing to low external input farming, (3) regrounding agriculture upon nature, (4) pluriactivity, (5) new forms of cooperation, and (6) feedback loops between inputs and outputs.

6. PRONAF-Jovem (Programa Nacional Agricultura Familiar–Jovem, or National Program of Family Farming–Youth) is an outgrowth of other PRONAF programs that provide agricultural credit. As detailed in chapter 2, these other PRONAFs are connected to the institutionalization of cattle ranching as the dominant form of land use in the region.

Chapter 7

1. We were singing a modified version of a popular song by Dominguinhos called "I Miss My Sweetheart" ("Eu Só Quero Um Xodo").

2. Oziel Alves Perreira, or Oziel, as he is frequently referred to, is a highly symbolic martyr within the MST. Oziel was one of the activists killed during the massacre of Eldorado dos Carajás. Various schools throughout Brazil, including the municipal school in the 17 de Abril settlement, are named after him. The MST memorializes Oziel, and the massacre that transpired at the S-curve, and in the process creates a legacy where his political participation is tied to education.

3. Scholars of adult education have long focused on informal learning within social movements. See Finger (1989), Foley (1999), Kilgore (1999), Overwien (2000), and Gouin (2009) for important debates.

4. In its more conventional usage, *formação* can be defined simply as training.

5. Nonformal education means different things in different historical and geographic contexts. In the first world, nonformal education is most frequently used to denote educational programs that are outside of school, such as at a nature center. In the developing world, nonformal education has frequently been used as part of a social justice agenda to "improve the participant's power and status either by adding to his or her stock of skills and knowledge or by altering basic attitudes and values toward work and life" (La Belle 1984: 80). In Latin America, nonformal education has a long history, existing since the 1920s, as part of community-based programs, literacy education, vocational training, extension education, popular education, community schooling, and female-dominated social movements (La Belle 2000: 21). Nonformal education can also be integrated as part of the state's larger educational system. Nicaragua's Sandinista government, which institutionalized nonformal education as part of its efforts to base its restructured educational system in the revolution's ideals of social justice, exemplifies how nonformal education can be institutionalized in emancipatory contexts (Arnove and Dewees 1991).

6. Many within the MST's encampments and settlements would not self-identify as activists. Rather than joining the movement out of an ideological desire to advance social transformation, these are marginalized individuals who have a basic desire for land, dignity, and a better life.

7. In describing the importance of both the encampment and settlement as pedagogical places, Raul's perspective tracks scholarship on the significance of autonomous spaces in which activists construct "futures in the present" (Cleaver 1979). Like Sitrin's (2012) account of Argentine factory occupations following the fiscal default of 2001, MST encampments provide a spatial arena in which to forge new social relations, including experiments with neighborhood self-management.

8. Analyses of social reproduction in education highlight how the education system reproduces the dominant societal structures, norms, and career pathways (Bowles and Gintis 1976; Bourdieu and Passeron 1977; Willis 1977; Apple 1982; Althusser 1984). Education implicitly prepares working-class students for working-class jobs, and students in general learn to uncritically accept the basic structure of society (Carnoy 1985).

9. Clarice's perspective parrots Marx's writings in *Capital*, that "by thus acting on the external world and changing it, he at the same time changes his own nature" (1967: 177).

10. See, for example, Blaikie (1989), Fairhead and Leach (1996), Forsyth (2003), and Latour (2004).

11. As Gonçalves (2005) describes in his treatise *Amazônia, Amazônias*, these are "movements of re-existence, because they don't only struggle against those that kill and deforest, but for a certain form of existence, a certain type of life and production, differentiated by modes of experience, action, and thought" (130; my translation).

12. Over the past century the imminent demise of the peasantry has been forecast by capitalists, development practitioners, and intellectuals, "indeed, by virtually everyone but the peasants themselves" (Desmarais 2007: 195). Hobsbawm (1994: 289), for example, writes that "the most dramatic and far-reaching social change of the second half of this (last) century, and the one which cuts us off or ever from the world of the past, is the death of the peasantry." This is what Araghi (1995) terms the "disappearance thesis" of the agrarian question: the idea that as capitalism spatially expands, transforming rural areas, the peasantry will inevitably disappear, consumed by capital and turned into wage laborers or capitalist farmers.

13. Clarice's analysis here is synonymous with Gramsci's understanding of common sense, which "is not a single unique conception, identical in time and space . . . it takes different forms. Its most fundamental characteristic is that it is a conception, which even in the brain of one individual is fragmentary, incoherent, and inconsistent, in conformity with the social and cultural position of those masses whose philosophy it is" (Gramsci 1971: 419).

14. Clarice's critical analysis of common sense also shares striking similarities with that of Franz Fanon (1967: 18), who suggests that colonial relationships shape the colonized people's subjectivities, forming an "inferiority complex, which rested in their souls."

15. See Crehan (2002) for an in-depth exploration of Gramsci's conception of culture.

References

Akram-Lodhi, A. Haroon, and Cristobal Kay. 2012. "The Agrarian Question: Peasants and Rural Change." In *Peasants and Globalization: Political Economy, Agrarian Transformation and Development*, edited by A. H. Akram-Lodhi and C. Kay, 3–34. London: Routledge.

Alfred, Taiaiake. 2009. "Restitution Is the Real Pathway to Justice for Indigenous Peoples." In *Response, Responsibility, and Renewal*, edited by Jonathan Dewar, Gregory Younging, and Mike DeGagne, 179–87. Ottawa: Aboriginal Healing Foundation.

Almeida, Anna Luiza Ozorio de. 1992. *The Colonization of the Amazon*. Austin: University of Texas Press.

Althusser, Louis. 1984. "Ideology and Ideological State Apparatuses." In *Essays on Ideology*, edited by Ben Brewster, 1–41. London: Verso.

Altieri, Miguel A., and Cynthia I. Nicholls. 2008. "Scaling up Agroecological Approaches for Food Sovereignty in Latin America." *Development* 5, no. 4: 472–80.

Altieri, Miguel A., and Victor Manuel Toledo. 2011. "The Agroecological Revolution in Latin America: Rescuing Nature, Ensuring Food Sovereignty and Empowering Peasants." *Journal of Peasant Studies* 38, no. 3: 587–612.

Andreoni, Manuela, and Christine Hauser. "Fires in Amazon Rain Forest Have Surged This Year." *New York Times*, August 21, 2019. www.nytimes.com/2019/08/21/world/americas/amazon-rainforest.html.

Apple, Michael W. 1982. *Culture and Economic Reproduction in Education*. London: Routledge & Kegan Paul.

Araghi, Farshad. 1995. "Global Depeasantization, 1945–1990." *Sociological Quarterly* 36, no. 2: 337–68.

Araujo, Severina G. 2004. "O PRONERA e os Movimentos Socias: Protagonismo do MST." São Paulo: A Educação na Reforma Agrária em Perspectiva.

Arnold, David. 1984. "Gramsci and Peasant Subalternity in India." *Journal of Peasant Studies* 11, no. 4: 155–77.

Arnove, Robert F., and Anthony Dewees. 1991. "Education and Revolutionary Transformation in Nicaragua, 1979–1990." *Comparative Education Review* 35, no. 1: 92–109.

Arthur, Mikaila Mariel L. 2009. "Thinking Outside the Master's House: New Knowledge Movements and the Emergence of Academic Disciplines." *Social Movement Studies* 8, no. 1: 73–87.

Badgley, Catherine, Jeremy Moghtader, Eileen Quintero, and Emily Zakem. 2007. "Organic Agriculture and the Global Food Supply." *Renewable Agriculture and Food Systems* 22, no. 2: 86–108.

Balée, William. 1998. "Introduction." In *Advances in Historical Ecology*, edited by William Balée, 1–17. New York: Columbia University Press.

Banaszak, Lee Ann. 2010. *The Women's Movement Inside and Outside the State.* New York: Cambridge University Press.

Barcello, Sérgio B. 2012. "A Jornada de Agroecologia ea Ampliação das Pautas e Mobilização Política nos Movimentos Sociais Rurais." *Antropolítica: Revista Contemporânea de Antropologia* 32: 149–69.

Bartels, Bradley, and Ruben Donato. 2009. "Unmasking the School Re-zoning Process: Race and Class in a Northern Colorado Community." *Latino Studies* 7, no. 2: 222–49.

Bastos, Corecha. 2002. *A Atuação do MST (Movimento dos Trabalhadores Rurais Sem Terra) na Eestrutura Jurídica-agrária do Pará.* Belém: Cejup.

Belle, Thomas J. L. 1984. "Liberation, Development, and Rural Non-formal Education." *Anthropology & Education Quarterly* 15, no. 1: 80–93.

Bernstein, Henry. 1996. "Agrarian Questions Then and Now." *Journal of Peasant Studies* 24, nos. 1–2: 22–59.

———. 2004. " 'Changing Before Our Very Eyes': Agrarian Questions and the Politics of Land in Capitalism Today." *Journal of Agrarian Change* 4, nos. 1/2: 190–225.

———. 2014. "Food Sovereignty via the 'Peasant Way': A Sceptical View." *Journal of Peasant Studies* 41, no. 6: 1031–63.

Bevington, Douglas, and Chris Dixon. 2005. "Movement-Relevant Theory: Rethinking Social Movement Scholarship and Activism." *Social Movement Studies* 4, no. 3: 185–208.

Bhaba, Homi K. 1994. *The Location of Culture.* London: Psychology Press.

Biersack, Aletta, and James B. Greenberg. 2006. *Reimagining Political Ecology. New Ecologies for the Twenty-First Century.* Durham, NC: Duke University Press.

Blaikie, Piers. 1989. "Explanation and Policy in Land Degradation and Rehabilitation for Developing Countries." *Land Degradation & Development* 1, no. 1: 23–37.

Borges, Juliano Luis. 2010. "A Crise do Produtivismo e a Transicao Agroecologica no. Movimento dos Trabalhadores Rurais Sem Terra-MST." VIII Congreso Latinoamericano de Sociología Rural, Porto das Galinhas.

Bourdieu, Pierre, and Jean Claude Passeron. 1977. *Reproduction in Education, Society and Culture.* Beverly Hills, CA: Sage.

Bowles, Samuel, and Herbert Gintis. 1976. *Schooling in Capitalist America.* New York: Basic Books.

Branford, Sue, and Oriel Glock. 1985. *The Last Frontier: Fighting over Land in the Amazon.* Totowa, NJ: Zed Books.

Branford, Sue, and Jan Rocha. 2002. *Cutting the Wire: The Story of the Landless Movement in Brazil.* London: Latin America Bureau.

Breitenbach, Fabiane Vanessa. 2011. "A Educação do Campo no. Brasil: uma História que se Escreve entre Avanços e Retrocessos." *Espaço Academico* 11, no. 121: 116–23.

Brenner, Neil. 2005. *New State Spaces: Urban Governance and the Rescaling of Statehood.* New York: Oxford University Press.

Brown, J. Christopher, and Mark Purcell. 2005. "There's Nothing Inherent about Scale: Political Ecology, the Local Trap, and the Politics of Development in the Brazilian Amazon." *Geoforum* 36, no. 5: 607–24.

Byres, Thomas J. 1996. *Capitalism from Above, Capitalism from Below: An Essay in Comparative Political Economy.* London: Macmillan.

Caldart, Roseli Salete. 2006. *Movement of the Landless Rural Workers (MST): Pedagogical Lessons.* São Paulo: Vieira.

Camini, Isabela. 2009. *Escola Itinerante: na fronteira de uma nova escola.* São Paulo: Expressão Popular.

Campelo, Daniel Alvez. 2014. "Public Policies for Brazilian Family Farming in a Semiarid Climate: From Combat to Coexistence." *Revista Brasileira de Pós-Graduação* 10, no. 21: 851–73.

Campos, María T., and Daniel Nepstad. 2006. "Smallholder, the Amazon's New Conservationists." *Conservation Biology* 20, no. 5: 1553–56.

Carnoy, Martin. 1985. "The Political Economy of Education." *International Social Science Journal* 37, no. 2: 157–73.

Cash, David W. 2001. " 'In Order to Aid in Diffusing Useful and Practical Information': Agricultural Extension and Boundary Organizations." *Science, Technology, & Human Values* 26, no. 4: 431–53.

Castro-Gomez, S. 2007. "The Missing Chapter of Empire: Postmodern Re-organization of Coloniality and Post-Fordist Capitalism." *Cultural Studies* 2, nos. 2–3: 428–48.

Chin, Christine N., and James H. Mittleman. 1999. "Conceptualizing Resistance to Globalization." In *Globalization and the Dilemmas of the State in the South*, edited by F. Adams, S. D. Gupta, and K. Mengisteab, 33–49. London: Palgrave Macmillan.

Cleary, Daniel. 1993. "After the Frontier: Problems with Political Economy in the Modern Brazilian Amazon." *Journal of Latin American Studies* 22, no. 2: 331–49.

Cleaver, Harry. 1972. "The Contradictions of the Green Revolution." *American Economic Review* 62, nos. 1/2: 177–86.

———. 1979. *Reading Capital Politically*. Brighton: Harvester.

Coleman, Simon, and Pauline von Hellermann, eds. 2012. *Multi-sited Ethnography: Problems and Possibilities in the Translocation of Research Methods*. London: Routledge.

Comilo, Maria Edi da Silva, and Elias Canuto Brandão. 2010. "Educação do Campo: a Mística como Pedagogia dos Gestos no. MST." *Revista Eletrônica de Educação. Ano III*.

Connor, D. J. 2008. "Organic Agriculture Cannot Feed the World." *Field Crops Research* 106, no. 2: 187–90.

———. 2013. "Organically Grown Crops Do Not a Cropping System Make and Nor Can Organic Agriculture Nearly Feed the World." *Field Crops Research* 144: 145–47.

Coulthard, Glen Sean. 2014. *Red Skin, White Masks: Rejecting the Colonial Politics of Recognition*. Minneapolis: University of Minnesota Press.

Crehan, Kate. 2002. *Gramsci, Culture and Anthropology*. Berkeley: University of California Press.

———. 2016. *Gramsci's Common Sense: Inequality and Its Narratives*. Durham, NC: Duke University Press.

Crowther, Jim, and Mae Shaw. 1997. "Social Movements and the Education of Desire." *Community Development Journal* 32, no. 3: 266–79.

Desmarais, Annette. A. 2007. *La Vía Campesina: Globalization and the Power of Peasants*. Halifax: Fernwood.

Edelman, Marc. 2013. "What Is a Peasant? What Are Peasantries? A Briefing Paper on Issues of Definition." Paper presented at the First Session of the Intergovernmental Working Group on a United Nations Declaration on the Rights of Peasants and Other People Working in Rural Areas, Geneva, Switzerland.

Escobar, Arturo. 2010. "Latin America at a Crossroads: Alternative Modernizations, Post-liberalism, or Post-development?" *Cultural Studies* 24, no. 1: 1–65.

Fairhead, James, and Melissa Leach. 1995. "False Forest History, Complicit Social Analysis: Rethinking Some West African Environmental Narratives." *World Development* 23, no. 6: 1023–35.

———. 1996. *Misreading the African Landscape: Society and Ecology in a Forest-Savanna Mosaic*. New York: Cambridge University Press.

Fajans, Jane. 2012. *Brazilian Food: Race, Class, and Identity in Regional Cuisines*. New York: Bloomsbury.

Falzon, Mark Anthony, ed. 2009. *Multi-sited Ethnography: Theory, Praxis and Locality in Contemporary Social Research*. New York: Ashgate.

Fanon, Franz. 1967. *Black Skin, White Masks*. Translated by C. L. Markmann. New York: Grove.

Fearnside, Philip M. 2001. "Land-Tenure Issues as Factors in Environmental Destruction in Brazilian Amazonia." *World Development* 29, no. 8: 1361–72.

Feierman, Steven M. 1990. *Peasant Intellectuals: Anthropology and History in Tanzania*. Madison: University of Wisconsin Press.

Ferguson, Bruce G., Miriam Aldasoro, Omar F. Geraldo, Mateo Mier y Terán Giménez Cacho, Helda Morales, and Peter Rosset. 2019. "Special Issue Editorial: What Do We Mean by Agroecological Scaling?" *Agroecology and Sustainable Food Systems* 43, nos. 7–8: 722–23.

Fernandes, Bernardo Mançano. 2009. "Sobre a Tipologia de Territórios." In *Territórios e Territorialidades: Teoria, Processos e Conflitos*, edited by Marcos A. Saquet and Eliseu S. Sposito, 197–215. São Paulo: Expressão Popular.

Finger, Matthias. 1989. "New Social Movements and Their Implications for Adult Education." *Adult Education Quarterly* 40, no. 1: 15–22.

Flowers, Rick, and Elaine Swan. 2012. "Pedagogies of Doing Good: Problematisations, Authorities, Technologies and Teleologies in Food Activism." *Australian Journal of Adult Learning* 52, no. 3: 532–71.

Foley, Griff. 1999. *Learning in Social Action: A Contribution to Understanding Informal Education*. New York: Zed Books.

Forsyth, Tim. 1996. "Science, Myth, and Knowledge: Testing Himalayan Environmental Degradation in Thailand." *Geoforum* 27: 375–92.

———. 2003. *Critical Political Ecology: The Politics of Environmental Science*. London: Routledge.

Foucault, Michel. 2008. "Of Other Spaces" (1967). In *Heterotopia and the City*, edited by Michiel Dehaene and Lieven De Cauter, 13–31. London: Routledge.

Foweraker, Joe. 1981. *The Struggle for Land: A Political Economy of the Pioneer Frontier in Brazil from 1930 to the Present Day*. New York: Cambridge University Press.

FREC (Forum Regional do Educação do Campo). 2011. *5a Conferençia Regional De Educação do Campo do Sul e Sudeste do Pará*. Marába, Brazil: Caderno de Textos.

Free Association. 2011. *Moments of Excess: Movements, Protest and Everyday Life*. London: PM Press.

Freire, Paulo. 1973. *Pedagogy of the Oppressed*. New York: Continuum.

Gadotti, Moacir. 1992. "Brazil: Conflicts between Public and Private Schooling and the Brazilian Constitutions." In *Education, Policy, and Social Change*, edited by Daniel A. Morales-Gómez and Carlos Alberto Torres, 111–29. Westport, CT: Greenwood.

Garfield, Seth. 2014. *In Search of the Amazon: Brazil, the United States, and the Nature of a Region*. Durham, NC: Duke University Press, 2014.

Gaztambide-Fernández, Rubén A. 2012. "Decolonization and the Pedagogy of Solidarity." *Decolonization: Indigeneity, Education & Society* 1, no. 1: 41–67.

Golubchikov, Oleg. 2010. "World-City-Entrepreneurialism: Globalist Imaginaries, Neoliberal Geographies, and the Production of New St Petersburg." *Environment and Planning A* 42: 626–43.

Gnoatto, Antonio. 2006. "Pedagogia da Alternancia; Uma proposta de educaca e desenvolvimento no. campo." Sociedade Brasileira de Economia e Sociologia Rural: XLIV Congresso da Sober, Fortaleza.

Godlewska, Anna. 2013. "Dislocation Pedagogy." *Professional Geographer* 65, no. 3: 384–89.

Goldman, Mara J., Paul Nadasdy, and Matthew D. Turner. 2011. *Knowing Nature: Conversations at the Intersection of Political Ecology and Science Studies*. Chicago: University of Chicago Press.

Gonçalves, Carlos Walter P. 2005. *Amazônia, Amazônias*. São Paulo: Editora Contexto.

Gouin, Rachel. 2009. "An Antiracist Feminist Analysis for the Study of Learning in Social Struggle." *Adult Education Quarterly* 59, no. 2: 158–75.

Grain. 2014. "Hungry for Land: Small Farmers Feed the World with Less Than a Quarter of All Farmland." www.grain.org/article/entries/4929-hungry-for-land-smallfarmers-feed -the-world-with-less-than-a-quarter-of-all-farmland.

Gramsci, Antonio. 1971. *Selections from the Prison Notebooks*. London: Lawrence and Wishart.

———. 1977. *Selections from Political Writings (1910–1920)*. Translated by J. Mathews. Cambridge: Cambridge University Press.

———. 1994. *Gramsci: Pre-prison Writings*. Cambridge: Cambridge University Press.

Grande, Sandy. 2015. *Red Pedagogy: Native American Social and Political Thought*. Lanham, MD: Rowman & Littlefield.

Gray, Ian, Tony Dunn, and Emily Phillips. 1997. "Power, Interests and the Extension of Sustainable Agriculture." *Sociologia Ruralis* 37, no. 1: 97–113.

Green, Duncan. 2003. *Silent Revolution: The Rise and Crisis of Market Economics in Latin America*. London: Latin American Books.

Greenberg, James, and Thomas Park. 1994. "Political Ecology." *Journal of Political Ecology* 1, no. 1: 1–12.

Gruenewald, David A. 2003. "The Best of Both Worlds: A Critical Pedagogy of Place." *Educational Researcher* 32, no. 4: 3–12.

Guthman, Julie. 2008. "Bringing Good Food to Others: Investigating the Subjects of Alternative Food Practice." *Cultural Geographies* 15: 431–47.

———. 2011. " 'If They Only Knew': The Unbearable Whiteness of Alternative Food." In *Cultivating Food Justice: Race, Class, and Sustainability*, edited by A. H. Alkon and J. Agyeman, 263–81. Cambridge, MA: MIT Press.

Hall, Anthony. 1990. "Land Tenure and Land Reform in Brazil." In *Agrarian Reform and Grassroots Development: Ten Case Studies*, edited by Roy L. Prosterman, Mary N. Temple, and Timothy M. Hanstad, 205–32. Boulder, CO: Lynne Rienner.

Halvorsen, Sam. 2015. "Taking Space: Moments of Rupture and Everyday Life in Occupy London." *Antipode* 47, no. 2: 401–17.

Hammond, John L. 2004. "The MST and the Media: Competing Images of the Brazilian Landless Farmworkers' Movement." *Latin American Politics and Society* 46, no. 4: 61–90.

———. 2013. "The Significance of Space in Occupy Wall Street." *Interface: A Journal for and about Social Movements* 5, no. 2: 499–524.

Hecht, Susanna B. 1993. "The Logic of Livestock and Deforestation in Amazonia." *BioScience* 43, no. 10: 687–95.

Hecht, Susanna, and Alexander Cockburn. 1989. *The Fate of the Forest: Developers, Destroyers and Defenders of the Amazon*. London: Verso.

Hempel, Lamont C. 1996. *Environmental Governance: The Global Challenge*. New York: Island Press.

Hennessy, C. Alistair. 1978. *The Frontier in Latin American history*. Albuquerque: University of New Mexico Press.

Hobsbawm, Eric. 1992. "The Crisis of Today's Ideologies." *New Left Review* 192: 55–64.

———. 1994. *Age of Extremes: The Short Twentieth Century, 1914–1991*. London: Abacus.

Hoelle, Jeffery. 2014. "Cattle Culture in the Brazilian Amazon." *Human Organization* 73, no. 4: 363–74.

Hollander, Jocelyn A., and Rachel L. Einwohner. 2004. "Conceptualizing Resistance." *Sociological Forum* 19, no. 4: 533–54.

Holston, Jeffery. 2011. "Contesting Privilege with Right: The Transformation of Differentiated Citizenship in Brazil." *Citizenship Studies* 15, nos. 3–4: 335–52.

Holt-Gimenez, Eric, and Annie Shattuck. 2011. "Food Crises, Food Regimes and Food Movements: Rumblings of Reform or Tides of Transformation?" *Journal of Peasant Studies* 38, no. 1: 109–44.

IBGE (Instituto Brasileiro de Geografia e Estatística). 2006. *Agricultural Census*. Rio de Janeiro.

IFPA-CRMB (Federal Institute of Pará-Rural Campus of Marabá). 2011. *Projeto Político Pedagógico*. Marabá: Ministério da Educação.

Issa, Daniela. 2007. "Praxis of Empowerment: Mística and Mobilization in Brazil's Landless Rural Worker's Movement." *Latin American Perspectives* 153, no. 34: 124–38.

Jasanoff, Sheila, ed. 2004. *States of Knowledge: The Co-production of Science and the Social Order*. London: Routledge.

Jenkins, J. Craig. 1983. "Resource Mobilization Theory and the Study of Social Movements." *Annual Review of Sociology* 9: 527–53.

Jessop, Bob. 2005. "Gramsci as a Spatial Theorist." *Critical Review of International Social and Political Philosophy* 8, no. 4: 421–37.

Karriem, Abdurazack. 2009. "The Rise and Transformation of the Brazilian Landless Movement into a Counter-hegemonic Political Actor: A Gramscian Analysis." *Geoforum* 40, no. 3: 316–25.

Katzenstein, Mary Fainsod. 1998. "Stepsisters: Feminist Movement Activism in Different Institutional Spaces." In *The Social Movement Society: Contentious Politics for a New Century*, 195–216. Lanham, MD: Rowman & Littlefield.

Kilgore, Deborah W. 1999. "Understanding Learning in Social Movements: A Theory of Collective Learning." *International Journal of Lifelong Education* 18, no. 3: 191–202.

La Belle, T. J. 1984. "Liberation, Development, and Rural Nonformal Education." *Anthropology & Education Quarterly* 15, no. 1: 80–93.

———. 2000. "The Changing Nature of Non-formal Education in Latin America." *Comparative Education* 36, no. 1: 21–36.

Larner, Wendy. 1998. "Hitching a Ride on the Tiger's Back: Globalization and Spatial Imaginaries in New Zealand." *Environment and Planning D: Society and Space* 16, no. 5: 599–614.

Latour, Bruno. 2004. *Politics of Nature: How to Bring the Sciences into Democracy*. Cambridge, MA: Harvard University Press.

Lave, Jean, and Ettiene Wenger. 1991. *Situated Learning: Legitimate Peripheral Participation*. Cambridge: Cambridge University Press.

La Vía Campesina. 2017. "Peasant Agroecology Schools and the Peasant-to-Peasant Method of Horizontal Learning." https://viacampesina.org/downloads/pdf/en/TOOLKIT _agroecology_FINAL.pdf.

Lefebvre, Henri. 1991. *The Production of Space*. Translated by D. Nicholson-Smith. Cambridge, MA: Blackwell.

Leitner, Helga. 2004. "The Politics of Scale and Networks of Spatial Connectivity: Transnational Interurban Networks and the Rescaling of Political Governance." In *Scale and Geographic Inquiry*, edited by Eric Sheppard and Robert B. McMaster, 236–56. New York: John Wiley.

Lisansky, Judith Matilda. 1990. *Migrants to Amazonia: Spontaneous Colonization in the Brazilian Frontier*. Boulder, CO: Westview.

Lloro-Bidart, Teresa. 2015. "A Political Ecology of Education in/for the Anthropocene." *Environment and Society: Advances in Research* 6: 128–48.

———. 2016. "A Feminist Posthumanist Political Ecology of Education for Theorizing Human-Animal Relations/Relationship." *Environmental Education Research* 23, no. 1: 111–30.

Loftus, Andrew. 2012. "Gramsci, Nature, and the Philosophy of Praxis." In *Gramsci: Space, Nature, Politics*, edited by Michael Ekers, Gillian Hart, Sam Kipfer, and Andrew Loftus, 178–96. London: John Wiley.

López, Ramón, and Alberto Valdés. 2000. "Fighting Rural Poverty in Latin America: New Evidence of the Effects of Education, Demographics, and Access to Land." *Economic Development and Cultural Change* 49, no. 1: 197–211.

Mahar, Dennis J. 1979. *Frontier Development Policy in Brazil: A Study of Amazônia*. New York: Praeger.

Maldonado-Torres, Nelson. 2011. "Thinking through the Decolonial Turn: Post-continental Interventions in Theory, Philosophy, and Critique—An Introduction." *Transmodernity: Journal of Peripheral Cultural Production of the Luso-Hispanic World* 1, no. 2: 1–15.

Marcus, George. 1995. "Ethnography in/of the World System: The Emergence of Multi-sited Ethnography." *Annual Review of Anthropology* 24: 95–117.

Marinho, D. L. 2016. *Rompendo as Cercas e Construindo Saberes: A Juventude na Construção da Educação Profissional do Campo no Sudeste do Pará* [Breaking Fences and Constructing Knowledges: Youth and the Construction of Professional Educação do Campo in Southeastern Pará]. Recife: Imprima.

Marsick, Victoria J., and Karen E. Watkins. 1990. *Informal and Incidental Learning in the Workplace*. New York: Routledge.

Marx, Karl. 1867/1967. *Capital*. Translated by S. Moore and E. Aveling. New York: International.

Marx, Karl. 1964. *The Economic and Philosophic Manuscripts of 1844*. Edited by Dirk Struik. New York: International.

Massey, Doreen. 1999. *Power-Geometries and the Politics of Space-Time*. Heidelberg: University of Heidelberg.

Maxey, Ian. 1999. "Beyond Boundaries? Activism, Academia, Reflexivity and Research." *Area* 31: 199–208.

Mayo, Peter. 2008. "Antonio Gramsci and His Relevance for the Education of Adults." *Educational Philosophy and Theory* 40, no. 3: 418–35.

McAdam, Doug, and David A. Snow. 1997. *Social Movements: Readings on Their Emergence, Mobilization, and Dynamics*. Los Angeles: Roxbury.

McCarthy, John, and Mayer Zald. 1977. "Resource Mobilization and Social Movements: A Partial Theory." *American Journal of Sociology* 82, no. 6: 1212–41.

McCune, Nils, Juan Reardon, and Peter M. Rosset. 2014. "Agroecological Formación in Rural Social Movements." *Radical Teacher* 98: 31–38.

McCune, Nils, and Marlen Sánchez. 2019. "Teaching the Territory: Agroecological Pedagogy and Popular Movements." *Agriculture and Human Values* 36, no. 3: 595–610.

McMichael, Phillip. 1997. "Rethinking Globalization: The Agrarian Question Revisited." *Review of International Political Economy* 4, no. 4: 630–62.

———. 2006. "Reframing Development: Global Peasant Movements and the New Agrarian Question." *Canadian Journal of Development Studies* 27, no. 4: 471–83.

———. 2010. "Agrofuels in the Food Regime." *Journal of Peasant Studies* 37, no. 4: 609–29.

———. 2014. "Historicizing Food Sovereignty." *Journal of Peasant Studies* 41, no. 6: 933–57.

Meek, David. 2015a. "Learning as Territoriality: The Political Ecology of Education in the Brazilian Landless Workers' Movement." *Journal of Peasant Studies* 42, no. 6: 1179–1200.

———. 2015b. "Taking Research with Its Roots: Restructuring Schools in the Brazilian Landless Workers' Movement upon the Principles of a Political Ecology of Education." *Journal of Political Ecology* 22: 410–28.

Meek, David, Katie Bradley, Bruce Ferguson, Lesli Hoey, Helda Morales, Peter Rosset, and Rebecca Tarlau. 2017. "Food Sovereignty Education across the Americas: Multiple Origins, Converging Movements." *Agriculture and Human Values* 36, no. 3: 611–26.

Meek, David, and Rebecca Tarlau. 2016. "Critical Food Systems Education (CFSE): Educating for Food Sovereignty." *Agroecology and Sustainable Food Systems* 40, no. 3: 237–60.

Mignolo, Walter D. 2009. "Epistemic Disobedience, Independent Thought and Decolonial Freedom." *Theory, Culture & Society* 26, nos. 7–8: 159–81.

Mignolo, Walter, and Christopher E. Walsh. 2018. *On Decoloniality: Concepts, Analytics, Praxis*. Durham, NC: Duke University Press.

Mintz, Sidney. 1973. "A Note on the Definition of Peasantries." *Journal of Peasant Studies* 1, no. 1: 91–106.

Molina, Monica. 2003. "A Contribuiçã do Pronera na Construção de Políticas Públicas de Educação do Campo e Desenvolvimento Sustentável." Dissertation, Centro de Desenvolvimento Sustentável, Universidade de Brasília.

Moll, Lois, and Richard Ruiz. 2005. "The Educational Sovereignty of Latino/a Students in the United States." In *Latino Education: An Agenda for Community Action Research*, edited by Pedro Pedraza and Melissa Rivera, 295–320. Mahwah, NJ, Lawrence Erlbaum.

Moore, Donald S. 1998. "Subaltern Struggles and the Politics of Place: Remapping Resistance in Zimbabwe's Eastern Highlands." *Cultural Anthropology* 13, no. 3: 344–81.

Moraes, Marli, and Elizabete Witcel. 2014. "The 'Responsibility' of Being Educators in a Social Movement School / O 'ofício' de Ser Educadoras em uma Escola em Movimento (Translated and Edited by Rebecca Tarlau and Nisha Thapliyal)." *Postcolonial Directions in Education* 3, no. 1: 42–56.

Moran, Emilio F. 2019. "Government-Directed Settlement in the 1970s: An Assessment of Transamazon Highway Colonization." In *The Dilemma of Amazonian Development*, edited by Emilio F. Moran, 297–317. London: Routledge.

Morgan, Kevin, and Jonathan Murdoch. 2000. "Organic vs. Conventional Agriculture: Knowledge, Power and Innovation in the Food Chain." *Geoforum* 31, no. 2: 159–73.

MST. 2018. "Seminário debate desafios e avanços da educação do campo na Paraíba." October 31. https://mst.org.br/2018/10/31/seminario-debate-desafios-e-avancos-da-educacao -do-campo-na-paraiba/.

Munarim, Antonio. 2008. "Trajetória do Movimento Nacional de Educação do Campo no. Brasil." *Educação*, January/April, 57–72.

Ndlovu-Gatsheni, Sabelo J. 2015. "Decoloniality as the Future of Africa." *History Compass* 13, no. 10: 485–96.

Neumann, Roderick P. 2005. *Making Political Ecology*. London: Hodder Arnold.

Nicholls, Walter J. 2007. "The Geography of Social Movements." *Geography Compass* 1, no. 3: 607–22.

Novo, Andre, Kees Jansen, Maja Slingerland, and Ken Giller. 2010. "Biofuel, Dairy Production and Beef in Brazil: Competing Claims on Land Use in São Paulo State." *Journal of Peasant Studies* 37, no. 4: 769–92.

Ogle, Ha Thi Anh Dao, Mulokozi Generose, and Britta Leif Hambraeus. 2001. "Micronutrient Composition and Nutritional Importance of Gathered Vegetables in Vietnam." *International Journal of Food Sciences and Nutrition* 52, no. 6: 485–99.

Ondetti, Gabriel. 2008. *Land, Protest, and Politics: The Landless Movement and the Struggle for Agrarian Reform in Brazil*. University Park: Pennsylvania University Press.

———. 2016. "The Social Function of Property, Land Rights and Social Welfare in Brazil." *Land Use Policy* 50: 29–37.

Overwien, Bernd. 2000. "Informal Learning and the Role of Social Movements." *International Review of Education* 46, no. 6: 621–40.

Peluso, Nancy Lee, and Michael J. Watts, eds. 2001. *Violent Environments*. Ithaca, NY: Cornell University Press.

Pérez, Emma. 1999. *The Decolonial Imaginary: Writing Chicanas into History*. Bloomington: Indiana University Press.

Pettinicchio, David. 2012. "Institutional Activism: Reconsidering the Insider/Outsider Dichotomy." *Sociology Compass* 6, no. 6: 499–510.

Pirbhai-Illich, Fatima, Pete Shauneen, and Fran Martin, eds. 2017. *Culturally Responsive Pedagogy: Working towards Decolonization, Indigeneity and Interculturalism*. New York: Springer.

Plank, David Nathan. 1996. *The Means of Our Salvation: Public Education in Brazil, 1930– 1995*. Boulder, CO: Westview.

Quijano, Anibal. 2007. "Coloniality and Modernity/Rationality." *Cultural Studies* 21, nos. 2–3: 168–78.

Ribeiro, Marlene. 2008. "Pedagogia da Alternância na Educação Rural/do Campo: Projetos em Disputa." *Educação e Pesquisa* 34, no. 1: 27–45.

Robbins, Paul. 2004. *Political Ecology: A Critical Introduction.* Malden, MA: Blackwell.

Rocha, A. Charles De Oliveira. 2010. *O Movimento dos Trabalhadores Rurais Sem Terra no. Pará: da Luta Posseira à Construção de um Bloco Histórico Camponês (1984–2009).* Belem, Brazil: Universidade Federal do Pará.

Rocheleau, Diane E. 2008. "Political Ecology in the Key of Policy: From Chains of Explanation to Webs of Relation." *Geoforum* 29, no. 2: 716–27.

Roos, Nanna, Mohammed M. Islam, and Shakuntala H. Thilsted. 2003. "Small Indigenous Fish Species in Bangladesh Contribution to Vitamin A, Calcium and Iron Intakes." *Journal of Nutrition* 133, no. 11 (Suppl. 2): 4021S–26S.

Rosing, Howard. 2012. "Demystifying the Local: Considerations for Higher Education Engagement with Community Food Systems." *Journal of Agriculture, Food Systems, and Community Development* 2, no. 4: 79–84.

Rosset, Peter. 1999. "The Multiple Functions and Benefits of Small Farm Agriculture in the Context of Global Trade Negotiations." Policy Brief No. 4, Food First: The Institute for Food and Development Policy.

Rosset, Peter Michael, and Maria Elena Martinez-Torres. 2012. "Rural Social Movements and Agroecology: Context, Theory, and Process." *Ecology and Society* 17 (3): article 17. www .ecologyandsociety.org/vol17/iss3/art17.

Rule, P. 2004. "Dialogic Spaces: Adult Education Projects and Social Engagement." *International Journal of Lifelong Education* 23, no. 4: 319–34.

Sack, Robert S. 1986. *Human Territoriality: Its Theory and History.* New York: Cambridge University Press.

Sampson, Devon. 2019. "Productivism, Agroecology, and the Challenge of Feeding the World." *Gastronomica: The Journal of Food and Culture* 18, no. 4: 41–53.

Schmink, Marianne, and Charles H. Wood. 1991. *Frontier Expansion in Amazonia.* Gainesville: University Press of Florida.

Schwarzmantel, John. 2014. *The Routledge Guidebook to Gramsci's Prison Notebooks.* New York: Routledge.

Scott, James C. 1987. *Weapons of the Weak: Everyday Forms of Peasant Resistance.* New Haven, CT: Yale University Press.

Scott, Roy Vernon. 1971. *The Reluctant Farmer: The Rise of Agricultural Extension to 1914.* Champaign: University of Illinois Press.

Seufert, Verena, Navin Ramankutty, and Jonathan Fole. 2012. "Comparing the Yields of Organic and Conventional Agriculture." *Nature* 485: 229–32.

Shanin, Teodor. 1973. "The Nature and Logic of the Peasant Economy 1: A Generalisation." *Journal of Peasant Studies* 1, no. 1: 63–64.

Shiva, Vandana. 1993. *Monocultures of the Mind: Perspectives on Biodiversity and Biotechnology.* New York: Palgrave Macmillan.

Silva, H. W. S. 2003. "Formação e resistência do MST no pará." Mestrado em Sociologia, Universidade Federal do Pará, Belém.

Silva, Lourdes Helena da, Vânia Aparecida Costa, and Walquíria Miranda Rosa. 2011. "A Educação de Jovens e Adultos em áreas de Reforma Agrária: Desafios da Formação de Educadores do Campo." *Revista Brasileira de Educação* 16, no. 46: 149–270.

Simmons, Cynthia. 2004. "The Political Economy of Land Conflict in the Eastern Brazilian Amazon." *Annals of the Association of American Geographers* 94, no. 1: 183–206.

———. 2005. "Territorializing Land Conflict: Space, Place, and Contentious Politics in the Brazilian Amazon." *GeoJournal* 64, no. 4: 307–17.

Simmons, Cynthia S., Robert T. Walker, Eugenio Y. Arima, Stephen P. Aldrich, and

Marcellus M. Caldas. 2007. "The Amazon Land War in the South of Pará." *Annals of the Association of American Geographers* 97, no. 3: 567–92.

Sitrin, Marina. 2012. *Everyday Revolutions: Horizontalism and Autonomy in Argentina.* London: Zed.

Smith, Neil. 2010. *Uneven Development: Nature, Capital, and the Production of Space.* Athens: University of Georgia.

Snelgrove, Corey, Rita Kaur Dhamoon, and Jeff Corntassel. 2014. "Unsettling Settler Colonialism: The Discourse and Politics of Settlers, and Solidarity with Indigenous Nations." *Decolonization: Indigeneity, Education & Society* 3, no. 2: 1–32.

Soja, Edward W. 1996. *Thirdspace: Expanding the Geographical Imagination.* New York: Blackwell.

Sparovek, Gerd, and Rodrigo Fernando Maule. 2009. "Negotiated Agrarian Reform in Brazil." In *Agricultural Land Redistribution: Towards Greater Consensus*, edited by Hans Binswanger-Mkhize, Camille Bourguignon, and Rogier van den Brink, 291–308. Washington, DC: World Bank.

Stahelin, Nicolas. 2017. "Spatializing Environmental Education: Critical Territorial Consciousness and Radical Place-Making in Public Schooling." *Journal of Environmental Education* 48, no. 4: 260–69.

Stott, Philip Anthony, and Sian Sullivan. 2000. *Political Ecology: Science, Myth and Power.* London: Arnold.

Suh, Doowon. 2011. "Institutionalizing Social Movements: The Dual Strategy of the Korean Women's Movement." *Sociological Quarterly* 52, no. 3: 442–71.

Sumner, Jennifer. 2013. "Food Literacy and Adult Education: Learning to Read the World by Eating." *Canadian Journal for the Study of Adult Education* 25, no. 2: 79–92.

Tarlau, Rebecca. 2013. "Soviets in the Countryside: The MST's Remaking of Socialist Educational Practices in Brazil." In *Logics of Socialist Education,* edited by Tom Griffiths and Zsuzsanna Millei, 53–72. Dordrecht: Springer.

———. 2015. "Education of the Countryside at a Crossroads: Rural Social Movements and National Policy Reform in Brazil." *Journal of Peasant Studies* 42, no. 6: 1157–77.

Tarrow, Sidney G. 1998. *Power in Movement: Social Movements and Contentious Politics.* New York: Cambridge University Press.

Tilly, Charles. 2000. "Spaces of Contention." *Mobilization: An International Journal* 5, no. 2: 135–59.

Torres, Carlos A., and Daniel Schugurensky. 2002. "The Political Economy of Higher Education in the Era of Neoliberal Globalization: Latin America in Comparative Perspective." *Higher Education* 43, no. 4: 429–55.

Tsing, Anna L. 2005. *Friction: An Ethnography of Global Connection.* Princeton, NJ: Princeton University Press.

Tuck, Eve, Marcia McKenzie, and Katie McCoy. 2014. "Land Education: Indigenous, Post-colonial, and Decolonizing Perspectives on Place and Environmental Education Research." *Environmental Education Research* 20, no. 1: 1–23.

Tuck, Eve, and K. Wayne Yang. 2012. "Decolonization Is Not a Metaphor." *Decolonization: Indigeneity, Education & Society* 1, no. 1: 1–40.

Tuhiwai Smith, Linda. 2012. *Decolonizing Methodologies: Research and Indigenous Peoples.* London: Zed Books.

Vanden, Henry E. 2007. "Social Movements, Hegemony, and New Forms of Resistance." *Latin American Perspectives* 34, no. 2: 17–30.

Van der Ploeg, Jan Douwe. 2008. *The New Peasantries: Struggles for Autonomy and Sustainability in an Era of Empire and Globalization.* London: Earthscan.

———. 2012. "The Drivers of Change: The Role of Peasants in the Creation of an Agroecological Agriculture." *Agroecologia* 6: 47–54.

Veiga, Ilma Passos Alencastro. 2005. *Projeto Político-pedagógico da Escola*. Rio de Janeiro: Papirus Editora.

Velásquez Runk, Julie, Gervacio Ortíz Negría, Leonardo Peña Conquista, G. Mejía Peña, F. Peña Cheucarama, and Yani Cheucarama Chiripua. 2010. "Landscapes, Legibility, and Conservation Planning: Multiple Representations of Forest Use in Panama." *Conservation Letters* 3: 167–76.

Vergara-Camus, Leandro. 2009. "The Politics of the MST Autonomous Rural Communities, the State, and Electoral Politics." *Latin American Perspectives* 36, no. 4: 178–91.

Weis, Timothy. 2010. "The Accelerating Biophysical Contradictions of Industrial Capitalist Agriculture." *Journal of Agrarian Change* 10, no. 3: 315–41.

Wenger, Ettiene. 1998. *Communities of Practice: Learning, Meaning, and Identity*. Cambridge: Cambridge University Press.

Willis, Paul. 1977. *Learning to Labor: How Working Class Kids Get Working Class Jobs*. New York: Teachers College Press.

Wittman, Hannah. 2010. "Agrarian Reform and the Environment: Fostering Ecological Citizenship in Mato Grosso, Brazil." *Canadian Journal of Development Studies* 29, nos. 3–4: 281–98.

Wolf, Eric. 1969. *Peasant Wars of the Twentieth Century*. New York: Harper Torch.

Wolford, Wendy. 2003. "Families, Fields, and Fighting for Land: The Spatial Dynamics of Contention in Rural Brazil." *Mobilization: An International Journal* 8, no. 2: 157–72.

———. 2004. "This Land Is Ours Now: Spatial Imaginaries and the Struggle for Land in Brazil." *Annals of the Association of American Geographers* 94, no. 2: 409–24.

———. 2005. "Agrarian Moral Economies and Neo-liberalism in Brazil: Competing Discourses and the State in the Struggle for Land." *Environment and Planning A* 37: 241–61.

———. 2010. *This Land Is Ours Now: Social Mobilization and the Meanings of Land in Brazil*. Durham, NC: Duke University Press.

Wright, Angus, and Wendy Wolford. 2003. *To Inherit the Earth: The Landless Movement and the Struggle for a New Brazil*. Oakland, CA: Food First!

Wright, Erik Olin. 2013. "Transforming Capitalism through Real Utopias." *Irish Journal of Sociology* 21, no. 2: 6–40.

Zimmerer, Karl S., and Thomas J. Bassett. 2003. *Political Ecology: An Integrative Approach to Geography and Environment-Development Studies*. New York: Guilford.

Index